African American Chronology

AFRICAN AMERICAN CHRONOLOGY

CHRONOLOGIES OF THE AMERICAN MOSAIC

Kwando M. Kinshasa

GREENWOOD PRESS
Westport, Connecticut • London

Library of Congress Cataloging-in-Publication Data

Kinshasa, Kwando Mbiassi.
   African American chronology : chronologies of the American mosaic / Kwando M. Kinshasa.
      p. cm.
   Includes bibliographical references and index.
   ISBN 0–313–33797–7 (alk. paper)
   1. African Americans—History—Chronology. I. Title.
E185.K48   2006
973'.049607300202—dc22   2006011700

British Library Cataloguing in Publication Data is available.

This book is included in the African American Experience database from Greenwood
Electronic Media. For more information, visit www.africanamericanexperience.com.

Library of Congress Catalog Card Number: 2006011700
ISBN: 0–313–33797–7

First published in 2006

Greenwood Press, 88 Post Road West, Westport, CT 06881
An imprint of Greenwood Publishing Group, Inc.
www.greenwood.com

Printed in the United States of America

The paper used in this book complies with the
Permanent Paper Standard issued by the National
Information Standards Organization (Z39.48-1984).

10 9 8 7 6 5 4 3 2 1

CONTENTS

PREFACE

The *African American Chronology* is a compilation of events and circumstances experienced by people of African ancestry within the American social and political construct. By utilizing this data-filled format, the reader is exposed to a series of so-called historical waves as the tenor of the times changes from decade to decade and century to century. Starting from the 15th century, when the first recorded arrival of Africans occurred, up to the early years of the 21st century, the reader senses the importance of chronicled social experiences that are presented not as isolated incidents but as a result of previous social experiences that provided a knowledge base for succeeding generations. As a result, historical data that underscores the importance of a particular event will also be framed by substantive historical information to enhance the reader's contextual understanding of the chronicled event. With this as a primary understanding, other factors are important to recognize about the *African American Chronology.*

Utilizing a format that subdivided centuries into years, subject areas, and dates, an array of experiences were inserted into 49 areas, such as religion, migration, slavery, war, business, media, and education. In this regard, subject categories are indicated by abbreviations, such as CENS for census, GOV for government, and MIL for military. Though these categories contain information that relates to a specific year and month, methodologically speaking they provide the reader with the ability to follow the increase or decline of any specific social activity over a number of years and centuries. For example, the sudden appearance of African American inventors in the latter years of the 19th century may be more indicative of African American's enhanced social mobility than increased educational opportunities. A closer study of accompanying events within the same time period would help to provide an answer.

Throughout the *Chronology,* a number of sidebars are provided to facilitate further historical and contextual information about the chronicled subject or event. Similarly, a glossary presents the reader with a listing of terms, organizational names, pseudonyms, and acronyms from a number of subject areas along with their accompanying definitions.

Significant to any chronology is its bibliography and index; there one will find a listing of historical sources, names, and significant events utilized by the author. In this instance, data was acquired from well-known to lesser-known textbooks, journals, and online databases. However, in almost every instance, this process also necessitated close scrutiny for historical reliability and viable interpretation.

A major task, however, was acquiring and then selecting the proper data for the *Chronology*. This process required access to research journals, history books, newspaper articles, online research engines, and the author's personal recollections of events. The selection process of material was itself critical due to the fact that each generation of African Americans and each decade tended to have its own dynamic ethos and pathos. Recognizing this was important when inserting an incident or events that represented this reality. Furthermore, historical research indicates to the chronicler that significant events often occur simultaneously and in two or more different subject areas. Being aware of this and then choosing the proper sequence of events is important.

Another important aspect within this *Chronology* was recognizing the variant self-defining racial terminologies used by Africans within American society over the past three centuries. In this regard, as a result of evolving assimilation, acculturation, and discriminatory trends in American culture and history, the Africans from the earliest periods up to the present era have redefined themselves in relationship to their social or political status. As a result, the *Chronology* reflects modifications in racial labeling in the following manner: the terms *African, black, Negro,* and *colored* are used up to the post–Civil War era. From 1868 onward, however, when the 14th Amendment to the U.S. Constitution converted the former slaves and native-born people of African descent into citizens, the term African Americans is used.

An easily recognizable aspect of the *Chronology* is its ability to underscore for the reader those waves of social concerns in African American history that were associated with the larger society. For example, in the 1880s up to the 1930s, a major issue was lynching, political disenfranchisement, agricultural development, and migration, all of which helped establish the basis for the founding of the National Association for the Advancement of Colored People (NAACP). In a later era, it was a lack of civil rights, education, and business development that provided the context for Rev. Dr. Martin Luther King Jr. and other civil rights leaders to change the very construct of U.S. government. This development is chronicled in a manner that reveals the connective sinews of historical events.

ABBREVIATIONS

ABOL	Abolition	JOUR	Journalism
AGRI	Agriculture	LAW	Laws and Legislation
ARTS	Art and Performing Arts	LIT	Literature
ASSO	Associations	MANU	Manumission
BUSI	Business	MARR	Marriage
CDIS	Civil Disobedience	MED	Media
CENS	Census	MEDI	Medicine
CIVI	Civil Rights	MIGR	Migration
CRAF	Handcrafts	MILI	Military
CRIM	Crime	MUS	Music
CULT	Culture	OBIT	Obituary
ECON	Economics	POLI	Politics
EDUC	Education	POPU	Population
EMAN	Emancipation	REBE	Rebellion
EMIG	Emigration	RELI	Religion
ENTE	Entertainment	REPA	Reparations
EXP	Explorers	REVO	Revolts
EXPO	Exploration	SCIE	Science
FAMI	Family	SETT	Settlers
FINA	Finance	SLAV	Slavery
FOOD	Food and Drink	SPOR	Sports
GOV	Government	TERR	Terrorism
HHC	Health and Health Care	WAR	War
HOUS	Housing	WORK	Jobs and Employment
INVE	Inventions		

FIFTEENTH AND SIXTEENTH CENTURIES

1492

EXPO. African sailors, soldiers, servants, and settlers arrive in the Americas in the latter part of the century along with Europeans. These first Africans are from Spain rather than Africa and are known as Ladinos. Juan las Canarias is an African sailor who served on Christopher Columbus's flagship, the *Santa Maria,* during the first transatlantic voyage in 1492.

1496

EXPO. Juan Garrido is a free African who made his way from Seville, Spain, to Hispaniola around 1496. He becomes well known for his exploits with Ponce de León's Caribbean expeditions and later joins Hernán Cortés in Mexico, fighting in the epic battles at Tenochtitlán.

1526

EXPO. Luis Vasquez de Ayllon arrives with 100 enslaved African laborers and 500 Spaniards in 1526. Ayllon establishes the town of San Miguel de Gualdape, near present-day Sapelo Sound in Georgia. The colony fails after two months because of illness, Indian hostility, and a slave rebellion. Although the Spanish colony fails and is abandoned, many of the Africans escape to the forest and choose to remain there in freedom with the Native Americans.

1528

EXPO. Estevanico de Dorantes, an African gun bearer, scout, slave, and soldier, sets out with Panfilo de Naravez in an expedition to Florida. Estevanico (Esteban) is one of only four survivors out of the original group of 400. They spend eight years walking overland from Florida to Mexico, and Esteban is probably the first non-Indian person seen by many Native Americans. After arriving in Mexico, the four tell the Spanish authorities of their incredible journey but also about a large, opulent Indian civilization to the north. This information helps reinforce a pre-Columbian Spanish myth about the Seven Cities of Gold. The imperial viceroy in Mexico authorizes Esteban to guide an expedition of explorers and missionaries to these Seven Cities of Gold. During the expedition, Esteban separates himself from the group and heads north, traveling through present-day Arizona and New Mexico. On May 29, 1539, he finally reaches the Hawikuh people, one of six—not seven—pueblos of the people today known as the Zuni. In a dispute, he is killed in a Zuni town on the upper Rio Grande in 1538. This ends the first military expedition on the North American continent in which a person of African heritage is involved.

1540

EXPO. A free black Spaniard serves as the interpreter on Francisco Coronado's expedition through southwestern North America. He, along with two other Africans, stays behind in New Mexico when Coronado returns to Mexico. The interpreter lives with missionaries at Quivira and eventually becomes a Franciscan friar.

1565

SETT. Africans both free and enslaved are a part of the founding Spanish colony of St. Augustine, in present-day Florida. This is the first permanent settlement by nonindigenous people in North America. The Africans come from the Caribbean and South America as well as from West Africa and make up about 10 percent of the town's population.

SEVENTEENTH CENTURY

1606

CENS. The first recorded birth of an African in North America occurs in St. Augustine, Florida.

1607

SETT. Jamestown becomes the first permanent English colony in North America. Financed by the Virginia Company of London and located in the Chesapeake region of the British colonies, it is named after Queen Elizabeth I (1558–1663) of England. The colony contains a number of people of African descent.

1619

MIGR. In August 1619, there are some 32 Africans (5 men and 17 women) reported to be living in the English colony. They were all "in the service of sev[er]al planters." Nothing is known about how they arrived or from where they had come. Also in August, a Dutch warship that earlier attacked a Portuguese slave ship and captured 17 men and 3 women from Angola is moored at Hampton Roads, near the mouth of the James River. For many years, historians believe that they are the first Africans to arrive in British North America. Actually, the Africans are a part of a group of 300 taken from Angola by the Portuguese slaver ship on its way to Vera Cruz in New Spain (Mexico). The Dutch ship, with the help of an English freighter, capture the human cargo and trade them to Virginian officials in return for provisions. The Africans are accorded the status of indentured servants. Some of them, however, are retained by the Dutch, whereas others are "put to work upon public lands to support the governor and officers of the government." There is no evidence that any of the Africans are made slaves, whereas evidence that they are servants is abundant.

1621

MIGR. Anthony Johnson arrives in Jamestown, Virginia, in 1621 from England, though his original home is probably Angola. He is one of 4 blacks among 56 inhabitants on the Bennett plantation, where he labors to survive.

1623

MIGR. The English ship *Swan* arrives in Virginia with a number of immigrants, including a black man named Pedro.

Angolans and earlier Africans in Jamestown are regarded to be *unfree* but not slaves. Those Angolans who bear names such as Pedro, Isabella, Antoney, and Angelo are generally converted to Christianity. According to English custom at that time, Christians cannot be enslaved. Once the unfree, or indentured, servants have worked off their purchase price, they are able to regain their freedom. Antoney and Isabella marry in Jamestown.

William Tucker is the first recorded birth of an African child in the English colony of Jamestown, Virginia.

1624

FAMI. Antoney and Isabella become the parents of William, whom their master may have baptized in the local Church of England. William is the first documented birth of a child of African parents in English North America. He is born free.

The first African slaves are brought to Manhattan, New Amsterdam. Two years later, the Dutch establish Fort Amsterdam in present-day New York. Africans build the fort and perform other labors in the settlement. When necessary, they join with the militia to fight the indigenous population.

1625

FAMI. Anthony Johnson, a servant, marries a Negro woman named Mary, who at that time is the only woman residing at the Bennett Plantation in Jamestown, Virginia.

POPU. Virginia's census indicates that the African population is relatively small. There are 23 Africans compared to a combined 1,227 whites and Native Americans. Of this number, there are 11 males, 10 females, and 2 children, all of whom live in 6 of the 23 settlements in the colony. This indicates that the black population decreased from 1619 and now represents about 2 percent of the total population.

1626

POPU. Eleven black males are identified in the census records of New Amsterdam. Imported by the Dutch West Indian Company, they represent about 5 percent of the non-Native American population. Responding to the pleas of these males, the Dutch import three women, who are identified as *Angolans*.

1634

SLAV. Enslaved Africans arrive in the British colonies of Massachusetts and Maryland.

1635

WORK. Anthony Johnson, who escaped death in an earlier attack by the native population on the British township of Jamestown, is released from indentured service. Johnson, like other freemen of his time, scrambles to acquire wealth in the form of livestock and human beings.

1638

MIGR. The *Desire*, an English ship from Salem, Massachusetts, returns to Boston from the West Indies with cotton, tobacco, and several Africans.

1639

MILI. Africans, free or enslaved, in Virginia are, by law, denied the right to carry weapons. The fear of armed slave insurrection is extremely high.

1640

SLAV. A Virginia court decides that three servants who escaped to Maryland should suffer the following consequences: One of the escapees is Dutch, another is a Scot, and a third, named John Punch, is of African descent. Following their capture and return to Virginia, their terms of service are extended by four years, but Punch's term is to last the rest of his life.

1641

RELI. Under Dutch rule, there are at least 40 black members of Bouweire Chapel in New Amsterdam, present-day New York City. Two Africans, Anthony van Angola and Lucie d'Angola, are married in the Dutch church in New Amsterdam.

SLAV. The Massachusetts Body of Liberties becomes the first British colonial court to officially sanction the institution of slavery in British North America.

1643

MILI. An Indian threat near the Dutch colony of New Amsterdam allows the enslaved Africans to be armed with tomahawks and short spikes to assist the Dutch colonists in fighting the Indians.

Abraham Pearse is listed among those capable of bearing arms in the Plymouth, Massachusetts, colony. He is probably a free black, but the evidence is not clear.

1644

POLI. In February, Dutch Negroes, as they are called, file a petition for freedom, the first black protest in North America. The petition granted by the Council of New Netherlands frees the blacks because of they have "served the Company seventeen or eighteen [years]" and were previously "promised their freedom." The 11 blacks cited are: Paul d'Angola, Big Manuel, Little Manuel, Manuel de Gerrit de Rens, Simon Congo, Anthony Portuguese, Garcia, Peter Santome, John Francisco, Little Anthony, and John Fort Orange. They each receive a parcel of land in what is now Greenwich Village in New York City.

1647

MIGR. The first group of blacks to arrive in the Dutch colony of New Amsterdam do not spend their entire lives in servitude and not all are laborers. Dutch records indicate that a land grant was given to one Jan Negro, "who came with the privateer."

1648

SLAV. The governor of Virginia orders rice planted on the advice of "our Negroes," who tell whites that conditions in Virginia are as favorable to the production of the crop as "in their Country."

1649

MIGR. Colonial officials report that Virginia is the home to "about fifteen thousand English and of Negroes brought thither, three hundred good servants." Africans brought into the colony were not all enslaved. Many were considered servants because they could be manumitted. This changed in the 1680s, when statutory slavery was established.

1650

SLAV. Connecticut gives statutory recognition to slavery.

1651

AGRI. Anthony Johnson receives 250 acres on July 24 under the colonial government's so-called headright system, which encourages population growth by awarding 50 acres of land for every new servant a settler brings to Virginia. This means that Johnson becomes the master of five servants, some of whom are white. He and his relatives eventually bring 11 more servants to the colony and receive 650 additional acres.

Richard Johnson, who migrates to Virginia or other colonial courts, is freed as a matter of course. Johnson arrived as a carpenter and a free man with a signed contract of indenture. Within two years, he is again a free man who now acquires pounds, property, and servants.

1652

SLAV. In Rhode Island, African servitude for life, though not sanctioned by law, is widely practiced. A law is passed, however, declaring that no black or white man can serve a master for longer than 10 years or past the age of 24, as long as they are under servitude before the age of 14.

On May 10, John Johnson, a free black, is granted 550 acres in Northampton County, Virginia, for importing 11 persons.

On November 21, Richard Johnson, a free black, is granted 100 acres of land in Northampton County for importing two persons.

1654

WORK. Plantation owner Anthony Johnson files and wins a lawsuit against his black servant, John Casor, who claims that Johnson has kept him in servitude seven years longer than he should have. Johnson counters that he is entitled to Casor for life. Not pressing the issue for fear of a successful countersuit by Casor, Johnson briefly relents in his claim. Shortly thereafter, Johnson claims that his white neighbor, Robert Parker, has detained Casor under the pretense that Casor is a free man. The court rules in Anthony Johnson's favor by returning Casor to him and forcing the neighbor to pay court costs. This case helps establish slavery as a legally binding institution in Virginia as well as indicates the lifestyle of some black Virginians.

1658

REVO. Africans and Indians in Hartford, Connecticut, decide to make a bid for their freedom by destroying several houses of their masters.

1660

MILI. The colonial assembly of Connecticut bars blacks from military service.

The record from a Virginian court of the discharge of Francis Pryne is an example of the discharge certificate of black servants: "I Mrs. Jane Elkonhead … have hereunto sett my hadn yt ye aforesd Pryne [a Negro] shall bee discharged from all hindrance of servitude (his child) or any [thing] yt doth belong to ye sd Pryne estate. Jane Elkonhead."

1661

SLAV. Virginia's House of Burgesses recognizes blacks servants will be maintained throughout their lives. Essentially, this is statutory recognition of slavery.

1662

SLAV. Virginia's House of Burgesses decrees that a child's social condition, free or nonfree, is determined by the mother's social status. This is opposite to English common law, which assumes that a child's status is determined by the father's status. This change in the law allows slave masters to sexually exploit enslaved African women without fear of having to acknowledge any children that might result after such contacts.

Virginia law decrees, "if any Christian shall commit Fornication with a Negro man or woman, hee or shee soe offending" should pay double the usual fine.

1663

SLAV. Maryland enacts a law that proclaims Negroes to be servants *durante vita,* meaning "for life." Essentially, this is statutory recognition of slavery.

South Carolina offers original settlers 20 acres for every African male slave and 10 acres for every African woman brought into the colony in the first year.

In Virginia, on September 13, where scarcely 1,000 enslaved blacks reside, enslaved blacks and white bondsmen in Gloucester County plan an attempted insurrection. John Berkenhead, a slave belonging to a John Smith, discloses the plot. The informer is given his freedom and 5,000 pounds of tobacco for his faithful service. So impressed are colonial officials with the magnitude of this plot, and so grateful are whites for deliverance from its dire consequence, a resolution is passed making September 13 a day of remembrance.

1664

FAMI. On September 20, Maryland bans interracial marriages.

SLAV. The colonial assembly of New York recognizes the existence of slavery in which persons have willingly sold themselves into bondage.

1669

LAW. Virginia's House of Burgesses exempts slave masters from felony charges if they kill a slave while administrating punishment.

1670

MIGR. British planters arriving in South Carolina from Barbados bring with them enslaved Africans. Consequently, Africans living in the low country of the Carolinas are never indentured servants but chattel labor.

SLAV. The Maryland legislature proclaims that the conversion of slaves to Christianity will not affect their status. Masters now feel that they can import Africans, convert them to Christianity, and thus justify the act of holding them in slavery.

1672

SLAV. King Charles II of England charters the Royal African Company. For almost half a century, this company dominates the transatlantic slave trade and thereby becomes the single most important slaver in the world.

1676

REBE. Enslaved Africans are the majority population in the tobacco-producing Chesapeake Bay colonies of Delaware, Maryland, and Virginia. A diminishing class of white indentured farm laborers and a growing number of Africans provide the basis for this social transformation.

Nathaniel Bacon, an English-born aristocrat who recently migrated to Virginia, issues a "Declaration of the People" in July that indicates a level of populist resentment against the rich and frontier hatred of Indians. His declaration indicts the colony's royal governor, William Berkley, for unjust taxes, installing favorites into positions of authority, monopolizing the beaver trade, and for not protecting the western frontier from Indian attacks. Bacon's followers are white indentured servants, former indentured servants who resent the control exercised by the tobacco-planting elite. Evidence suggests that the rank and file of both Bacon's rebel army and governor Berkley's official army are not as enthusiastic as their leaders for a confrontation. In fall, Bacon, age 29, becomes ill and dies from dysentery. The rebellion does not last long after his demise; however, an English warship with 30 guns, cruising the York River, uses intimidation to force the remaining 400 armed Englishmen and Negroes—a mixture of freemen, servants, and slaves—to surrender their arms, except for 80 Negroes and 20 Englishmen who insist on retaining their weapons. They are eventually tricked into doing so, whereupon the slaves and servants are returned to their masters. That Bacon had appealed to both poor black and white colonials indicates that there is some level of interaction by lower classes to confront the master class.

1682

SLAV. The colonial assembly of South Carolina recognizes statutory slavery.

1683

CRAF. Juan Merino is a 46-year-old free African who came to St. Augustine, Florida, from Havana, Cuba, as a convict in 1675. He works as a master charcoal burner in the royal forge, burning charcoal and making and repairing weapons. By 1683, he has opened his own forge, where he does blacksmithing for the royal armorer and private citizens. Merino is also listed as second lieutenant in the St. Augustine black militia. Ex-governor de Hita Salazar notes that, "If we had not gotten a black convict from Havana and a mulatto exiled from Havana, both

of whom know something of weapons and charcoal making, we would have found ourselves in necessity."

MILI. The St. Augustine, Florida, garrison has a black militia company. Its members come from throughout Latin America and Africa and include both free blacks and slaves. Some officers in fact are slaves. Black soldiers in colonial Florida serve in military maneuvers and often perform the critical functions of scouting and information-gathering on the frontier, sometimes alone and sometimes in groups that include Indians and Spanish soldiers. Chrispin de Tapia, a free black, is listed as a corporal in the St. Augustine black militia.

1684

SLAV. The colonial assembly of New York officially recognizes the existence of slavery as a legitimate institution.

1686

SLAV. South Carolina forbids blacks to engage in any kind of trade and prohibits them from leaving their masters' plantations without written permission.

1691

MARR. In Westmoreland County, Virginia, Hester Tate, a white indentured servant, and her husband, James Tate, an enslaved black, have four children; one is apprenticed to her master and the other three to his.

To curtail the growth of a mulatto class, particularly through intermixture and intermarriage of black men and white women, a Virginian law declares that the woman be fined or sold into service for five years, or given five years of added time, and the mulatto be bound out for 30 years. Generally, colonial assemblies fear that having free white mothers might allow persons of mixed races to sue and gain their freedom, thereby creating a legally recognized mixed-race class. Such a class, wealthy whites also fear, would blur the distinctions between dominant and subordinate races and weaken white supremacy. These colonial assemblies did little to prevent white male masters from sexually exploiting their black slaves, however, because the offspring of such liaisons take on the social status of the enslaved woman.

1693

POLI. King Charles II of Spain issues a royal proclamation on the status of runaways to Florida. Word of the Spanish proclamation spreads quickly among blacks living in the Carolinas, and the number of escapees steadily increases as they battle slave catchers, hunger, and dangerous swamps. This is, in fact, the first underground railroad, more than a century before the Civil War.

1695

FOOD. Isavel de los Rios is a free black woman who lives in St. Augustine and sells fresh baked *rosquetes* (spiral rolls), sugar syrup, and possibly other provisions from her home. In a court case against several Apalachee Indians, Isavel and Captain Chrispin de Tapia, a free black man who runs a grocery store, claim that Apalachee customers have given them counterfeit money for the purchase of rolls and other goods.

EIGHTEENTH CENTURY

1700

SLAV. The total New England population is approximately 90,000, of which 1,000 are Africans. The total enslaved African population in British North America, however, is 28,000, of which 23,000 live in the southern colonies.

The colonial assembly of Pennsylvania gives statutory recognition of slavery.

1704

EDUC. On February 28, Elias Neau, a Frenchman, opens a school for blacks in New York City. Most white slave owners immediately fear this attempt to educate slaves as a possible incitement of expectations among the growing black enslaved class in New York City.

1708

REVO. Seven whites are killed in a revolt by enslaved blacks in Newton, Long Island (New York). Colonial authorities put down the revolt and then hang two black males and an enslaved Indian. A black woman is burned alive.

1712

SLAV. In Louisiana, a shrewd French capitalist, Antoine Crozat, is awarded the exclusive right to bring blacks from Africa by ship once each year for a 15-year period. In addition, he is granted the power to establish a governing body that soon becomes known as the Superior Council. Within four years, his company fails to fulfill its commitment.

South Carolina requires all slaves when traveling to another plantation to carry a pass.

REVO. In New York, 27 Africans taking revenge for "hard usage" set fire to an outhouse. When the white men arrive to put out the fire, the rebels attack them with muskets, hatchets, and swords. They kill nine white males and wound six. Shortly thereafter, local militia units capture the rebels, six of whom kill themselves. The other 21 are brutality executed.

1713

SLAV. England secures the Asiento, the exclusive right to take enslaved Africans to British colonies in the Caribbean and to the North American mainland. In this manner, England's commerce is able to dominate the entire world with its strengthened navy and almost unlimited resources in capital investments to satisfy a growing demand for slaves in North America and throughout the world. New England ports, particularly in Boston, Salem, Providence, and New London, bustle with activity as outgoing ships are loaded with rum, fish, and dairy products and incoming ships are loaded with Africans, molasses, and sugar. Until the American Revolution, the slave trade was vital to the economic life of New England.

1715

SLAV. The colonial assembly of North Carolina gives statutory recognition of slavery and passes antimiscegenation laws preventing marriage or legal cohabitation between whites and blacks.

Two ragged, hungry, and frightened Frenchmen who arrive in New Orleans from Natchez report that Indians had massacred a French garrison. Rumors suggest that New Orleans will also be attacked. This fear is so great that Governor Perier in one of his dispatches reports: "I am extremely sorry to see, from the manifestations of such universal alarm, that there is less of French courage in Louisiana than anywhere else. Fear [so] … uncontrollable … that the insignificant nation of the Chouachas … became a subject of terror…. This induced me to have them destroyed by our Negroes, who executed this mission with as much promptitude as secrecy. This example given by our Negroes, kept in check all the small nations up the river … I have ordered that a certain number of Negroes be sent to make entrenchments around the city of New Orleans."

This law also eliminates any recognition of marriage between enslaved blacks.

WAR. Approximately 400 blacks and 600 whites join in the defeat of a group of Indians in the Yamassee War in South Carolina and northern Georgia. Once the war scare subsides, blacks are barred from military units.

1717

SLAV. The Mississippi Company receives a 25-year commercial and governmental contract in Louisiana to search for precious minerals. The company is to concern itself with the development of agriculture and is obligated to transport to the colony 6,000 white inhabitants and 3,000 Africans. With these actions, the Africans (primarily from Senegambia) become a fixed and essential element in the population of Louisiana.

1721

SLAV. Whites in Charleston, South Carolina, organize the Negro Watch to enforce a curfew on its black population. Watchmen are allowed to shoot recalcitrant Africans on sight.

1723

REVO. On April 13, the governor of Massachusetts issues a proclamation on fires that have broken out, claiming that "villainous and desperate" blacks have confessed to setting them deliberately. On April 18, the Rev. Joseph Sewell of Boston preaches a sermon on the fires, supposing them to be purposely set by blacks. On the April 19, the selectmen of Boston make a report of 19 articles, the ninth of which declares that "if more than two Indians, Negro or mulatto servants, or slaves be found in the streets, or highways, or in or about the town, idling or lurking together, unless in the service of their masters or employers, they should be punished at the House of Corrections."

1724

EMAN. The Superior Council of Louisiana adopts royal regulations pertaining to the governing of slaves known as the Black Code of Louisiana. In this body of laws, there are also provisions allowing slave owners to free slaves. This right falls to owners older than 25 years old. The permitted methods are either by last will and testament or by the execution of a deed between the slave and master. In emancipating slaves, the owner is required to secure permission from the Superior Council before such an action is declared legal. This provision is purposely made stringent to prevent private emancipations from proliferating without governmental supervision and control.

1731

POPU. On November 9, Benjamin Banneker is born free in Ellicott's Mills, Maryland. He is the son of a mixed-race mother and an African father. His grandmother, Molly Welsh, came to America as an indentured servant, worked off her indenture, and bought a farm and two slaves. She later freed the slaves and married one of them. Banneker's mother, Mary, was one of four children born to this union, and she, too, married an African native. Banneker will create the first American-made clock.

1736

MILI. Black soldiers constitute almost 19 percent of a Spanish force assembled in Mobile, Alabama, for an assault on Natchez warriors. Among this group is a separate company of black soldiers with free blacks serving as officers. This is probably the first occasion that blacks serve as officers in a colonial military unit in North America.

1738

MIGR. Fugitive slaves begin to refuge with the Creek people of Georgia and the Spanish in Florida.

More than 100 blacks reach St. Augustine, Florida. Spanish authorities establish the fort and community of Gracia Real de Santa Teresa de Mose about two miles north of the town. The captain of the fort is Francisco Menendez, who was first appointed captain of the St. Augustine slave militia in 1726. Like the other Mose officers, Menendez is an escaped slave. The recently freed soldiers move to the frontier with their families, where they build Fort Mose and a small adjacent town. The fort is built about two miles north of St. Augustine, across marsh and open land. There are 38 households of men, women, and children at Mose.

1739

REVO. The Stono rebellion begins when a group 20 enslaved blacks who recently arrived from Angola strike a violent but abortive blow for liberation at Stono Bridge, South Carolina, a few miles outside of Charleston. Under the leadership of an African named Jemmy or Tommy, they brake into a warehouse, stealing guns and ammunition. Killing the warehousemen, the Angolans leave the men's severed heads on the building steps and flee toward Florida. Other slaves join the Angolans until their numbers reach about 100. Sacking white plantations and killing approximately 30 more whites, they stop to celebrate their victories and beat drums to attract other slaves to the revolt. Soon, planters aided by Indians attack the rebels, killing 44 of them and routing the rest, including their leaders, who remain at large for up

to 30 years. The rebellion results in the deaths of more than 60 people. Fewer than 25 whites' lives are taken, and property damage is localized, but the episode represents a new dimension in overt African resistance to enslavement.

1740

POPU. The Carolina low country that becomes a major producer of rice has 40,000 slaves, who constitute 90 percent of the population in the region around Charleston.

REVO. Charleston, South Carolina, authorities the arrest of 150 slaves and hangs 10 each day to quell the spirit of rebellion. The governor enacts the Negro Act, a series of restrictions on blacks in South Carolina. One of the act's more brutal provisions states that if a slave is condemned to death, he is to be executed in such manner and in such time and place as should be a means of deterring others from committing the same offense.

1741

REVO. New York is a thriving town not more than one mile long and a half-mile wide, with a population of 12,000. One-sixth of these are of African heritage or recently imported from Africa. A few are free, but the vast majority are enslaved. Far fewer than half of the whites own slaves, who are distributed in lots that average ten slaves to each family. In March and April, a series of suspicious fires and reports of impending insurrection by enslaved Africans in New York City create an atmosphere of white racial hysteria that results in the deaths of 30 blacks and 4 whites.

1746

LIT. Lucy Terry Prince, of African birth, is brought to British colonial North America, sold into slavery, learns to read and write, and eventually becomes a trailblazer in the African American tradition. Her poem "Bars Fight, August 28, 1746" chronicles an Indian attack against white colonists at Deerfield, Massachusetts. The poem also examines the tensions between whites and the indigenous population in colonial America and indicates the poet's awareness and concern about the existing political climate.

POPU. St. Augustine, Florida, has a population of 1,500, including about 400 black people.

Absalom Jones, who will become a major religious leader, is born on November 6.

1750

POPU. The enslaved population of British North America reaches approximately 236,000.

REVO. On September 30, Crispus Attucks, who will become instrumental in the anticolonial struggle against England 20 years later, escapes from his slaveholder in Framingham, Massachusetts.

SLAV. The colonial assembly of Georgia recognizes statutory slavery.

1753

RELI. On July 18, Lemuel Haynes, the first black minister to serve a white congregation, is born.

1758

LIT. On April 17, Frances Williams publishes a collection of Latin poems.

1759

EMIG. On January 17, Paul Cuffe, who will become an emigration leader, is born near Dartmouth, Massachusetts.

1760

LIT. Jupiter Hammon, a poet, is born a slave in British North America, living in New York. He utilizes his reading and writing abilities as a clerk in the store owned by the Lloyd family, his owners. He moves to Connecticut with his owners during the American Revolution and returns to Long Island with the family after the war. His poem "An Evening Thought: Salvation by Christ with Penitential Cries" stresses the role of religion in one's life while tangentially attacking the institution of slavery. It is published on December 25.

RELI. Richard Allen, future bishop of the African Methodist Episcopal Church, is born in slavery in Philadelphia.

SCIE. On May 1, physician James Durham is born in Philadelphia, Pennsylvania. Born enslaved, Durham learns the fundamentals of reading and writing. Though he is owned by a number of doctors, he continues to learn about the profession of medicine. Eventually, a Scottish physician in New Orleans buys Durham and then hires him out in 1783 to perform medical services. Once manumitted, he returns to Philadelphia, where he is lauded by prominent local doctors when he saves the lives of more yellow-fever victims than most doctors in colonial Philadelphia. Returning to New Orleans a free man, he has a flourishing practice until 1801, when the city restricts his practice because he is "unlicensed and untrained."

WAR. Deborah Sampson Gannett is born on December 17, in Plymouth, Virginia. Gannett will later disguise herself as a man to fight in the American Revolution on the side of the rebels.

1763

MIGR. Fort Mose, and its African community of Gracia Real de Santa Teresa de Mose in Florida, is abandoned at the conclusion of the French and Indian War, the American phase of the Seven Years' War. The resulting Treaty of Paris gives Florida to England and Cuba to Spain. All of the inhabitants of the former Spanish colony leave their homes and sail to Cuba, including the people of Mose and the 86 Indians who live in St. Augustine. Some of the residents of Mose settle in the Matanzas province. Once again, they are forced to start a new life in an unfamiliar land.

1766

WORK. James Forten Sr. is born on September 2 in Philadelphia. As a youth, Forten participates in the American Revolution as a sailor on an American ship, the *Royal Louis*. He is eventually captured and held prisoner by the British on a prisoner-of-war ship in New York City. Released during a prisoner exchange, he returns home to Philadelphia to establish the first major black-owned sail-making business. Forten also becomes an organizer of the American Anti-Slavery Society and a strong supporter of woman suffrage.

1767

MUS. "Yankee Doodle" is a hit song in *The Disappointment; or The Force of Incredulity,* by Andrew

Barton, the first ballad opera published in America. It is sung by the opera's leading character, a free black called Racoon. Played by a white actor in blackface, Racoon has a white mistress and equal status with comic Irish and Scottish characters. It is believed that Brazillai Lew is the real ragtag fifer in Archibald Willard's iconic revolutionary painting *The Spirit of '76*. Brazillai Lew plays in New York City at George Washington's first inauguration. His Bunker Hill powder horn can be found in Chicago's DuSable Museum of African American History.

1768

CIVI. In September, British troops are dispatched to Boston to awe the population. Shortly after their arrival, these troops fight an intense battle with a large group of black and white citizens on the common. The Boston *Journal of the Times* reports the fight, noting, "to behold Britons scourged by Negro drummers was a new and very disagreeable spectacle."

1770

EDUC. On June 28, Quakers open a school for blacks in Philadelphia, Pennsylvania. This occurs as a result of Quaker reformer Anthony Benezet's suggestion that the Philadelphia Society of Friends (Quakers) establish a coeducational Negro School. The institution is open to enslaved and free blacks of all ages, offering them instruction in reading, writing, arithmetic, and Christian doctrine. James Bringhurst, a master carpenter and one of the school's trustees, notes that the students are highly intelligent and possess tenacity.

REBE. On March 2, three British soldiers in Boston, Massachusetts, become involved in a fight with rope makers. The soldiers are driven off but return with reinforcements, including a tall black man who sides with the redcoats. This infuriates a white Bostonian, who shouts, "You black rascal, what have you to do with white people's quarrels?" The black man responds, "I suppose I may look on." He looks on and throws a number of punches. Despite his help, the soldiers are forced to give ground. Beaten and frustrated, they leave, shouting curses and yelling threats.

On March 5, British redcoats armed with cudgels and tongs emerge from the Murray's Barracks near the town's common. They are almost immediately faced with a crowd composed largely "of saucy boys, Negroes and mulattoes, Irish Teagues and outlandish Jack Tars," who begin insulting the British soldiers. In the center of this crowd stands an imposing 47-year-old figure, Crispus Attucks, who is a Massachusetts native, an escapee from slavery, and sailor who has sailed the seas. In the ensuing battle, his voice rises, telling other Bostonians, "Don't be afraid," "They dare not fire," and "Fire! Fire and be damned!" These challenges are followed by sticks and bricks aimed at the soldiers. Private Hugh Montgomery is hit with a stick, whereupon he lifts his musket, aims, and fires into the crowd, killing Crispus Attucks. Other British soldiers then fire into the crowd, and seven more patriots are shot. Attucks will be revered as the first "American patriot" to give his life in the cause for freedom and independence from England.

SCIE. Benjamin Banneker constructs his own clock. Banneker was born free in Maryland in 1731 and had access to his white neighbors' library, where he studied Latin and Greek and acquired a working knowledge of German and French. He will gain international fame as a mathematician and astronomer.

1773

LIT. Phillis Wheatley publishes her first collection of writings entitled *Poems on Various Subjects, Religious and Moral*. Printed in England, her collection introduces an ever-expanding international audience to her work. In this writing, she focuses on the contrast, as a black woman in colonial America, between slavery and freedom. In one particular poem, she explores the meaning of Africa to the African in America and considers the importance of religion in this regard. Captured, enslaved, and then transported to British North America, she is eventually purchased in 1761 by John and Susanna Wheatley, who provide her with the opportunity to study Latin, astronomy, history, geography, the Bible, and poets John Milton and Alexander Pope. Wheatley's book is the second publication by a woman in the American colonies.

Phillis Wheatley seated at desk with pen and paper, 1773. Courtesy of Library of Congress.

POLI. On April 20, 1773, a committee of enslaved Africans in Boston submits a petition to the delegate to the Massachusetts General Court from the town of Thompson. The petition underscores the irony of white Americans who contend that England desires to enslave them when, in fact, Africans are the only group that is enslaved by law and custom within the nation. Recognizing the potentiality for black freedom and countervailing entrenched racial prejudice among whites, the authors of the petition announce that if they gain their freedom they will emigrate from America to Africa.

RELI. The first known black church is founded in Silver Bluff, South Carolina. The church grows out of regular worship services held as early as the 1750s. Conceived first as a nondenominational church that services both blacks and whites, it formally organizes as the Silver Bluff Baptist Church with Rev. Walt Palmer as its first preacher.

1774

SLAV. Some delegates in the Continental Congress view the institution of slavery as inconsistent with its fight with England and conclude that current hostilities exist because of England's insistence on the continuation of slavery. This perspective will facilitate the Continental Congress to pass an agreement not to import enslaved Africans after December 1, 1775. This agreement, particularly among southern delegates, is not interpreted as an antislavery proposition but as only a temporary measure against England.

The Colonial Assembly of Massachusetts bans the importation of Africans as slaves, thereby becoming the first American colony to enact such a policy.

1775

ASSO. On March 6, the British Army Lodge No. 441 of Freemasons attached to a regiment under General Gage at Fort Independence, Massachusetts, initiates 15 blacks, including Prince Hall, a young man who had come from Barbados 10 years earlier. On July 3, African Lodge No. 1 is organized in Boston by a group of black Masons.

LIT. Phillis Wheatley publishes her poem to George Washington entitled "To His Excellency General Washington."

MILI. On May 10, black patriots participate in the first military action by American rebel forces in the capture of Fort Ticonderoga by Ethan Allen and the Green Mountain Boys.

On July 10, Horatio Gates, George Washington's adjutant general, issues an order excluding blacks from the Colonial army.

In her poem "To His Excellency General Washington," Phillis Wheatley cautions, "Proceed, great chief, with virtue on thy side, thy ev'ry action let the goddess guide. A crown, a mansion, and a throne that shine, With gold unfading, WASHINGTON! be thine."

On October 8, the Council of General Officers in the American Continental army decides to prohibit the enlistment of enslaved and free blacks.

On October 23, the Continental Congress passes a resolution effectively barring all blacks from the army.

After receiving encouragement from black veterans and alarmed about Lord Dunmore's November proclamation offering to liberate slaves who join the British forces, on December 31, George Washington rescinds his earlier ban on blacks in the Continental army and signs an order that allows the reenlistments of those free blacks with "prior military experience."

REBE. In April, an irregular militia force known as minutemen begin to stockpile arms in the villages surrounding Boston. When Paul Revere rides through the countryside, he alerts both black and white patriots. Black minutemen, most notably Lemuel Haynes, Peter Salem, and Pomp Blackman, gather with white patriots at Lexington and the bridge at Concord to face the British. Peter Salem, a slave, had marched in from the nearby town of Framingham as a private in the company of Capt. Simon Edgel. Armed, like other patriots, with a flintlock musket, Salem fires and loads through the brief fight until British Major Pitcairn calls for a retreat, and the Redcoats march back to Boston.

In June, British soldiers under the command of Major Pitcairn storm up Breed's Hill (often erroneously called Bunker Hill). They are repulsed in their initial attacks by determined patriots, one of whom is Peter Salem, who "took aim at major Pitcairn as he was rallying the British troops, and shot him thro the head." The major falls dead just as he shouts to his men, "The day is ours." Soon afterward, white patriot soldiers from a number of New England colonies raise reward money for Peter Salem for his bravery, and the black hero is presented to General Washington as the man who killed Pitcairn. After the war, Salem settles in Leicester, Massachusetts, where he barely earns a living weaving cane seats for chairs. He dies in the poorhouse in Framingham in 1816. Almost 70 years later, citizens of the town erect a monument to Peter Salem's memory. Salem Poor, another black fighter at Breed's Hill, is also honored for his heroics in that battle.

At Breed's Hill (Bunker Hill), scores of black patriots, such as soldier-fifer Brazillai Lew, a veteran of Ticonderoga, keep American patriots' morale high by playing "There's Nothing Makes the British Run Like Yankee Doodle Dandy." On July 9, George Washington bans black enlistment in the Continental army.

On November 7, Lord John Murray Dunmore, the last and deposed royal governor of Virginia, issues a proclamation offering to liberate slaves who join "His Majesty's Troops … for the more speedily reducing this colony [British North America] to a proper sense of their duty to His Majesty's crown and dignity." Throughout the war, other British and loyalist commanders follow his example, recruiting thousands of black men who work and sometimes fight in exchange for their freedom. In all, more blacks become active loyalists than patriots during the war. For every free black who supports the American patriots, four are loyalists in support of Great Britain.

SLAV. On April 14, the Pennsylvania Quakers organize the first abolitionist society in the American colonies.

1776

LAW. On January 16, the Continental Congress supports Washington's order to enlist free blacks.

Thomas Jefferson's second draft of the Declaration of Independence is adopted on July 4. The antislavery passage in the first draft is rejected by southern planters and northern mercantilists who fear its future economic and political implications.

Peter Salem is commended by 14 officers who say he "behaved like an experienced officer, as well as an excellent soldier. To set forth particulars of his conduct would be tedious…. In the person of this said Negro centers a brave and gallant soldier."

> In response to Dunmore's proclamation, George Washington is quoted as saying, "If that man, Dunmore is not crushed before the spring he will become the most dangerous man in America. His strength will increase like a snowball running down hill. Success will depend on which side can arm the Negro faster."

Consequently, the following paragraph was eliminated:

> He [England's King George] has waged cruel war against human nature itself, violating its most sacred rights of life and liberty in the persons of a distant people who never offended him, captivating and carrying them into slavery in another hemisphere, or to incur miserable death in their transportation thither. This piratical warfare, the opprobrium of *infidel* powers, is the warfare of the Christian king of Great Britain. Determined to keep open a market where MEN should be bought and sold, he has prostituted his negative [veto] for suppressing every legislative attempt to prohibit or to restrain this execrable commerce; and that this assemblage of horrors might want no fact or distinguished die, he is now exciting these very people to rise in arms among us, and to purchase that liberty of which he deprived them, by murdering the people upon whom *he* also obtruded them; thus paying off former crimes committed against the *liberties* of one people, with crimes which he urges them to commit against the *lives* of another.

MILI. On the night of December 24–25, black soldiers Prince Whipple and Oliver Cromwell accompany George Washington in the crossing of the Delaware River and participate in the surprise attack on the Hessian mercenary troops in the service of the British army at Trenton, New Jersey.

1777

RELI. In an era of alleged egalitarianism among white Baptists, Methodists, and Episcopalians, separate but not independent black churches appear in some areas of the South. Usually headed by black pastors, they are clearly subordinate to white church hierarchies and policies. The first of these churches emerge in Georgia, South Carolina, and Virginia. In December, what is now the oldest continuing-service black church, the First African Baptist Church, is established in Savannah, Georgia. Its first pastor, George Leile, born enslaved in Virginia, was brought as a child to Georgia by speculators and sold to a Henry Sharpe, a deacon in a Baptist church in Kiokee, Burke County. Feeling that he was called to become a preacher, Leile began so-called silent preaching but was hesitant about going to the local white church. His owner, Sharpe, encouraged his participation in the church and eventually had him baptized. The church granted him a license, and Deacon Sharpe gave him permission to travel from plantation to plantation up and down the Savannah River by way of a bateau, a light, flat-bottom boat, preaching the Christian Gospel to the slaves. He was ordained on May 20, 1775.

SLAV. On July 2, Vermont becomes the first American colony to abolish slavery.

WAR. Gen. George Washington extends the enlistment terms of all free blacks by one year in order to help fill the depleted ranks of the Continental army. Because the states consistently fail to meet their quotas of manpower for the army, the Continental Congress authorizes the enlistment of all blacks, free and slave.

During and after the winter at Valley Forge, Pennsylvania, enslaved and free blacks are welcomed into the Continental army. Most of the estimated 5,000 black soldiers fight in integrated units. Among the blacks who survive Valley Forge are Salem Poor, veteran of Bunker (Breed's) Hill; Timothy Prince, veteran of the Battle of Long Island; Prince Whipple and Oliver Cromwell, who crossed the Delaware River with George Washington and participated in the attack on Trenton, New Jersey; and Nero Hawley.

1778

WAR. The First Rhode Island regiment, an elite all-black unit, musters into service. It consists of 197 black enlisted men, free and slave, and is commanded by white officers. Baron von Closen describes the regiment as "the most neatly dressed, the best under arms, and the most precise in its maneuvers." In February, the Rhode Island legislature announces that any slave volunteering for the new battalion would be "free," with the same wages and bounties as regular soldiers. Commanded by Col. Christopher Greene, one of George Washington's best young officers, the Rhode Island regiment receives its baptism of fire at the battle of Rhode Island (Newport) on August 29, successfully defeating three assaults by veteran Hessian troops. Rhode Island is the only battleground during the American Revolution where blacks are conspicuous as a distinct racial group.

1779

HOUS. Jean Baptiste Pointe DuSable, the free-born son of a French mariner and an African slave born in St. Marc, Saint Domingue (now Haiti), builds the first permanent home on the north bank of the Chicago River, approximately where the Tribune Building stands today. His house is a well-constructed building consisting of five rooms and all of the modern conveniences of the day. DuSable then establishes a prosperous trading post and rapidly becomes known as far away as Wisconsin and Detroit. The trading post consists of a mill, bakery, dairy, smokehouse, workshop, poultry house, horse stable, barn, and several other smaller buildings. This post becomes the main supply station for white trappers, traders, woodsmen, and the indigenous population. He also maintains a large supply of carpentry tools, which indicates he might also have hired a number of workers for field work and building construction. His post also becomes the main site for merchant trading, from which DuSable sends wheat, breads, meats, and furs to other trading posts in Detroit and Canada. DuSable becomes a man of wealth in a relatively short period of time.

WAR. On July 15, Pompey Lamb, a local slave in Stony Point, New York, guided General Anthony Wayne and his army in a night attack against a British strong point on the Hudson river.

1780

EDUC. The African Union Society of Newport, Rhode Island, is formed as the first self-help organization for Africans in North America. These newly freed men retain their African pride and tradition by blending English and African names for themselves and their children. The records of the organization list men with names such as Occramar, Nubia, Cuffe, Yama, and Cudjo.

RELI. Lemuel Haynes, who distinguished himself at the battle at Fort Ticonderoga, begins to preach at a Congregational church in Connecticut. Haynes is the first person of African heritage to become the minister of a predominately white congregation.

1781

LAW. An enslaved woman known as Mum Bett receives an arm wound when she attempts to protect her sister from her owner's wife, who attacks them with a hot kitchen shovel. Outraged by this attack, Bett leaves the owner's house and refuses to return. Instead, she engages the legal assistance of Theodore Sedgwick Sr., who submits a legal suit for her freedom on the basis of Massachusetts's new bill of rights. The jury decides in her favor and demands that the slave owner, Col. John Ashley, pay Bett 30 shillings in damages. At this point, Mum Bett changes her name legally to Elizabeth Freemen. Shortly thereafter, the Massachusetts Supreme Court declares slavery unconstitutional throughout the state.

MIGR. On September 4, 44 settlers, including 26 who are descendants of Africans, establish the city of Los Angeles.

1783

LAW. Quok Walker leaves his owner and begins living as a free person. In response, his owner seeks a court order to force Walker's return. This case leads to the Massachusetts Supreme Court's ruling that, "slavery is as effectively abolished as it can be by the granting of rights and privileges wholly incompatible and repugnant to its existence." This decision encourages other Massachusetts slaves to sue for their freedom or leave their masters and, in effect, abolishes slavery in that state.

MIGR. From April through November, 29,000 loyalist blacks who joined, supported, or sympathized with the British cause during the American Revolution leave the new United States for Nova Scotia, Canada. The great majority of these emigrants sailed from April through November and arrived in Nova Scotia at Port Roseway, Annapolis Royal, and Port Mouton. In August alone, 5,339 persons apply at the adjutant general's office for passage. Among the emigrating blacks are many who were born in Africa and who reached America in the holds of ships, whereas others are only a generation removed from such an experience.

MILI. On June 5, Oliver Cromwell, a 24-year-old black farmer from New Jersey and a soldier in the American Revolution, receives an honorable discharge signed by George Washington, with the notation that he earned "the Badge of Merit for six years' faithful service." Having crossed the Delaware River with Washington in a successful surprise attack on British forces in Trenton, New Jersey, he sees combat in most of the major battles of the war.

SCIE. James Derham purchases his freedom from his physician owner. He eventually opens his own practice in New Orleans.

1785

ABOL. On September 28, David Walker is born in Wilmington, North Carolina.

1787

ASSO. On April 12, Richard Allen and Absalom Jones organize the Philadelphia Free African Society.

On May 6, Prince Hall's application to the Grand Lodge of England to establish a chapter of black Masons is accepted. Hall becomes the master of African Lodge No. 459 in Boston, Massachusetts.

EDUC. On October 17, Boston blacks, organized and led by Prince Hall, petition the legislature for equal school facilities.

On November 1, the African Free School opens as the first free school in New York City. Its stated purpose is to give mutual aid to members in distress. Soon after, blacks organize themselves into beneficial, missionary, temperance, tract, educational, welfare, and other reform societies.

LAW. On September 17, the Constitution of the United States of America is adopted, and its pro-slavery aspects are underscored by a number of articles and sections. Article I, Section 2 indicates that, when counting a state's population to determine taxation, people "bound to Service for a Term of Years" will be counted as three-fifths of a person. Delegates to the Constitutional Convention omit the words *slave, slavery,* and *Africans* from the document. Included are clauses that, shrewdly protect the enslavement of "persons." In this regard, Article I, Section 9 of the Constitution states that "the Migration or Importation of such Persons as any of the States now existing shall think proper to admit" will not be banned by Congress until 1808. In assuring that runaway slaves will be viewed as escaped property or fugitives, the delegates include Article IV, Section 2, proclaiming that, "No person held to Service or Labour in one State, under the Laws thereof," can gain freedom by escaping into a free state.

On July 13, the Northwest Ordinance is enacted. Migrants settling in areas across the Appalachian Mountains and lands east of the Mississippi River make slavery a contested issue. In 1784, Thomas Jefferson proposed that the region be divided into separate territories and prepared for statehood. He also proposed that after 1800 slavery be banned from the entire region as well as from Spanish Florida northward to British Canada. His proposals failed to pass Congress by one vote. Congress agreed to adopt what it calls the Northwest Ordinance, which provides for the orderly sale of land, support for public education, territorial government, the eventual formation of new states, and the immediate banning of slavery. The ordinance does not apply, however, to lands south of the Ohio River that are open to slavery. By preventing slaveholders from legally transporting their slaves northward across the Ohio River, slavery is technically banned from part of the United States. This becomes the first legal North-South separation of the country based on slavery. The first governor of the territory, however, forces those blacks who were enslaved before the adoption of the Northwest Ordinance to remain so. Consequently, in new territories north of the Ohio River, such as Illinois and Indiana, blacks remain in involuntary servitude well into the nineteenth century.

1789

SCIE. Benjamin Banneker correctly predicts the solar eclipse.

Freed slave Olaudah Equiano publishes his autobiography, *The Interesting Narrative of the Life of Olaudah Equiano, or Gustavus Vasa*. Born in eastern Nigeria in 1745, Equiano spends his early life as a slave and endures a forced conversion to a Euro-Christian-Calvinistic lifestyle. The autobiography chronicles his experiences during the French and Indian War and the battle at Quebec in 1759, his manumission in 1766, his involvement in England's antislavery movement, and his major role in the establishment of Sierra Leone in West Africa as a new home for emancipated British slaves.

1790

EDUC. Charleston, South Carolina's, Brown Fellowship Society is established at the suggestion of the rector of the Protestant Episcopal St. Philips's Church. In addition to its benevolence, one of the purposes of this society is to maintain schools for "Negro children," particularly those of its members.

LAW. United States federal law limits the granting of naturalized citizenship to "any alien, being a white person."

POPU. The first federal census indicates that there are nearly four million inhabitants in the United States of America. Among these are more than 750,000 people of African heritage, of whom 697,624 are counted as slaves and 59,557 are listed as free. The vast majority of these inhabitants of African heritage—some 89 percent—live in the southern Atlantic states, where the plantation system makes the largest demand for slave labor. Slavery as an institution is dying rapidly in New England, and states such as Maine, Vermont, and Massachusetts report no enslaved population; Connecticut's 2,648 enslaved blacks represent the bulk of New England's slave population.

1791

ASSO. Prince Hall is refused a full charter by American Mason's to form an African Mason lodge. Hall then requests and receives approval from British Masons, thereby creating a unique situation whereby under an English charter he becomes the provincial grand master of North America. He quickly authorizes the establishment of black lodges in cities such as Philadelphia, Boston, and Providence.

SCIE. On August 19, Benjamin Banneker publishes his first edition of 10 annual almanacs based upon his observations and mathematical calculations.

1792

ARTS. Frank (Francis) Johnson, composer and bandleader, is born in Philadelphia, Pennsylvania.

ASSO. A black female mutual aid society, the Philadelphia Female Benevolent Society of St. Thomas, assumes the welfare functions of the city's Free African Society. Though ostensibly

---

On March 12, the Georgetown *Weekly Ledger* notes that the commission that made the original survey of Washington, DC, consisted of Benjamin Banneker, "an Ethiopian whose abilities as surveyor and astronomer already prove that Mr. [Thomas] Jefferson's concluding that that race of men were void of mental endowment was without foundation." Banneker's participation on the commission makes him the first black civilian employee of the United States government.

secular, these organizations foster notions of Christian moral character. Similarly, these societies maintain middle-class standards, self-improvement, a refrain from fornication, adultery, drunkenness, and other "disreputable behavior."

LAW. On February 12, the U.S. Congress passes the first Fugitive Slave Law that designates escaped slaves as fugitives and allows their extradition back to their owners. This law is derived from Article IV, Section 2 of the U.S. Constitution.

MIGR. A colony of 1,200 formerly enslaved blacks who supported England during the American Revolution and later relocated to Nova Scotia are resettled, upon their request, in Freetown, Sierra Leone.

RELI. Richard Allen, Absalom Jones, and other blacks are prohibited from praying in the white-dominated St. George's Church in Philadelphia, Pennsylvania. Recalling the incident, Allen indicates that the group of blacks left the church, rented a storeroom, and held their own services.

On October 11, Antoine Blanc founds the first black Catholic order of nuns.

The Free African Society takes the lead in a campaign to raise funds for a new church for the black community. Though interrupted by a yellow fever epidemic in the city, the campaign succeeds, and Richard Allen is authorized to purchase a lot at the corner of Lombardi and Sixth Streets. After Allen reaches an agreement with the seller of the lot, the committee decides to buy a different lot on Fifth Street, leaving Allen personally responsible for the first lot, which eventually becomes the site for Mother Bethel Church.

SCIE. The first edition of Benjamin Banneker's annual almanac is published. Often compared with Benjamin Franklin's *Poor Richard's Almanac,* Banneker's publication discusses aspects of astronomy, mathematics, and other scientific subjects.

1794

INVE. On March 13, Eli Whitney receives a patent for the cotton gin. The device easily and efficiently removes seeds from the cotton plant, thereby making cotton easier to process into a number of products. This technological innovation has a direct impact on the production, distribution, and national and international demand for cotton products as well as on increased demands for additional enslaved laborers by southern planters. For example, as a direct result of the cotton gin, England's demand for American cotton rises from 3,000 to 178,000 bales between 1790 and 1810.

RELI. On May 5, Richard Allen and 11 other black Methodists make final plans for a separate house of worship. They purchase a frame structure, a former blacksmith shop, and move it to the lot Allen had purchased at Sixth and Lombardi Streets in Philadelphia. Hired carpenters make the building suitable for church meetings, and by July, Allen is satisfied when Bishop Asbury dedicates Bethel African Church.

Differences as to whether the new black Church in Philadelphia will be Episcopalian or Methodist split the religious black community. Richard Allen, a committed Methodist, refuses to join the new St. Thomas Episcopal Church. On August 12, the African Church in Philadelphia joins the Protestant Episcopal Church of America. Absalom Jones, despite his own Methodist leanings, accepts the pastorate and is eventually ordained the first black Episcopal priest in the United States.

1796

ASSO. Forty-four blacks in Boston, Massachusetts, organize the African Society. Its declared objectives are to be benevolent and to accept "no one into the society who shall commit any injustice or outrage against the laws of their country." Having earlier sought full integration into the social, political, and economic arenas of American society, they conclude that a better strategy is to establish their own institutions.

Richard Allen's wife, Sarah, forms the Benevolent Daughters mutual aid society.

EDUC. Prince Hall, failing to convince Boston's city council to provide schools for black students, establishes a school in his own home and that of his son, Primus.

RELI. On August 6, Absalom Jones is ordained a deacon in the Protestant Episcopal Church in Philadelphia.

1797

ASSO. Prince Hall helps establish and organize the African Grand Lodge of North America in Philadelphia, Boston, and Providence, thereby becoming a pioneer in the development of black interstate organizations. These lodges are known colloquially as the Prince Hall Masons.

On June 17, Prince Hall publishes his last public speech presented before the Boston African Lodge. In this speech, he condemns assaults by white mobs upon black people and notes the importance of events occurring in Haiti that could be instructive for American blacks.

Paul Cuffe utilizes his own money to establish a school for African and Indian children at New Bedford, Massachusetts. He travels throughout the northeastern states urging other blacks to start self-help organizations and mutual benefit societies.

BUSI. James Forten, who served at the age of 15 in the American Revolution as a powder boy for a canon crew on the American privateer *Royal Louis,* is reputed to be the wealthiest free black in the new United States after amassing a fortune of about $100,000—a large sum at the time.

CIVI. Sojourner Truth, whose original name is Isabella, is born a slave in the Dutch-speaking region of Hurley, New York.

NINETEENTH CENTURY

1800

MANU. An enslaved African carpenter named Denmark Vesey wins a prize of $1,500 in the Charleston, South Carolina, East-Bay Street Lottery, which he uses to purchase his freedom from his master for $600, much less than his market value.

MIGR. On May 7, the so-called Father of Chicago, Jean Baptiste Pointe DuSable, sells his property for a mere $1,200 and leaves his home in Chicago.

POLI. On May 10, the man who will become the first black governor of a state (Louisiana), Pinckney Benton Stewart Pinchback, is born.

POPU. The African population in the United States reaches 1,002,037, nearly 18.9 percent of the total population.

RELI. Zion African Methodist Episcopal Church is dedicated on September 7 in New York City.

REVO. On May 9, the antislavery leader and insurgent John Brown is born in Torrington, Connecticut.

On August 30, Gabriel Prosser and an unknown number of enslaved and free blacks and sympathetic whites conspire to rebel against the institution of slavery. Taught to read by the wife of his owner, Gabriel believed that God, speaking to him through the Bible, had told him to free his people, and he imitated the Biblical character Samson by refusing to cut his hair. The 24-year-old Gabriel oversaw the making of weapons and bullets and eventually recruited more than a thousand slaves from at least three counties around Richmond, Virginia. On August 20, he assembles his rebels near a brook on his owner's property and prepares to march six miles to Richmond, but the plan is thwarted by both nature and treachery. As the rebels gather, a storm washes out the roads and bridges to Richmond, and the plot is then revealed by two slaves to their owner, Mosby Sheppard of Richmond, who informs the governor of Virginia, James Monroe, of the impending attack. Later, Monroe states in a message to the State Assembly that the revolt probably included slaves from Richmond and its neighborhood as well as the adjacent counties of Hanover, Caroline, Louisa, Chesterfield, and the neighborhood of Point of Fork. According to Gabriel's testimony, he estimates that some 10,000 blacks were directly involved in the conspiracy. All the whites were to be killed except the French, the Quakers, and the Methodists, who were to be spared because they were believers in liberty. The poor white men who held no slaves were also to be spared because they were expected to join the revolt. The attack was expected to spread to Petersburg with the assistance of the Catawba Indians. If these plans could not be implemented, they were to retreat to the Virginia mountains and commence guerrilla attacks against plantations while constructing a new social-political order. Once the plot is revealed, Gabriel flees and is not captured until September 24 as he attempts to escape in the schooner *Mary*. Again, his whereabouts are revealed by two unsympathetic free black sailors. After his conviction, he is executed on October 7 with 15 other rebels. A total of 41 blacks are executed.

On October 2, Nathaniel Turner, leader of a major slave uprising 31 years later, is born in Southampton County, Virginia.

Denmark Vesey purchases his freedom in Charleston, South Carolina. A carpenter by trade who earns $1.50 per day, Vesey goes on to organize slaves intent on rebellion 22 years later.

SLAV. On November 29, the state of Ohio outlaws slavery.

1803

EXPO. An enslaved African named York travels with Meriwether Lewis and William Clark in their exploration of the newly acquired Louisiana Territory purchased from France. Described as a large powerful man he is valued on the expedition due to his hunting and fishing skills. Upon completion of the expedition, Clark emancipates York, and legend has him returning to the western interior, where he becomes a chief of a native ethnic group.

SLAV. South Carolina reopens its ports to the African slave trade, utilizing Latin America and the West Indies to satisfy increased labor demands by southern plantation owners and both domestic and foreign mercantilists specializing in rice and cotton.

1804

LAW. On January 5, the Ohio legislature passes the first of a succession of northern black laws that restrict the rights and movements of free blacks in the North. Most northern states pass similar black laws. The constitutions of three states—Illinois, Indiana, and Oregon—bar black settlers.

1806

INVE. On March 17, inventor Norbert Rillieux is born.

1807

ARTS. Ira Frederick Aldridge, celebrated Shakespearean actor, is born on July 24 in New York City. His parents are co-called free Negroes and, though poor, are able to see that Ira receives an education at the New York African Free School. Aldridge studies briefly at the University of Glasgow in Scotland but returns to enter the New York amateur theater. He makes his professional debut as the first black actor at the Royal Coburg Theatre in London on October 10, 1825, playing the role of Prince Oroonoko of Africa, who is sold into slavery and then becomes a rebel, in the play *The Revolt of Surinam; or A Slave's Revenge*. Aldridge tours the British Isles for 27 years, starring in about 60 roles in melodrama, romantic drama, operetta, comedy, and Shakespearean works. He becomes the first actor to be knighted when Duke Bernhard of Saxe-Meiningen bestows on him the Royal Ernestinischen House Order in 1858. He is best known for his portrayal of Shakespearean characters: "the black Othello, the white Macbeth, the hurt and maddened old king Lear, the splenetic villain, Richard III, his sympathetic portrayal of vilified Jewish patriarch, Shylock—and Mungo the West Indian house slave, in [the] operetta *The Padlock* by Bickerstaffe, singing, dancing, playing guitar, mixing protest with comedy of the oppressed." After his death in 1867, his grave in Lodz, Poland, is a national shrine cared for by the Polish Artists of both Film and Theatre. His name is inscribed with other Shakespearean celebrities at the Shakespeare Memorial Theatre at Stratford-upon-Avon, England.

EDUC. The first black school in Washington, DC, is opened by three former slaves.

SLAV. On March 2, Congress, following the mandate of the U.S. Constitution, bans the importation of slaves into the United States or its territories after January 1, 1808.

1808

SLAV. Federal law supported by the Constitution prohibits the legal importation of enslaved Africans. An estimated 250,000, however, are imported illegally until the beginning of the Civil War in 1861.

1809

RELI. On July 5, a group of 18 blacks under the leadership of Rev. Thomas Paul establishes the Abyssinian Baptist Church in New York City.

1810

BUSI. The American Insurance Company of Philadelphia, Pennsylvania, is established as the first insurance company managed by blacks.

On March 26, explorer and businessman William A. Leidesdorff is born in St. Croix to a Danish father and an African mother. He becomes a merchant captain first in New York and then in New Orleans, where he becomes a wealthy cotton broker. In 1838, he makes additional contacts with merchants who trade in the Hawaiian Islands. He eventually sails to the islands and establishes his own trade mission between Hawaii and Yerba Buena in California. From Hawaii come sugar and from Yerba Buena, animal hides. In 1841, Leidesdorff builds San Francisco's City Hotel and its first shipping warehouse. By befriending Emanuel Victoria, the so-called black governor of Alta California, Leidesdorff becomes a Mexican citizen. Victoria grants Leidesdorff Rancho Rio de Americanos on the site of Folsom, California. Among the several business ventures he founded, he has the distinction of launching the first steamboat to sail on San Francisco Bay on November 15, 1847. His steamer *Stka* makes the trip from San Francisco to Santa Clara and then to Sonoma.

POPU. The United States population is 7,239,881, of which 1,377,808 (19%) are people of African heritage.

SPOR. In December, Tom Molineaux, former slave turned boxer, achieves international prominence by challenging British heavyweight champion Tom Cribb. The fight for the heavyweight championship of England occurs at Copthorne, near East Grinstead, England. After 19 rounds, Molineaux has Crib in trouble on the ropes. Cribb's supporters enter the ring, and during the melee Molineaux has one of his fingers broken. Molineaux continues to fight and in the 28th round appears to knock out Cribb. Cribb's seconds complain, however, that Molineaux has been hiding lead bullets in his fists. While this accusation is being disproved, Cribb recovers and is able to continue. Molineaux remains the favorite but unluckily slips and hits his head on one of the ring posts. He fights on but by the 39th round is unable to defend himself, and Cribb is declared the

winner. The fight makes Molineaux a celebrity in England and earns him a place in boxing history.

1811

RELI. On February 24, Bishop Daniel A. Payne, reformer and educator of the African Methodist Episcopal (AME) Church, is born.

REVO. Between January 8 and 10, Charles Deslondes, a free mulatto from Santo Domingo, leads more than 400 slaves in a rebellion outside New Orleans. They destroy several plantations and kill at least two whites, including the son of Major Andry, the owner of the plantation where the rebellion begins. Fleeing to the woods, the rebels are followed by superior armed whites who capture then summarily execute 66 of them; the severed heads of the executed are strung up at intervals from New Orleans to the Andry plantation. The next day, Governor William Claiborne calls out additional troops, including a battalion of the Free Men of Color, or Corps d'Afrique, to quell any possible additional slave uprising.

1814

CIVI. Daniel Reaves Goodloe, emancipationist, is born.

MILI. On September 21, Andrew Jackson issues a proclamation at Mobile, Alabama, urging free blacks "to rally around the standard of the eagle" in the War of 1812. A large number of black sailors fight with Matthew Perry and Isaac Chauncey in the battles on the upper lakes and are particularly effective at the battle of Lake Erie. Two battalions of black soldiers fight with Andrew Jackson when he defeats the British at the battle of New Orleans on December 18, 1814.

1815

MIGR. Paul Cuffe, a wealthy free black, starts a campaign to resettle other free blacks in Sierra Leone, the West African British colony. He utilizes his own ship to transport the first 34 migrants.

1816

MILI. On July 27, the first of three Seminole wars begins at Fort Blount, also known as Fort

Negro, on Apalachicola Bay, Florida, when it is attacked by U.S. troops. The fort, which is held by escaped black slaves and Indians, is taken after several days of siege. A young surgeon with the infantry, Marcus Buck, reports, "We were pleased with their spirited opposition, though they were Indians, negroes and our enemies."

RELI. On April 10, Richard Allen becomes the first African in the United States to become a bishop when he is elected by the General Convention of the African Methodist Episcopal Church in Philadelphia, Pennsylvania.

SLAV. On December 28, the American Society for Colonizing Free People of Colour of the United States, better known as the American Colonization Society (ACS), is formed in Washington, DC, by prominent white slaveholders and sympathizers such as Henry Clay, Bushrod Washington, Francis Scott Key, and John Randolph. Its appeal to free blacks is that white Americans will never relinquish slavery as an institution, and, therefore, emigration from the United States to Africa is a better sociopolitical option. In this regard, the ACS purchases territory near Cape Mesurado, West Africa, for the settlement of free American blacks.

1817

OBIT. Paul Cuffe, entrepreneur and emigrationist, dies at the age of 58 in Westport, Massachusetts.

SLAV. In January, Philadelphia blacks hold a series of meetings at Bethel Church to protest colonization plans by the American Colonization Society "to drive free blacks out of America."

It is speculated that on February 14, Frederick Douglass, the most prominent black leader of the nineteenth century, is born in Tuckahoe, Talbot County, Maryland.

1818

ARTS. Frank Johnson becomes the first black musician to publish sheet music in the United States. Johnson is also the first black to tour the country and give formal band concerts. His first racially integrated concerts in U.S. history are produced during the 1843–44 concert season.

The African Grove Company, the first all-black acting troupe, debuts in New York City on September 21. The company began from the efforts of a retired steamship steward, William Henry Brown, who constructed a tea garden in the back of his house in Lower Manhattan and called it the African Grove. His teahouse served refreshments and provided vocal and instrumental entertainment in the evenings. One of the main artists to perform at the African Grove was James Hewlett, who introduced dramatic events. The dramatic ensemble becomes known as the African Company, the first black theatrical company. The first performance is Shakespeare's *Richard III,* staged in an upper apartment of the African Grove. *Othello* also become a popular production. Ira Aldridge, the celebrated black Shakespearean actor, begins his career here and later becomes one of the greatest actors of his age.

MIGR. The American Colonization Society (ACS) charters the ship *Elizabeth* for an expedition to resettle blacks in West Africa. With ACS support, African Methodist Episcopal Bishop Daniel Coker leads the first 86 blacks from America to colonize land south of Sierra Leone, which will eventually become Liberia. Their arrival is less than harmonious with the indigenous population.

MILI. On April 18, Andrew Jackson, at the head of an American military force, defeats a force of Seminoles (blacks and Indians) at the battle of Suwanee, ending the First Seminole War.

OBIT. Absalom Jones dies at the age of 71 in Philadelphia, Pennsylvania.

Jean Baptiste Pointe DuSable, the founder of Chicago, dies almost penniless and is buried in a Catholic cemetery in St. Charles, Missouri.

SCIE. James Hall becomes the first known free black to graduate from an American college of medicine, the Medical College of Maine.

1820

LAW. The U.S. Congress enacts the Missouri Compromise, which permits Missouri to become a slave state but allows Maine, which had previously been a part of Massachusetts, to enter the Union as a free state, thereby maintaining a sectional and voting balance in Congress. A critical aspect of this compromise is that slavery is banned above the north 36°30′ latitude line in the Louisiana territory.

POPU. The population of the United States is 9,638,453, of which 1,771,656 (18.4%) are people of African heritage.

On February 6, the *Mayflower of Liberia* sails from New York City to Sierra Leone with 86 blacks. It arrives on March 9.

SLAV. Harriet Tubman is born a slave with the slave name Araminta on the Eastern Shore of Maryland.

On May 15, the U.S. Congress declares that foreign slave trading is an act of piracy punishable by death.

1821

RELI. On March 14 in New York City, James Varick, Peter Williams, George Collins, Christopher Rush, and a number of other blacks withdrew from the John Street Methodist Episcopal Zion Church and formed the African Methodist Episcopal Church in New York City.

1822

EDUC. On July 15, the first public schools for blacks open in Philadelphia, Pennsylvania.

POLI. On September 27, Hiram R. Revels, who will become the first black United States senator, is born in Fayetteville, North Carolina.

RELI. On July 30, James Varick is consecrated as the first bishop of the African Methodist Episcopal Zion Church.

REVO. Denmark Vesey, who 20 years earlier purchased his own freedom and who maintains a flourishing business, employs several men, and owns his own home, organizes a slave revolt for which he has actively prepared since his manumission. The attack is aimed at first securing Charleston, South Carolina's, arsenal on Meeting Street, where arms and ammunition are held. Additional columns of armed slaves are to attack the city from different directions and secure key points in the downtown areas and then fire specific buildings.

The original day of the attack is July 14 but is changed to June 16, a Sunday and a day on which large numbers of blacks come into town without molestation from slave patrols. A loyal slave learns of the conspiracy, however, and in turn will informs his master and betrays the plot two days before the planned attack. Even with the arrest of Denmark Vesey and other leaders, those who are not captured attempt to reorganize an attack but again are stopped on July 5 by the arrests of important leaders such as Gullah Jack and John Drayton. Under torture, only bits of the plot are revealed to the authorities, and to this day, details of the plans are vague. Sentenced to death on June 29, 1822, Denmark Vesey and 37 other conspirators keep secret many aspects of the plot, even though they endure severe torture. On July 2, Vesey and five of his aides are hanged at Blake's Landing in Charleston, South Carolina. Weeks after their deaths, however, hundreds of other blacks are tortured and killed by local whites.

1823

EDUC. Alexander Lucius Twilight becomes the first free black college graduate at Middlebury College in Vermont, where he receives an AB degree. Twilight later obtains a public office.

1824

MIGR. In mid-August, 60 black emigrants depart Philadelphia on the ship *Charlotte Corday* and sail 10 days later on the *De Witt Clinton* from New York City to Haiti.

1824

ARTS. American black actor Ira Aldridge begins a career in Europe as a Shakespearean actor.

1826

EDUC. On September 6, John B. Russwurm graduates from Bowdoin College in Maine and becomes the third black to receive a BA degree in the United States.

MED. On February 16, the first newspaper printed in West Africa, *The Liberia Herald,* is published by C. L. Force, an African American from Boston, Massachusetts.

Prior to the sailing of the *De Witt Clinton,* Rev. Peter Williams urges the emigrants to "go to that highly favored, and as yet only land, where the sons of African appear as a civilized, well-ordered, and flourishing nation. Go, remembering that the happiness of millions of the present and future generations, depend upon your prosperity, an that your prosperity depends much upon yourself."

1827

LAW. The state of New York abolishes slavery.

MED. On March 16, Samuel Cornish and John B. Russwurm begin publication of the first black newspaper, *Freedom's Journal,* in New York City. The two editors maintain a difference of opinions on the question of black emigration from the United States to Africa and the American Colonization Society (ACS). Cornish calls for independent action by blacks against slavery in the United States and views the ACS's plan to foster black colonization in Africa as an attempt to eliminate free blacks from the United States through emigration. He also sees himself and other blacks as Americans rather than Africans. Russwurm, however, contends that white Americans will never relinquish full rights to blacks and that their only recourse is to establish a government in Africa. He eventually emigrates from the United States to West Africa and helps establish the colony of Monrovia, which will become Liberia.

SLAV. Isabella (Sojourner Truth) escapes to an antislavery family who purchases her freedom.

1829

CRIM. White mobs attack blacks in Cincinnati, Ohio, during a three-day race riot. Approximately 1,000 are force to flee the city and resettle in Canada.

LIT. David Walker publishes his *Appeal to the Colored Citizens of the World* (in pamphlet form), in which he aggressively calls for blacks to revolt against slavery by declaring, "that one good black can put to death six white men." Born free, of a free mother and slave father, David Walker learns to read and write while very young and, when possible, reads extensively on the subjects of revolution and resistance to oppression. When he is

about 30 years old, he leaves the South, claiming, "If I remain in this bloody land, I will not live long. As true as God reigns, I will be avenged for the sorrows which my people have suffered." In 1827, he becomes an agent for the newly published *Freedom's Journal,* the black abolitionist paper. To earn a living, he runs a secondhand clothing store. His *Appeal,* first published in *Freedom's Journal* in 1828, has a great impact upon both enslaved and free blacks in at least three ways: First, it liberates other abolitionists who dare not use such fiery rhetoric by allowing them to demand a more immediate elimination of slavery, by any means necessary. Second, it helps instill pride in blacks to support and formulate a more militant form of resistance to slavery than verbal abolitionism. Third, once this pamphlet circulates throughout the southern states and is read secretly to the South's enslaved black population, white slave owners become fearful of encirclement, fearful of slave rebellions within their own state borders, and fearful of the possible duplicity of those blacks whom they earlier discounted.

1830

ASSO. On September 20, the First National Black Convention meets at Philadelphia's Bethel African Methodist Episcopal Church and elects Richard Allen president. Thirty-eight delegates from eight states attend the fist national meeting of blacks. One of their resolutions proclaims a boycott of slave-produced goods.

POPU. The population of the United States is 12,866,020, of which 2,328,642 (18.1%) are people of African heritage.

RELI. On April 6, James Augustine Healy, who will become the first black Roman Catholic bishop in the United States, is born to an enslaved mother and an Irish planter on a plantation near Macon, Georgia.

1831

ABOL. On January 1, William Lloyd Garrison publishes the first issue of the abolitionist journal the *Liberator*.

ASSO. From June 6 to 11, the Second National Black Convention meets in Philadelphia. Fifteen delegates from five states attend.

OBIT. On March 26, Bishop Richard Allen dies at the age of 71 in Philadelphia.

REVO. On August 21, near the southeastern border of Virginia, in Southampton County, near a neighborhood known as Cross Keys, Nathaniel Turner and a band of 60 to 70 rebels kills 57 white men, woman, and children in a relatively quick and deadly attack. The first slave owner killed is Turner's owner, Joseph Travis. Two days later, on August 23, the insurgents meet their fist stiff opposition. A number of insurgents are killed and the rest scatter in the face of the superior weaponry of local farmers. Turner escapes from the area and lives off the land and dodges capture for six weeks until he is captured on October 30. He is hanged in Jerusalem, Virginia, on November 11.

1832

ASSO. On January 6, the New England Anti-Slavery Society is organized at the African Baptist Church on Boston's Beacon Hill.

The Third National Black Convention meets in Philadelphia with 29 delegates from eight states. Henry Sipkins of New York is elected president.

1833

ABOL. On December 4, white abolitionist William Lloyd Garrison forms the American Anti-Slavery Society (AASS) an Adelphi Hall in Philadelphia, Pennsylvania. Its stated purpose is to secure an immediate, uncompensated emancipation and equal rights for blacks in the United States. Interestingly, the society also proclaims that it will never resort to violence in its fight against oppression.

ARTS. Black actor Ira Aldridge debuts as Othello on a stage in London, England.

ASSO. From June 3 to 13, the Fourth National Black Convention meets in Philadelphia with 62 delegates from eight States. Abraham D. Shadd of Pennsylvania is elected president.

EDUC. On June 27, Prudence Crandall, a well-known Quaker grade-school teacher opens a school in Canterbury, Connecticut. The local villagers attempt to burn it down. When state officials pass a law banning black schools, Crandall is arrested. After successfully appealing the decision, local whites again attack the school, forcing it to close. Their rational is that this is necessary "for the protection of the students."

On May 21, for the first time, black students enroll in classes at Oberlin College in Ohio.

1834

ASSO. From June 2 to 13, the Fifth National Black Convention meets in New York City. Fifty delegates from eight states participate.

Wealthy black shipbuilder James Forten helps structure the charter of the American Moral Reform Society, a biracial assimilationist organization that

---

Thomas Gray, Turner's counsel and to whom Turner supposedly makes a full confession, writes the following about Nat Turner:

The calm and deliberate composure with which he spoke of his late deeds and intentions, the expression of his fiend-like face, when excited with enthusiasms, still bearing the stains of the blood of innocence about him, clothed with rags, and covered with chains, yet daring to raise his manacled hands to heaven, with a spirit soaring above the attributes of man—I looked upon him and the blood curdled in my veins.

has as its intended social policy the advocacy of Christian education, temperance, economy, and universal liberty for all humankind.

The first Anti Slavery Convention of American Women meets in New York City; blacks make up 10 percent of the membership.

MED. David Ruggles opens the first black bookstore and publishing company in New York City. He also publishes the abolitionist pamphlet entitled *The "Extinguisher" Extinguished.*

MILI. The last organized group of black soldiers, the New Orleans Free Men of Color, is abolished. Only the navy continues to recruit blacks.

1834
INVE. On August 31, Henry Blair of Maryland is reputed to be the first black to receive a patent when he develops a seed planter.

1835
ASSO. The Sixth National Black Convention meets in Philadelphia, Pennsylvania, from June 1 to 5, with 35 delegates representing six states and the District of Columbia.

EDUC. A white mob determined to stop the education of black children and adults uses 100 yoke of oxen to pull a black schoolhouse into a swamp a half-mile outside of the town of Canaan, New Hampshire.

SLAV. Free blacks form a vigilance committee to assist fugitive slaves in New York City.

WAR. The Second Seminole War begins. The alleged beginning is the seizure of Chief Osceola's wife by U.S. troops. Whether this is myth or fact, a more basic hostility and distrust exist between the interracial Seminoles under Osceola's command and U.S. troops. A more fundamental disagreement is the Seminoles' realization that, after the first war, they had been tricked into signing an agreement that implied that they agreed to be relocated to Arkansas and Oklahoma.

1836
POLI. Alexander Lucius Twilight, a minister and educator, is elected to the Vermont legislature,

thereby becoming the first black in the United States to be elected to a public office.

1837
EDUC. On April 19, Cheyney State College, originally founded as a training school for black boys, is established in Pennsylvania.

MED. On March 4, Samuel Cornish, who opposes colonization to Africa or the Caribbean, changes the name of the *Weekly Advocate* newspaper to the *Colored American,* the second major black newspaper.

Elijah P. Lovejoy, a white abolitionist newspaper editor, is murdered on November 7 by a proslavery mob while defending his newspaper press in Alton, Illinois. Though he places his printing press in a warehouse to protect it from proslavery attack, the building is eventually torched.

POLI. On March 24, Canada officially recognizes black suffrage.

SLAV. William S. Whipper, a leading follower of abolitionist William Lloyd Garrison, is one of the first Americans to deal with the nonviolent philosophy, publishing in 1837 an "Address on Non-Resistance to Offensive Aggressive." In this essay, which precedes Henry David Thoreau's celebrated essay "On the Duty of Civil Disobedience" by 12 years, Whipper states, "The practice of nonresistance to physical aggression is not only consistent with reason, but the surest method of obtaining a speedy triumph of the principles of universal peace." Samuel Cornish opposes Whipper's argument by claiming, "We honestly confess that we have yet to learn what virtue there would be in using moral weapons in defense against kidnappers or a midnight incendiary with a torch in his hand."

WAR. By June the Third Seminole War rages. Osceola is the leader of black and red resistance to U.S. slaveholders' efforts to capture escaped slaves from Georgia and beyond. Though the Seminole nation shows signs of division, those who side with Osceola, such as Coacoochee, are prepared to defend their black brothers and sisters to the death.

On December 25, a Seminole force retreats in the face of the superior numbers of U.S. troops. When the troops enter into tall grass and trees, they are shot with accurate fire from hiding Seminoles. After the encounter, Taylor counts 28 U.S. dead and 112 wounded and only the Seminoles dead. The battle of Lake Okeechobee becomes the most decisive upset the United States has suffered in more than four decades of warfare in Florida and is particularly disturbing because it occurs at the hands of a small band of black Indian (Seminole) guerrilla fighters. Noted in this battle at Okeechobee is the black chief Cohia (or John Horse), who shares command with Alligator Sam Jones and Coacoochee (or Wild Cat).

1838

ABOL. Charles Lenox Remond begins his career as an antislavery agent. Remond is one of the first blacks to be employed by the antislavery movement as a lecturer.

MED. David Ruggles publishes the first black magazine, *Mirror of Liberty*, in New York City.

1839

POLI. On November 13, the Liberty Party is organized in Warsaw, New York, as the first antislavery political party. Samuel Ringgold Ward and Henry Highland Garnet are among the earliest supporters of the new political direction.

REBE. On July 2, 36 enslaved Africans (Mendi from present-day Nigeria) aboard the Spanish slaver *Amistad* rise up under the leadership of Joseph Cinque (birth name Singbe-Pi,h), kill the ship's captain, and attempt to sail back to West Africa. Due to improper use of the navigational equipment, they become stranded off the coast of Long Island, New York, and are eventually captured by a U.S. warship on August 26. With the understanding that the U.S. government has banned the importation of Africans as slaves, abolitionists such as Lewis Tappan, a merchant and industrialist, Rev. Joshua Leavitt, editor of the antislavery journal *Emancipator*, and Simon S. Jocelyn, an engraver active in the antislavery movement and eventually the lead attorney in the case, as well as a hesitant supporter of abolitionism, John Quincy Adams, prepare to bring the case to the United States Supreme Court.

SLAV. On September 3, Frederick Douglass escapes from slavery disguised as a sailor.

WAR. Gen. Sidney T. Jesup brokers a peace treaty with the Seminoles that permits them to migrate together to the Indian Territory in Arkansas and Oklahoma. On February 25, a large number of Seminoles are shipped westward from Tampa, Florida. Jesup is then relieved of his command and recalled to Washington, DC.

1840

EDUC. The Ecole des Orphelins Indigents (School for Needy Orphans) is founded in New Orleans primarily by three financially secure blacks: Thomy Lafon, Madame Couvent, and Aristide Mary.

On May 16, educator, founder of Lincoln University, and the first United States ambassador to the Republic of Liberia, James Milton Turner, is born.

POPU. The total black population in the United States reaches 2,873,648.

1841

ABOL. Frederick Douglass delivers his first antislavery speech in Nantucket, Massachusetts.

LAW. On February 22, John Quincy Adams, the lead defense attorney in *United States v. Amistad*, argues the case in the U.S. Supreme Court.

Blanche Kelso Bruce, the first black to serve a full term in the U.S. Senate, is born on March 1, in Prince Edward County, Virginia.

Senior Supreme Court Justice Joseph Story, in a decision rendered on March 9 in *United States v. Amistad*, writes that those Africans on board the *Amistad* are free individuals. Kidnapped and transported illegally, they had never been slaves. The Court ordered the immediate release of the *Amistad* Africans.

MED. The pioneer quarterly *African Methodist Episcopal Magazine* is published in Brooklyn, New York, in September.

REBE. On November 7, enslaved Africans led by a captured runaway slave, Madison Washington, revolt and successfully commandeer the slave ship

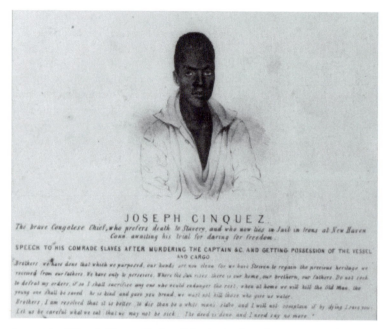

JOSEPH CINQUEZ.
The brave Congolese Chief, who prefers death to Slavery, and who now lies in Jail in Irons at New Haven Conn. awaiting his trial for daring for freedom.

SPEECH TO HIS COMRADE SLAVES AFTER MURDERING THE CAPTAIN &C. AND GETTING POSSESSION OF THE VESSEL AND CARGO

Brothers we have done that which we purposed, our hands are now clean, for we have Striven to regain the precious heritage we received from our fathers. We have only to persevere, Where the Sun rises there is our home, our brothers, our fathers. Do not seek to defeat my orders, if so I shall sacrifice any one who would endanger the rest, when at home we will kill the Old Man, the young one shall be saved he is kind and gave you bread, we must not kill those who give us value. Brothers, I am resolved that it is better to die than be a white man's slave, and I will not complain if by dying I save you. Let us be careful what we eat that we may not be sick. The deed is done and I need say no more.

A portrait of Joseph Cinque, leader of the Amistad revolt, awaiting trial in New Haven, Connecticut. Courtesy of Library of Congress.

Creole, which had set out from Hampton, Virginia, with a cargo of 134 Africans and bound for New Orleans. After the takeover, Washington changes the ship's destination to British-held Nassau, where the Africans are given asylum and set free. Frederick Douglass, who is familiar with Washington's antislavery speeches in Canada, captures this symbol of black bravery in a novel entitled *The Historic Slave.*

On November 25, 35 Africans who were aboard the *Amistad* return to West Africa.

1842

ABOL. On November 25, George Latimer in Boston becomes the first fugitive slave for whom Boston abolitionists successfully raise money to purchase his freedom.

SLAV. In response to the large number of black men in the U.S. Navy, a quota is imposed stating that no more than 5 percent of naval personnel can be black. South Carolina mandates that any black sailor who sets foot on South Carolina soil will be jailed.

1843

ABOL. Frederick Douglass, in the company of two white abolitionists, William A. White and George Bradburn, is attacked by an antiabolitionist crowd in the town of Pendleton, Indiana, after giving an antislavery speech. Shouting, "Kill the nigger! Kill the damn nigger!" the mob chases the three abolitionists out of town, with Douglass suffering a broken hand and White a head injury as the result of a thrown rock.

In June, Isabella Baumfree formally assumes the name Sojourner Truth (meaning "traveling preacher") and begins her career as an antislavery activist by leaving New York. In the late 1840s, Truth associates with the abolitionists and becomes a popular speaker, particularly on the question of race and gender. In a 1851 speech given at a woman's rights conference in Ohio, Truth, in response to a male heckler, asks the question, "Ain't I a woman?" and in doing so opens a political, philosophical, and cultural discussion that still resounds around the world in a variety of sociopolitical contexts some 150

During the *Amistad* trial, Justice Story states that it was "the ultimate right of all human beings in extreme cases to resist oppression, and to apply force against ruinous injustice."

In his fourth biography, *My Bondage, My Freedom,* Douglass recalls those moments before his flight from slavery:

> The last two days of the week—Friday and Saturday—were spent mostly in collecting my things together, for my journey. Having worked four days that week, for my master, I handed him six dollars, on Saturday night. I seldom spent my Sundays at home; and, for fear that something might be discovered in my conduct, I kept up my custom, and absented myself all day. On Monday, the third day of September, 1838, in accordance with my resolution, I bade farewell to the city of Baltimore, and to that slavery which had been my abhorrence from childhood. How I got away—in what direction I traveled—whether by land or by water; whether with or without assistance—must, for reasons already mentioned, remain unexplained.

years later. Sojourner Truth's simple but highly controversial question and speech address a number of social problems and their consequences as they pertain to slavery, human rights, the enslaved, and "free" women's rights. Those who hear her presentations are struck by her resounding voice and sense of dignity and purpose. During her subsequent career as an abolitionist speaker, she interacts with abolitionists such as Harriet Beecher Stowe, who writes about Truth in the *Atlantic Monthly* and the introduction to the *Narrative of Sojourner Truth.* At one point, Truth becomes involved with the Millerites, the precursors of the Seventh-Day Adventists.

ASSO. The National Black Convention meets in Buffalo, New York, on August 15 with approximately 75 delegates attending. Henry Highland Garnet gives a stirring address during which he essential calls for slave rebellion and a general strike by all slaves throughout the nation. In his presentation, billed as an "Address to the Slaves," he accepts the possibility that massive violence may occur but makes it known that he disagrees with the nonviolent approach to slavery favored by abolitionists such as Frederick Douglass.

Blacks participate for the first time in a national political convention sponsored by the Liberty Party in Buffalo, New York. Samuel R. Ward leads the convention in prayer, and Henry Highland Garnet serves as a member of the nominating committee. Rev. Charles R. Ray, co-editor of the *Colored American,* acts as one of the convention's secretaries.

LAW. On May 3, Macon B. Allen becomes the first African American to practice law when he passes the Massachusetts bar examination and is admitted to the bar.

1844

EDUC. On January 30, Richard Greener graduates from Harvard University as the first black person to do so.

INVE. The term *the real McCoy* emanates from the inventive life of Elijah J. McCoy, an inventor, master mechanic, and mechanical engineer. Born in Canada on May 2, 1844, the son of enslaved blacks who fled from Kentucky, Elijah develops a fascination with machines at a young age. His father encourages this aptitude and sends him to Scotland, where he studies mechanical engineering, completes his apprenticeship, and becomes a master mechanical engineer. Settling in the United States in 1870, the best job he can get is in Ypsilanti, Michigan, as a locomotive fireman on the Michigan Central Railroad. At that time, trains stop often to oil various moving parts. As fireman, McCoy finds this job tedious and inefficient. He studies the problem for two years and develops and patents a lubricating cup (patent no. 139,407) to supply oil to the train's engine and other mechanical parts while it is moving. During the following years, he develops, patents, and supplies other self-oilers for factories and on steamships and ocean liners (patent no. 129,843). This innovative development has an immediate impact on industries that require enhanced production from machines. His manufacturing standards are so high that competitors cannot match his products. According to legend, this is the source of the expression used to describe something that is not an imitation, the real McCoy.

1845

ARTS. On July 14, in the village of Greenbush, Albany, New York, Mary Edmonia Lewis is born to an African American father and a mother of Mississauga and African American descent. The Mississauga are a Chippewa (Ojibwa) ethnic group who lived on the Credit River reserve, which is now the city of Mississauga on Lake Ontario. Lewis attends Oberlin College in 1859 and almost immediately finds herself in a controversy, which has at its core racial bias, with other students and administrators that will lead to her marginalization and eventual withdrawal, though she is not expelled, from Oberlin. Only 18 years old, she leaves Oberlin in late February or early March 1863 for Boston, Massachusetts, to become a sculptor. The obstacles Edmonia Lewis overcomes are unparalleled among American artists. The art world of the day requires that the artist develop a particular style, which can make the work of one artist appear indistinguishable from that of another. Her adoption of neoclassicism, however, does not diminish the impact of Lewis's work, and she displays a unique style when compared to her contemporaries. Despite the obstacles of racism and prejudice she must overcome, her life is indeed one of triumph. Virtually ignored until the civil rights and feminist movements in the late 1960s, Edmonia Lewis emerges as an artist who captures in her art the dynamic issues of her time. Although she is often depicted as a religious artist, only one of her original religious statues, *Hagar*, is known in the United States, and other major works have not been located. Her copy of Michelangelo's *Moses*,

which retains the original's monumental character although in small scale, is in the Museum of American Art in Washington, DC. To her credit are works such as *Urania* (1862), Lewis's only signed drawing, which is created as a wedding gift for an Oberlin classmate marrying a former student on leave from the Union Army. Another important work is her marble sculpture *Colonel Robert Gould Shaw* (1866–67), the commanding officer of the heroic black Fifty-Fourth Massachusetts Volunteer Infantry during the attack on Fort Wagner, South Carolina, in summer 1863. Lewis sells 100 plaster copies of her sculpture, which enables her to go to Rome in 1865. In Rome, Lewis creates *Forever Free* (1867–68), which is the first sculpture by an African American that celebrates the Emancipation Proclamation. She borrows money to sculpt the statue in marble. Lewis's sculpture *Henry Wadsworth Longfellow* (1869), who is her hero because his *Song of Hiawatha* influenced her own attitudes about the American indigenous population, is a good example of how she formulated her working style. When she observes Longfellow walking in Rome, she follows him and sketches his face. When she has made enough drawings, she asks him to sit for the finishing touches. The result is an excellent example of a neoclassical bust. Longfellow's *Hiawatha* also inspires one of Lewis's better-known works, *The Old Indian Arrowmaker and His Daughter* (1872). Although the faces in this sculpture appear not to be indigenous, the garments, poses, and decorations reflect her own background among the Mississauga, the Chippewa people with whom she spent her childhood. Lewis memorializes the importance of the Native American craftsman as a maker of arrows to hunt food and for defense. Another popular sculpture by Lewis is *Hagar* (1869), the biblical Egyptian cast into the wilderness after bearing Abraham's child. Lewis identified with Hagar as a result of her experiences at Oberlin College. In the sculpture, Hagar has just heard an angel ask her, "What aileth thee, Hagar?" For Lewis, who has just become a Catholic, this question represents a hopeful future. Lewis's statue of the goddess of health, *Hygieia* (1874), is commissioned by Dr. Harriot Hunt for her grave in Mount Auburn Cemetery in Cambridge, Massachusetts.

Dr. Hunt is one of the first woman physicians and a pioneer feminist. One of Lewis's more controversial sculptures is *The Death of Cleopatra* (1875). Unlike William Wetmore's earlier depiction of Queen Cleopatra's suicide and calm contemplation of the deadly asp, Edmonia Lewis depicts Cleopatra seated in her throne after her suicide with her head turned tragically backward and over the left shoulder. She grasps the asp in her right hand, and the left arm extends downward outside the chair. This powerful full-size marble sculpture is exhibited at the 1876 Philadelphia Centennial Exposition and the Chicago Exposition of 1878. One of Lewis's later works is a bust of John Brown (1876), the fiery antislavery insurrectionist executed in 1859. Unfortunately, the bust is destroyed when a tornado strikes Wilberforce University Library in 1974. A photograph of the work survives, however. Where and when Edmonia Lewis dies remains a mystery.

MED. Frederick Douglass publishes the first of three autobiographies, *Narrative of Frederick Douglass.*

MEDI. On May 7, Mary Eliza Mahoney is born free in Dorchester, Massachusetts. She begins her outstanding nursing career as the first African American nurse to graduate from the New England Hospital for Women and Children (now Dimrock Community Health Center in Roxbury, Massachusetts) as an unofficial nurse's assistant.

POLI. William A. Leidesdorff is named subconsul to Yerba Buena, part of the Mexican territory that later becomes San Francisco.

1846

BUSI. William A. Leidesdorff opens the first hotel in San Francisco and eventually becomes the first self-made black millionaire in the United States.

ECON. In Philadelphia, 80 percent of employed black men perform unskilled labor. Barbers and shoemakers predominate among those black workers with skills. Only 0.5 percent hold factory jobs. Among employed black women, 80 percent either wash clothes or work as domestic servants. Three-quarters of the remaining 20 percent are seamstresses. By the 1850s, black women, too, lose work to Irish immigrants. A few become prostitutes. About 5 percent of black men and women are self-employed, selling food or secondhand clothing.

INVE. Norbert Rillieux, a New Orleans machinist and engineer, invents and receives a patent (# 4,879) for a vacuum-evaporating pan that revolutionizes the sugar-refining industry.

SLAV. During the Mexican War of 1846, David Wilmot, a Democratic Congressman from Pennsylvania, introduces a bill in Congress that prohibits slavery in any territory acquired from Mexico and is known as the Wilmot Proviso. The author of the bill explains that he wants neither slavery nor black people to taint territory that should be reserved for whites. Though this proviso never becomes law, southern whites view the proposal as a blatant attempt to prevent them from moving westward and enjoying the prosperity that an expanding slave system will afford them. They also feel any attempt to limit slavery is actually a veiled attempt to abolish it.

1847

ASSO. From October 6 to 9, the National Black Convention meets in Troy, New York, with more than 60 delegates from nine states attending. Nathan Johnson of Massachusetts is elected president of the convention.

MED. In December, Frederick Douglass publishes the first issue of the newspaper *North Star.*

POLI. On July 26, President Joseph Jenkins Roberts declares Liberia an independent West African Republic.

In September, William A. Leidesdorff is elected to San Francisco's town council, after receiving the third highest vote. One year later, he becomes the town's treasurer.

On September 10, John R. Lynch, the first African American speaker at a Republican National Convention, is born.

1848

ASSO. On September 6, the National Black Convention meets in Cleveland, Ohio, with

70 delegates attending. The convention elects Frederick Douglass as its president.

INVE. On September 4, Louis Latimer, inventor and engineer, is born.

LAW. In December, Benjamin F. Roberts files a suit on behalf of his daughter, Sarah, who is barred from attending a white school near her home in Boston, Massachusetts. William C. Nell, a Boston historian and abolitionist, collects money to fight this case and hires attorney Charles Summer.

OBIT. William A. Leidesdorff dies at age 38 in San Francisco.

POLI. On July 19 and 20, Frederick Douglass attends the first Woman's Right Convention at Seneca Falls, New York. He seconds the woman suffrage motion introduced by Elizabeth Cady Stanton.

SLAV. On August 6, Susie King Baker (later Taylor) is born a slave in Liberty County, Georgia.

In December, William and Ellen Craft escape from slavery in Georgia. Ellen Craft, who is light enough to be mistaken for a white person, impersonates a slave owner taking her personal slave northward on a visit.

1849

EDUC. Charles Reason becomes the first black professor in the United States to teach at a predominantly white university. He teaches French, Greek, Latin, and mathematics at New York Central University.

George Washington Williams, the first major black historian, is born on October 16 in Bedford Springs, Pennsylvania.

SLAV. In summer, Harriett Tubman escapes from slavery in Maryland. Over the years, she travels throughout the South and brings an estimated 300 enslaved blacks from the southern states.

1850

EDUC. Lucy Stanton Sessions is the first black woman in the United States to complete a collegiate course of study when she is graduated from Oberlin College in Ohio.

A Boston court hears Charles Summer's argument in the education case brought by Benjamin Robert on behalf of his daughter, Sarah, who was denied admittance into an all-white school. The court renders a precedent-setting "separate but equal" decision. This decision forces local abolitionists to stage the first sit-in demonstrations and wage a propaganda campaign against the decision. Eventually, the issue is resolved by the Massachusetts legislature, which passes a law banning school segregation.

Hallie Quinn Brown, a women's civil rights activist, is born on March 10 in Pittsburgh, Pennsylvania. Brown begins her activist career shortly after graduating from Wilberforce University in 1873. After teaching in South Carolina, Mississippi, and Ohio from 1873 to 1892, she is appointed dean of women at Tuskegee Institute. The following year, she accepts a professorship at Wilberforce University. Known as an effective elocutionist and lecturer, Hallie Brown travels throughout the United States and Europe from the late 1880s until her death in 1949, articulating the demands for woman suffrage and human and civil rights.

POLI. On September 18, the U.S. Congress passes a fugitive slave law as part of the Compromise of 1850.

POPU. The population of the United States is 23,191,876, of which 3,638,808 (15.7%) are of African heritage.

SLAV. On September 18, the Fugitive Slave Act is passed by the U.S. Congress as one component of the Compromise of 1850 that allows California to enter the Union as a free state, eliminates slave trading but not slavery in the District of Columbia, and allows New Mexico and Utah to be organized as territories without the mention of slavery. With Henry Clay as the main sponsor of this compromise, many hope that the issue of slavery will be finally settled. The U.S. Constitution provides proslavery advocates ample support through Article IV, Section 2 as well as the Fugitive Slave Laws of 1793 that provide ample authority for slave owners to recapture any runaway slaves.

1851

ABOL. In Boston, on February 15, federal marshals capture a black waiter who escaped from slavery and changed his name to Shadrach. During courtroom proceedings, a well-organized band of black men, led by Lewis Hayden, invades the courtroom and escapes with Shadrach. They send Shadrach to Canada through the underground network. He later becomes the owner of a well-known Montreal restaurant. Federal authorities file charges and indict four black men and four white men in the raid. In an early nineteenth-century example of jury nullification, a local jury refuses to convict them.

On September 11, in the town of Christiana, Pennsylvania, U.S. marshals, proslavery supporters, and Edward Gorsuch, who is attempting to recover two runaway slaves, confront a hostile and well-armed group of black abolitionists and a few white supporters who are determined not to turn in the two runaways. A battle ensues, resulting in the death of Gorsuch, the wounding of his son, and the injury of several black and white abolitionists. President Millard Fillmore sends a contingent of U.S. Marines to help capture the armed abolitionists. Eventually, 36 black men and 5 white men are arrested and indicted for treason by a federal grand jury. Due to the overall weakness of the government's case, the first trial ends in acquittal and the remaining cases are dropped.

On October 1, black and white abolitionists smash their way into a courtroom in Syracuse, New York, and rescue an escaped slave.

EDUC. Martin Delany, who becomes the foremost African nationalist and emigration advocate of his era, is dismissed from Harvard Medical School when white students petition Dean Oliver Wendell Holmes Sr. to rid the class of its three black members. Medical licenses not being required to practice medicine at that time in the United States, he returns home as Dr. Delany and begins his practice.

LIT. Abolitionist William C. Nell publishes the first extended work on the history of blacks in the United States military before the Civil War, *Services of Colored Americans in the Wars of 1776 and 1812*. A revised edition is published in 1855 and renamed *The Colored Patriots of the American Revolution*.

1852

EMIG. Martin R. Delany publishes *The Condition, Elevation, Emigration and Destiny of the Colored People of the United States,* considered to be the first major statement on black nationalism in the United States.

LIT. Harriet Beecher Stowe's novel *Uncle Tom's Cabin; or Life among the Lowly* is published in installments in the antislavery newspaper the *National Era*. Published in Boston, Massachusetts, it sells nearly 300,000 copies in the first year. The novel depicts the cruelty and inhumanity of slavery while appealing to the sentimentality of nineteenth-century white readers.

1853

ABOL. On April 20, Harriet Tubman begins her activities as an Underground Railroad antislavery agent.

ARTS. Elizabeth Taylor Greenfield is the first black concert singer in the United States. She also becomes the first black singer to perform for European royalty, when, on May 10, she sings before Queen Victoria of England.

ASSO. The National Black Convention meets in Rochester, New York, with 140 delegates from

---

In *The Condition, Elevation, Emigration and Destiny of the Colored People of the United States,* Martin R. Delany states, "We are a nation within a nation: as the Poles in Russia, the Hungarians in Austria, the Welsh, the Irish, and Scotch in the British dominions." In response to Delany's thoughts on race and nationalism, Frederick Douglass remarks, "I thank God for making me a man simply … but Delany always thanks Him for making him a black man."

The auction scene from a stage production of *Uncle Tom's Cabin,* 1901. Courtesy of Library of Congress.

nine states. James W. C. Pennington from New York is elected president of the convention. This is generally recognized as the largest and most representative of the early black conventions. Three major assertions at the convention include: (1) blacks' equal protection under the law, (2) citizenship rights, and (3) poor blacks' displacement in menial and unskilled jobs by European immigrants. The delegates even discuss establishing a black museum and library.

LIT. In March, Frederick Douglass publishes his novella *The Heroic Slave* in his newspaper *Frederick Douglass' Paper.* It is a depiction of the *Creole* slave ship revolt 12 years earlier. A few months after its initial publication, the novella is reprinted in *Autographs for Freedom,* an anthology of antislavery writings compiled by Julia W. Griffiths, the business manger of *Frederick Douglass' Paper,* to raise funds to support the paper.

William Wells Brown, the first black novelist in the United States, publishes *Clotel; or The Presidents Daughter: A Narrative of Slave Life in the United States.* He later writes the play *The Escape; or A Leap for Freedom* (1858) and the nonfiction work *The Rising Sun* (1873).

1854

ABOL. On May 24, Anthony Burns, who escaped from slavery in Virginia by stowing away in a ship bound for Boston, Massachusetts, and then found employment in a clothing store, is discovered and arrested by a deputy marshal. Recalling the Shadrach incident, the marshal places Burns in the federal courthouse under guard and in chains. Attempts by both black and white abolitionists to free Burns fail, and a deputy U.S. marshal is killed during the assault. President Franklin Pierce, a northern Democrat who enjoyed southern support in the 1852 elections, sends U.S. troops to Boston, including U.S. Marines, cavalry, and artillery, to secure Burns. A local abolitionist committee attempts to purchase Burns's freedom, but the U.S. attorney rejects that appeal. In June, with thousands of people quietly and tearfully lining the streets, church bells ringing, and buildings draped in black, Anthony Burns is forcibly marched through the streets to a waiting ship in

Boston Harbor that spirits him away to Virginia and slavery.

EDUC. On January 1, one of the first black colleges is chartered as Ashmun Institute in Oxford, Pennsylvania (later renamed Lincoln University). Its mission is to provide higher education to those of African descent.

EMIG. From August 24 to 26, the National Emigration Convention meets in Cleveland, Ohio, with more than 100 delegates attending. William C. Munroe is elected president of the convention.

LAW. On May 30, the Kansas-Nebraska Act repeals the Missouri Compromise of 1820 and allows voters in the Kansas and Nebraska Territories to decide whether to allow slavery. This formula, know as *popular sovereignty,* is problematic in that it creates the possibility for slavery to extend to other territories. The major proponent of this act is Stephen Douglas, who has presidential aspirations.

RELI. On June 10, James Augustine Healy, the first black Roman Catholic bishop, is ordained a priest in Notre Dame Cathedral in Paris, France.

SCIE. In August, John V. DeGrasse, a prominent physician, is admitted into the Massachusetts Medical Society.

1855

ABOL. John Brown joins antislavery forces in Kansas to fight proslavery settlers from Missouri. Brown forms a militia known as the Liberty Guards with his sixth son and a son-in-law. They eventually receive guns from Rev. Henry Ward Beecher (brother of Harriet Beecher Stowe), who like Brown believes, "Guns are a greater moral force in Kansas than the Bible."

ASSO. From October 16 to 19, the National Black Convention meets in Philadelphia, Pennsylvania, with more than 100 delegates from six states attending.

LIT. William C. Nell publishes a revised edition of *Colored Patriots of the American Revolution.*

1856

ABOL. After the torching of Lawrence, Kansas, by proslavery supporters, John Brown leads an attack at Pottawatomie Creek, Kansas, against proslavers in which five are killed. Brown is heralded by northern newspapers and demonized by southern papers as the leader of armed attacks against slavery.

EDUC. On April 5, Booker Taliaferro Washington is born a slave in Franklin County, Virginia.

The Methodist Episcopal Church establishes Wilberforce University in Cincinnati, Ohio. It is later transferred to the African Methodist Episcopal Church.

INVE. On April 23, Granville T. Woods, an inventor of more than 42 products, is born. One of the greatest electrical engineers in the United States, Woods never finishes elementary school and is self-taught. Having patented more than 100 electrical and mechanical inventions, many of his ideas are acquired by General Electric, Westinghouse, Bell, and Thomas Edison. One of his more notable inventions is a transmitter that delivers sound louder and clearer than any other device at that time. Patented on December 2, 1884 (no. 308,816), this device reduces the need for Morse code by combining the telegraph and the telephone. Woods also develops an electric egg incubator that increases the production of chicken eggs. Other patents awarded to Granville Woods also underscore his genius, including the automatic air brake system (June 10, 1902; patent no. 701,981), electric railway system (July 9, 1901; patent no. 678,086), roller coaster (December 19, 1899; patent no. 639,692), and steam boiler furnace (June 3, 1884; patent no. 299,894).

LAW. The U.S. Supreme Court accepts the case of Dred Scott, a slave owned by John Emerson, an army doctor in Missouri, who took Scott to Illinois and Fort Snelling in what is now Minnesota. Upon Emerson's death, Scott sued for his freedom based on the assumption that if slavery is illegal in Illinois, he became free once taken there by Emerson. Scott lost this first suit. He appealed to the U.S. Circuit Court where he lost again.

MEDI. On January 18, Daniel Hale Williams, a pioneer in surgery, is born.

1857

LAW. Dred Scott's final appeal is made to the United States Supreme Court in *Dred Scott v. Sandford.* Though Chief Justice Roger B. Taney has freed his own slaves, he is a strong supporter of slavery as a southern American institution. On March 6, Taney writes in the majority opinion that Dred Scott, like every other black person in the United States, cannot sue in a federal court because he is not a citizen of the country. Moreover, he argues that because, for more than a century, blacks in the United States have been considered inferior to whites and, therefore, have no rights to speak of, it is right and fair to enslave them. Historically, Taney is incorrect. Blacks, though treated unequally in many states, have enjoyed rights associated with citizenship since the ratification of the U.S. Constitution in 1789, have held title to property, have sued in courts, and have voted in some of the original 13 states.

1858

ASSO. From May 8 to 10, John Brown and 46 blacks and whites meet antislavery delegates at Chatham, Canada, to establish a new strategy against U.S. slavery. A major document emerges from this convention: (1) the *Provisional Constitution and Ordinances for the People of the United States,* which will provide an instrument for the government of a nation of liberated slaves by "amendment and reform" of the federal government. Along with a preamble and 48 articles that establish the structure of governance, the constitution by way of articles 23 and 27 provides for the creation of a national army. The printer and publisher of the constitution, William Howard Day, is a free black living in St. Catherine's,

Ontario, who also provides several recruits for John Brown's future activities.

Abraham Lincoln of Illinois gains national recognition as a possible antislavery supporter during his unsuccessful bid for the U.S. Senate. Running against Lincoln is Stephen Douglas, who in his reelection bid for senator debates Lincoln on a series of issues throughout the state. Slavery and its extension into or rejection from new territories is the main focus of debate for both candidates. In this regard, race becomes a lighting rod for both candidates, as when in a debate with Lincoln, Douglas states: "The signers of the Declaration [of Independence] had no reference to the Negro ... or any other inferior or degraded race when they spoke of the equality of men." He later asserts, "If you Black Republicans, think the Negro ought to be on social equality with your wives and daughters, ... you have a perfect right to do so.... Those of you who believe the Negro is your equal ... of course will vote for Mr. Lincoln." Abraham Lincoln, on the other hand, in a retort to Stephen Douglas's taunt quite bluntly states:

> I am not, nor ever have been in favor of bringing about in any way the social and political equality of the white and black races—that I am not nor ever have been in favor of making voters or jurors of Negroes, nor of qualifying them to hold office, nor to intermarry with white people; and I will say in addition to this that there is a difference between the races which I believe will forever forbid the two races living together on terms of social and political equality.

Lincoln may have won most of the debates in the minds of many voters, but Douglas is reelected senator.

LIT. *The Escape,* the first play by an American black, is published by William Wells Brown.

Upon hearing the Dred Scott decision, Frederick Douglass asserts: "My hopes were never brighter than now, ... the Supreme Court is not the only power in the world.... Judge Taney cannot bail out the ocean, annihilate the firm old earth or plunk the silvery star of liberty from our Northern sky."

1859

ARTS. On June 21, Henry Ossawa Turner is born in Allegheny (now the Pittsburgh Northside), Pennsylvania. His father, Rev. Benjamin Tanner, is a leader of a group of Pittsburgh African Americans who considered John Brown a hero. By giving his son the middle name Ossawa, the elder Tanner further expresses his admiration for John Brown, who in 1856 killed proslaver vigilantes attacking antislavery homesteaders in Osawatomie, Kansas. Shortening the name is mere prudence in Pittsburgh, a town less than 150 miles from slave territory and one that is violently proslavery. Through happenstance, Tanner and his son Ossawa are walking in a nearby park when they come across an artist painting a landscape. From that moment, Ossawa decides that drawing and painting will be his life work. Notable among his works are *The Battle of Life* (1884), a portrayal of an elk attacked by wolves; *The Thankful Poor* (1893–94), a depiction of an African American family of two at dinner; *The Banjo Lesson* (1893), a depiction of an old African American man giving a young boy his first lesson on how to play the banjo that represents the transference of knowledge, nurturance, and respect from one generation to another; *Daniel in the Lion's Den* (1895); *The Annunciation* (1898); *Jews at the Jerusalem Wailing Wall* (1897); *Two Disciples at the Tomb* (1906); and *Disciples on the Sea of Galilee* (1910). Tanner dies in his sleep in Paris, France, on May 25, 1937.

LIT. Martin R. Delany publishes his controversial novel *Blake: The Huts of America* in serial form in the *Anglo American Magazine*. In this novel, Delany depicts a growing revolutionary antislavery movement of ex-slaves who threaten the very existence of the U.S. government. The novel's presents a contrasting and more threatening image of slaves and their political potential than does Harriet Beecher Stowe's *Uncle Tom's Cabin*. Mysteriously, the last chapter of *Blake* is never

Holy Family by Henry Ossawa Tanner. Courtesy of Library of Congress.

After Dangerfield Newby's death, a letter from his enslaved wife is found in his coat pocket, providing part of his rationale for participating in John Brown's raid:

> Dear Husband; It is said master is in want of money. If so, I know not what time he may sell me, and then all my bright hopes of the future are blasted, for their [*sic*] has been one bright hope to cheer me in all my troubles, that is to be with you. If I thought I should never see you this earth would have no charms for me. Come this fall without fail money or no money, do all you can for me, witch [*sic*] I have no doubt you will. The children are well. The baby cannot walk yet. You must write soon and say when you think you can come.—Your affectionate wife, Harriet Newby.

published, and reasons surrounding its disappearance have intrigued historians for years.

The first novel published by a black woman in the United States, Harriet E. Wilson's *Our Nig; or Sketches from the Life of a Free Black,* is also the first novel by a black in the United States to examine the life of an ordinary black person in realistic detail.

REBE. In August, Frederick Douglass meets with John Brown in Chambersburg, Pennsylvania, where Brown attempts to convince Douglass to join his band of insurgents in an attack on Harpers Ferry, Virginia. Douglass declines to participate stating, "he [Brown] was going into a perfect steel trap, and that once in he would never get out alive."

On October 16, a group of 22 black and white insurgents, making up the Provisional Army of the United States and led by John Brown, attacks the United States Armory and Arsenal at Harpers Ferry, Virginia. With the express plan to free enslaved blacks at the facility, their attack is initially successful. Five black insurgents are among the attackers: Osborne Perry Anderson, Dangerfield Newby, Shields Green, John Copeland, and Lewis Sheridan Leary. The first raider to be shot and killed is Dangerfield Newby. On October 18, U.S. Marines from Washington, DC, under the command of Col. Robert E. Lee, successfully storm the buildings held by the insurgents, capturing and killing those not killed earlier, and rescue captives. Of the original attackers, Osborne Anderson is the only insurgent to successfully escape. On December 2, after a lengthy trial, John Brown is hanged in Charlestown, Virginia.

On December 16, John Copeland and Shields Green, two black insurgents in the attack on Harpers Ferry, are hanged in Charlestown, Virginia.

SLAV. In February, the Arkansas legislature requires free blacks to choose between emigration or enslavement.

SPOR. On November 15, A black baseball team called the Unknowns plays a team from Jamaica, New York.

1860

POPU. The population of the United States is 31,443,790, of which 4,441,830 (14.1%) are people of African heritage.

POLI. On November 6, as a result of the political splits within the Democratic Party over the question of slavery and the emergence of a new political party, the Constitutional Union party, the Republican candidate, Abraham Lincoln, wins the necessary popular vote as well as the Electoral College vote to become president of the United States. Lincoln's adamant rejection of the expansion of slavery into the western territories enrages southern Democrats.

On December 20, South Carolina declares itself an independent commonwealth and secedes from the United States of America.

WORK. George Monroe and William Robinson are two of the earliest black Pony Express riders in the West. Eastern mail is sent westward by railroad to St. Joseph, Missouri, then picked up by professional Pony Express riders who deliver the

Upon the election of Abraham Lincoln, one Georgia paper proclaims, "Let the consequences be what they may—whether the Potomac is crimsoned in human gore, and Pennsylvania Avenue is paved ten fathoms deep with mangled bodies … the South will never submit to such humiliation and degradation as the inauguration of Abraham Lincoln." Another white southerner, Arthur P. Haynes of South Carolina, in a letter to President James Buchanan asserts, "Slavery with us is no abstraction-but a great and *vital fact*. Without it our every comfort would be taken from us. Our wives, our children, made unhappy—education, the light of knowledge—all *all* lost and our *people ruined for ever. Nothing short of separation from the Union can save us.*"

mail to numerous stations. Changing horses along the way, the riders brave a hostile native population as well as robbers. Their route extends as far west as San Francisco. Monroe Meadows in Yosemite National Park is named after Monroe, who also becomes a noted stagecoach driver.

1861

EDUC. On the eve of the Civil War, there are 32,696 people of African heritage in educational institutions in the United States and its territories.

On September 16, a school for freedmen is founded at Fortress Monroe, Virginia, with a black teacher, Mary Peake.

POLI. By February 1861, an additional six southern states seceded from the United States of America: Mississippi, Alabama, Florida, Louisiana, Georgia, and Texas.

On February 4, seven seceding states form the Provisional Government of the Confederate States of America (CSA).

On February 8, Jefferson Davis of Mississippi is confirmed as the president of the CSA.

On March 4, President Abraham Lincoln warns that he will not tolerate the seven seceding states to withdraw from the United States and that any attempt at secession would be the "essence of anarchy." In a conciliatory manner he also states that he has no reason or intention to interfere with the institution of slavery.

On March 11, the Confederate Congress of America meets in Montgomery, Alabama, to adopt a constitution that declares illegal any law that impairs the right of property in slaves. The population of the 11 states that make up the Confederate States of America is 9,103,332

(5,449,462 white, 3,521,110 slaves, and 132,760 free blacks). The population of the 22 northern states that make up the Union is 22,339,989.

On August 6, the U.S. Congress passes the Confiscation Act, which authorizes the appropriation of property, including enslaved blacks of rebel slave owners.

In response to the Confiscation Act, on August 30, Union Gen. John C. Frémont (Republican candidate for president in 1856) declares that all slaves in Missouri belonging to Confederates are free. Lincoln, concerned that this proclamation by Frémont might push Missouri or Kentucky into the Confederacy, countermands the order and states only slaves actively used by the Confederates can be freed.

In the late months of the year, Union military forces carve out a tract of land around Beaufort and Port Royal, South Carolina, that remains under their control for the rest of the Civil War. Know as the Port Royal Experiment, the land is administered under the U.S. Treasury Department, which auctions off portions of the land for nonpayment of taxes to freedmen who purchase some of it. Northern businessmen buy most of it, however, and hire freemen to work on it. When former white owners try to repossess the land, they are generally turned away by freedmen. In at least one instance on a South Carolina Sea Island, whites are turned back by armed black men.

REPA. Callie House is born into slavery in Nashville, Tennessee. House proposes the first class action reparations suit against the U.S. government for unpaid slave labor by African Americans.

WAR. On April 12, Confederate batteries in Charleston, South Carolina, fire cannon shells on Fort Sumter in Charleston Harbor.

On April 15, President Lincoln called for 75,000 men to enlist in the military for 90 days to put down the southern rebellion. He rejects, however, the official participation of black soldiers.

Nicholas Biddle, a 65-year-old runaway slave from Pottsville, Pennsylvania, responds to President Lincoln's appeal for volunteers after the attack on Fort Sumter. Attaching himself to the Washington Artillerists and the National Light Infantry, he marches from Pottsville with the younger soldiers into Baltimore, Maryland. A pro-Confederate mob attacks the soldiers, and in particular Biddle. Struck in the face by a rock and bleeding profusely, Biddle and the other troops finally arrive in Washington, DC. After this incident, Biddle drops out of sight until his death but holds the distinction of shedding the first blood in the war for the Union.

In May, U.S. Gen. George B. McClellan declares to Virginia slave owners that any attempt at slave insurrection will be crushed.

On May 24, the U.S. commanding general for the Department of Virginia, Benjamin F. Butler, confronts Confederate Maj. John B. Cary during a truce and debates the future of three runaway slaves who sought protection in Union lines. Major Cary argues for their release, but General Butler insists on detaining them as "contraband of war." Though General Butler is given credit for first using the term *contraband* in reference to escaped slaves, it is actually used the day before by a *New York Tribune* reporter describing the plight of escaping blacks from Confederate-held territory.

On September 25, the secretary of the U.S. Navy authorizes the enlistment of slaves. Although they serve in integrated units, these black sailors hold ranks no higher than boy, the lowest rank possible. Early in the Civil War, however, they participate in a number of crucial battles in the seas off South Carolina.

WORK. Before the formation of the Confederate States of America (February 4, 1861) but after the secession of South Carolina (December 12, 1860), 82 free black men in Charleston petition Gov. Francis W. Pickens for any form of assignment in armed service to help defend the safety of South Carolina. Governor Pickens rejects the offer; however, white South Carolinians are pleased to know that they have a counterbalance to any possible slave rebellion during any possible conflict with the North.

Virginia impressment laws compel free black men to work on Confederate defenses around Richmond and Petersburg.

1862

CIVI. Ida B. Wells, reformer, publisher, civil rights activist, and early statistician on the lynching of African Americans, is born in Holly Springs, Mississippi.

EDUC. Mary Jane Patterson is the first black woman to receive a bachelor's degree from Oberlin College.

Charlotte Forten, the granddaughter of shipbuilder and Revolutionary War patriot James Forten, begins teaching and nursing in St. Helena's Island, South Carolina. She is a close friend of Col. Robert Gould Shaw, the commanding officer of the Fifty-Fourth Massachusetts Volunteer Infantry. Her diary documents the lifestyle and thoughts of black soldiers during the Civil War.

On August 22, in a reply to newspaper editor Horace Greeley, Abraham Lincoln expounds on his political priorities in preserving the Union when he states:

> My paramount object in this struggle is to save the Union, and is *not* either to save or destroy slavery. If I could save the Union with out freeing *any* slaves, I would do it; and if I could save it by freeing *all* the slaves, I would do it; and if I could do it by freeing some and leaving others alone, I would also do that…. I have here stated my purpose according to my view of *official* duty, and I intend no modification of my oft-expressed *personal* wish that all men, everywhere, could be free.

Concluding that the central issue in holding the Union together is the issue of slavery, Abraham Lincoln confides in his secretary of the navy, Gideon Welles: "We must free the slaves or ourselves be subdued. The slaves were undeniably an element of strength to those who had their service, and we must decide whether that element should be with us or against us … Emancipation would strike at the heart of the rebellion."

POLI. On March 6, President Abraham Lincoln sends a message to Congress suggesting that gradual and possible compensated emancipation might be in order. The border states of Missouri, Kentucky, Maryland, and Delaware reject any such proposal.

On March 13, Congress officially prohibits the return of fugitive slaves to their owners. Lincoln funds voluntary emigration of blacks from the United States to Haiti and Liberia.

On April 16, Congress abolishes slavery in Washington, DC, and enacts a bill to pay District of Columbia slave owners up to $300 for each slave they free as well as provide $100,000 in support for blacks' voluntary colonization of Haiti or Liberia.

On July 22, President Lincoln submits a draft of the Emancipation Proclamation to his cabinet.

On August 14, President Lincoln invites a handpicked group of freemen, who for the first time confer with a U.S. president on national policy relating to blacks in the United States. Lincoln's agenda for the meeting includes the viability of black colonization in Central America or Africa. Frederick Douglass and a number of other northern black leaders immediately condemn the meeting and any policy that forces emigration upon blacks. One participant in the meeting, James M. McPherson, recalls that Lincoln tells them that it is their duty to leave the United States and that staying will cause both races to suffer.

On September 22, President Lincoln issues a preliminary Emancipation Proclamation that, in effect, warns the Confederate states that he will free slaves in all states in rebellion on January 1, 1863, unless hostility to the federal government ceases. The preliminary proclamation is announced only after the Union Army is assured a military victory at the battle of Antietam in western Maryland, where 2,000 men, both Union and Confederate, are killed in a single day of battle.

In December, President Lincoln urges Congress to provide federal funds as compensation for states that abolish slavery before 1900.

SLAV. In April, Susie King Baker (who later is known as Susie King Taylor after her marriage to Sgt. Edward King of the Thirty-Third United States Colored Troops) and her uncle enlist in a newly formed regiment of black Union soldiers under the command of Maj. Gen. David Hunter. She is appointed laundress of the Thirty-Third U.S. Colored Troops (initially the First South Carolina Volunteers), but due to her reading and writing skills, her responsibilities grow to include nursing. Her written reminiscences help document the role black women play in the Civil War and Reconstruction.

WAR. In May, Gen. David Hunter unofficially begins organizing the first black regiment, the First South Carolina Volunteers. General Hunter then issues a proclamation freeing slaves in Georgia, Florida, and South Carolina. Lincoln revokes the proclamation.

On May 13, Robert Smalls pilots a Confederate steamer, the *Planter,* out of Charleston, South Carolina's, harbor into the waiting hands of Union forces. Smalls wins a substantial reward from Congress and is made captain of the *Planter* when it is refitted as a gunboat.

On July 17, Congress authorizes the president to accept blacks in the Union military.

In August, Gen. Benjamin F. Butler, who made the term *contraband* popular, calls for black volunteers from New Orleans after his Union forces capture the city. French-speaking black soldiers from the First Regiment of Louisiana Native Guards (Corps d'Afrique), having unsuccessfully offered their services to the Confederate Army, are now given a choice: either join the Union Army or be captured as contraband. This is not an easy choice because their history includes fighting in the War of 1812 under the command of Andrew Jackson, and they were invited to march in the 1861 New Orleans Confederate Grand Review. Earlier in the year, however, the Confederate War Department issued Special Order 60 that proclaimed all black troops and their white officers were outlaws of war.

On August 25, the U.S. Secretary of War Edwin M. Stanton authorizes Gen. Rufus Saxton to arm up to 5,000 slaves for military service.

In October, the Kansas Volunteers become the first black soldiers of the Civil War to engage in combat operations when they repulse a superior force of Confederate forces near Island Mound, Missouri. Later at Honey Springs, Missouri, they fight against Cherokees who have aligned themselves with the Confederate cause.

On December 22, 1861, white New York troops claim they have encountered about 700 armed black troops near Newport News, Virginia.

In May 1862, near Yorktown, Virginia, a black Confederate sharpshooter positions himself in a chimney and shoots several passing Union soldiers before he is finally killed.

1863

EDUC. On September 22, educator and civil rights organizer Mary Church Terrell is born in Washington, DC.

Wilberforce University in Ohio becomes the first college administered by black educators when Daniel Payne purchases the school for the African Methodist Episcopal Church. He becomes the university's first president.

MEDI. Alexander Thomas Augusta becomes the first black surgeon in the United States Army. Augusta joins the Union troops after graduating from Trinity Medical College.

POLI. On January 1, President Abraham Lincoln signs the Emancipation Proclamation that, in essence, frees enslaved blacks in Confederate states with the exception of 13 parishes (including New Orleans) in Louisiana, 48 counties in Virginia that will become West Virginia, and 7 counties (including Norfolk) in eastern Virginia. The proclamation does not apply to enslaved blacks in the border states of Missouri, Kentucky, Maryland, and Delaware.

In February, in response to President Lincoln's Emancipation Proclamation, Confederate President Jefferson Davis issues a counterproclamation, stating that all free blacks in the South will be considered slaves and that any black captured in a free state will be considered a slave upon capture.

WAR. On January 26, the U.S. War Department authorizes Gov. John A. Andrews of Massachusetts to recruit blacks for an official regiment. The Fifty-Fourth Massachusetts Volunteer Infantry becomes the first regiment recruited in the North.

In March, two black infantry regiments, the First and Second South Carolina Volunteers, capture and occupy Jacksonville, Florida, causing panic along the southern coastline of the Confederacy.

On May 1, the Confederate congress passes a resolution that brands black troops and their officers as criminals. This order confers a death sentence or slavery to any captured black Union soldier.

On May 22, the U.S. War Department establishes the Bureau of Colored Troops and launches an aggressive campaign to recruit black soldiers.

By June, Harriett Tubman organizes a spy ring in the South Carolina low country and in cooperation with the all-black Second South Carolina Volunteer Regiment helps facilitate a raid that destroys plantations and frees nearly 800 slaves, many of whom later join the Union Army. With a bandanna on her head and several front teeth missing, she moves unnoticed through rebel territory. This makes her invaluable as a scout and spy under the command of Col. James Montgomery of the Second Carolina Volunteers. As leader of a corps of local blacks, she makes several forays into rebel territory, collecting information. Armed with knowledge of the location of cotton warehouses, ammunition depots, and slaves waiting to be liberated, Colonel Montgomery makes several raids in southern coastal areas. Tubman leads the way on his celebrated expedition up the Combahee River in June. For three years' work, Harriett Tubman is paid only $200. She must support herself by selling pies, gingerbread, and root beer.

Mary Elizabeth Bowser works in the Confederate White House in Richmond, Virginia. She reports to Union agents conversations of President Davis and his subordinates. Bowser and Jim Pemberton, a slave who is also a part of the Union spy ring, escape when suspicion is aroused about their activities.

From July 13 to 17, hostility to the draft and the possibility of free black economic competition with whites in the labor market (particularly with the Irish), leads to one of the country's bloodiest racial conflicts, the New York City draft riots.

At 7:45 P.M. on July 18, 650 Union soldiers from the Fifty-Fourth Massachusetts Volunteer Infantry attack Fort Wagner, a Confederate fort bordering Charleston, South Carolina's, harbor. Their charge on the fort is not initially successful; however, by September the Confederates are forced to abandon Fort Wagner. Sgt. William H. Carney receives the Medal of Honor for his role in the attack and becomes the first black soldier to receive the military award.

During the attack on Fort Wagner by black Union soldiers, John Wilson Buckner, a free black Confederate soldier with a light complexion is wounded. Buckner is a member the Ellison family, a well-known and favored free black family from Stateburg, South Carolina. Considered a so-called honorary white man, he is wounded during the bombardment of the Fort Wagner just before the attack by the Fifty-Fourth Massachusetts Volunteer Infantry.

President Lincoln issues a so-called eye-for-an-eye order, warning the Confederate government that the Union will shoot one rebel prisoner for every black prisoner shot and will condemn one rebel soldier to hard labor for every black soldier sold into slavery. This order has very little impact upon the practices of rebel soldiers or their officers.

Black soldiers receive less pay than white soldiers primarily because of an assumption that they will work construction, transportation, cooking, and burial details but will not fight against Confederate soldiers. For example, a white private earns $13 per month, whereas a black soldier earns only $10 per month, of which $3 is taken for clothing expenses, giving him a total of $7 per month. The Fifty-Fourth Massachusetts Volunteer Infantry refuses to accept their pay until it equals that of whites.

In November, Sgt. William Walker of the Third South Carolina Volunteers and other black soldiers refuse to fight until they are given equal pay and other intolerable living conditions are improved. Walker is found guilt of mutiny.

In the last two years of the war, approximately 179,000 blacks join the Union Army and Navy, thereby providing 12 percent of all Northern troops. U.S. military records indicate that only 110 blacks serve as active commissioned officers during the Civil War, and two-thirds of these officers belong to the Louisiana Native Guards. Of this group of officers, one-fourth are chaplains or surgeons.

1864

ASSO. The Knights of Pythias is established on February 19.

On October 4, the Seventh National Black Convention meets in Syracuse, New York.

MED. In July, the *New Orleans Tribune* becomes the first daily black newspaper. Founded by Dr. Louis C. Roudanez, it starts as a triweekly publication but by October is published daily in both English and French.

MEDI. On March 1, 1864, Rebecca Lee Crumpler graduates from the New England Female Medical College and becomes the first black female physician.

The first black woman to practice dentistry professionally is probably Emile Roberts Jones of Connecticut. After her husband's death, she develops his dental practice into a large business concern.

George Washington Carver is born a slave in Diamond Grove, Missouri. He spends much of his early youth doing menial work in Missouri, Iowa, and Kansas. He spends a year at Simpson College and then, in 1891, enrolls at Iowa State University as the only black student. He excels academically and becomes the caretaker of the campus greenhouse, where he becomes fascinated with botany, mycology (the study of fungi), and cross-fertilization. In 1896, at the request of

Booker T. Washington, Carver leaves Iowa State University and becomes the director of Tuskegee Institute's agriculture program. Committing to work with both students and local farmers to make their products more viable, he strives to help farmers diversify their crops beyond cotton. He develops more than 100 different uses for the protein-rich peanut. He receives the National Association for the Advancement of Colored People's (NAACP's) Spingarn Medal in 1923. Though he never earns more than $1,200 per year, he gives more than $60,000 to the Tuskegee Institute before his death in 1943.

WAR. Confederate Gen. Patrick Cleburne suggests enlisting slaves in the rebel cause if they promise to remain loyal. He argues that this policy will appeal to potential foreign allies such as England and that it will disrupt the Union's enlistment of black southerners. Most southerners, however, abhor the idea of arming blacks, slaves or free. President Davis orders General Cleburne to cease and desist in these discussions or efforts.

On April 12, Confederate Gen. Nathan Bedford Forrest attacks and captures Fort Pillow, Tennessee. A combined force of 600 Eleventh U.S. Colored Troops and white Unionists of the Thirteenth Tennessee Cavalry face the onslaught of 1,500 attacking Confederate cavalry and ground forces. The resulting slaughter of 200 surrendering Union black and white soldiers turns the Mississippi River red with blood, or as Forrest notes in his report of the attack, the river is "dyed with blood of the slaughtered for 200 yards."

On April 18, the First Kansas Volunteers (black) are outnumbered by Confederate troops at Poison Spring, Arkansas. Southern troops fire on trapped and wounded black soldiers as Union forces retreat. Breaking out of the entrapment, they sustain heavy casualties. Of the 438 members of the First Kansas, 182 are killed or missing. None are taken prisoner. A sister unit, the Second Kansas Volunteers, swears to revenge the slaughter and take no Confederate prisoners in future battles.

On June 14, the U.S. Congress repeals all fugitive slave laws and grants black Union soldiers equal pay, arms, equipment, and medical services.

On June 25, President Abraham Lincoln signs a bill providing schools for black children.

On July 30, in a major military blunder, three white and one black Union divisions are soundly defeated in an attempt to explode an underground mine near Confederate forces. Later the same day, however, the Forty-Third United States Colored Troops captures 200 Confederate soldiers and two stands of colors. Decatur Dorsey of the Thirty-Ninth United States Colored Troops receives the Medal of Honor for his actions.

On August 5, John Lawson, a black gunner on Adm. David Farragut's flagship, exhibits extreme courage in the battle of Mobile Bay and receives the Medal of Honor.

From September 19 to 30, 13 black soldiers receive the Medal of Honor for gallantry in capturing the fortified Confederate entrenchments at New Market Heights, Virginia.

At Jenkins Ferry, Arkansas, the Second Kansas Volunteers charge into battle shouting "Remember Poison Spring!" Overrunning the rebel positions, they kill 150 Confederates and lose 15 of their own soldiers. One rebel is taken prisoner by mistake.

On December 3, the Twenty-Fifth Corps is formed as part of the Army of the James. It is the largest all-black unit in the history of the U.S. Army.

On December 15 and 16 outside of Nashville, Tennessee, in one of the most decisive battles of the Civil War, two brigades of black troops help crush one of the South's finest armies. Black troops open the battle and successfully engage the right side of the rebel line. On the second day, Col. Charles R. Thompson's black brigade makes a brilliant charge up Overton Hill. The Thirteenth United States Colored Troops sustain heavier casualties than any other regiment involved in the battle.

1865

AGRI. President Andrew Johnson moves to reverse the federal policy that distributes abandoned land to freedmen, particularly in the states of South Carolina and Georgia.

CULT. June 16 is celebrated by as Juneteenth, the day all Texas slaves are freed. Although the

Emancipation Proclamation was issued in 1863, slavery in Texas and southern states under Confederate control continue. When Gen. Gordon Granger arrives in Galveston with Union forces, however, he announces that all slaves in Texas are free, which represents one-third of the entire state population. Jubilation spreads throughout the enslaved populace. Texas and many other areas of the South celebrate this date annually as a holiday.

EDUC. On July 26, Patrick Francis Healy is the first black to be awarded a PhD after he passes his final examination at the University of Louvain in Belgium.

In September, three major black educational institutions are founded: Atlanta University, Shaw University, and Virginia Union University.

EXP. On August 8, Matthew A. Henson, the first known person to reach the North Pole, is born.

FINA. The Freedmen's Savings Bank and Trust Company is formed. Chartered by the U.S. Congress but not connected to the Freedmen's Bureau, the bank quickly holds thousands of accounts for black Civil War veterans, black churches, and fraternal and benevolent organizations. Most of its accounts are $50 or less. Though African Americans are the holders of most of the accounts, the board of trustees and directors are white.

POLI. On February 1, John S. Rock becomes the first black admitted to practice before the U.S. Supreme Court.

On February 12, Henry Highland Garnet is the first black to address Congress when he gives a memorial address to the House of Representatives on the abolition of slavery.

On April 14, President Abraham Lincoln is shot and critically wounded by John Wilkes Booth at the Ford Theatre in Washington, DC. Booth escapes from the theater and is later killed by police or commits suicide. Vice President Andrew Johnson becomes the 17th president of the United States and almost immediately reverses Gen. William Tecumseh Sherman's Special Field Order No. 15, which redistributed land to ex-slaves, and allows former Confederates and their supporters to repossess the land.

President Abraham Lincoln dies on April 15.

On May 11, Blacks in Norfolk, Virginia, hold a mass meeting to demand equal voting rights. Similar demands occur during conventions in Petersburg, Virginia, on June 6; Vicksburg, Mississippi, on June 19; Alexandria, Virginia, on August 3; Nashville, Tennessee, on August 7 to 11; Raleigh, North Carolina, on September 29 to October 3; Richmond, Virginia, on September 18; and Jackson, Mississippi, on October 7.

On May 13, one black Union regiment (the Sixty-Second United States Colored Troops) and two white Confederate regiments fight in the last action of the war at White's Ranch, Texas.

On October 19, Gen. O. O. Howard, head of the Freedmen's Bureau, tells a meeting of freedmen on Edisto Island that the government has decided to return confiscated Confederate plantations to southern white planters. This causes freedmen in South Carolina, Virginia, and other southern States to arm themselves against any move to repossess the land.

On December 24, six former Confederate soldiers and sympathizers found the Ku Klux Klan in Pulaski, Tennessee. Former Confederate General Nathan Bedford Forrest will become its first Grand Wizard.

SLAV. On December 6, Congress ratifies the Thirteen Amendment to the U.S. Constitution, thereby abolishing slavery as a legal U.S. institution. In what will become controversial language, however, the amendment states, "Neither slavery nor involuntary servitude, except as a punishment for crime whereof the party shall have been duly convicted, shall exist within the United States, or any place subject to their jurisdiction." The vote in the House of Representatives is 121 to 24.

On March 3, the U.S. Congress establishes the Bureau of Refugees, Freedmen, and Abandoned Lands (Freedmen's Bureau) to aid refugees and newly emancipated slaves.

The U.S. Congress charters the Freedmen's Savings Bank and Trust Company, whose aim is to provide financial support to the newly emancipated and free black population.

WAR. On January 16, Union Gen. William Tecumseh Sherman announces that freemen

Thomas Morris Chester, the only black correspondent of the entire civil war, publishes the following observations of the newly abandoned Confederate Congress Hall in a Philadelphia newspaper:

> The Union element in this city consists of Negroes and poor whites, …including all that have deserted from the army, or having survived the terrible exigencies which brought starvation to so many homes…. Not even the familiarity peculiar to Americans is indulged in, calling the blacks by their first or Christian names, but even masters are addressing their slaves as "Mr. Johnson," "Mrs. Brown," and "Miss Smith." A cordial shake of the hand and a gentle inclination of the body, approaching to respectful consideration, are evident in the greetings which now take place between the oppressed and the oppressor.

will receive land as a result of Special Field Order No. 15. This military proclamation states that a 30-mile block of land stretching some 245 miles along the Atlantic coast from Charleston, South Carolina, to Jacksonville, Florida, will be set aside for farming and development by the ex-slave population. The order provides that "each family would have a forty-acre plot on which to farm, and that military forces would protect their ownership of this land." Under the direction of Gen. Rufus Saxton, some 40,000 blacks on 40-acre tracts work rich farming land in the low country of South Carolina and Georgia. In South Carolina, black farmers receive possessor titles pending final action on the confiscated and abandoned lands of Confederates.

Confederate military forces abandon Charleston, South Carolina, on February 18. Union Forces led by the Twenty-First United States Colored Troops and followed by two companies of the Fifty-Fourth Massachusetts Volunteer Infantry capture the city.

On March 13 (though most white southerners reject the idea), the Confederate congress votes to enlist 300,000 black men between the ages of 18 and 45 to receive the same pay, equipment, and supplies as white soldiers. The new policy stipulates, however, that if the enlisted blacks are slaves, they will not be freed unless their owner consents and the state in which they serve agrees to their emancipation.

On April 2, after nearly six months of horrific fighting and stalemate, the Fifty-Fourth Massachusetts Cavalry enters Richmond, Virginia, as the first Union unit to do so.

On April 12, with elements of the Twenty-Fifth Corps and white Union soldiers chasing Confederate troops from Richmond to Appomattox, Virginia, Gen. Robert E. Lee's trapped army surrenders, thus officially ending the Civil War.

WORK. The Mississippi legislature enacts the Black Codes, a set of restrictions and regulations that monitor every aspect of the freedmen's life within Mississippi and other southern states. A major tenet of the codes is the arrest of so-called vagrants, or those blacks who are either unemployed or without shelter. Vagrancy is classified as a felony; thereby, under the Thirteenth Amendment to the U.S. Constitution, a vagrant is eligible for arrest and imprisonment, or "involuntary servitude." Such imprisonments provides free labor to planters for the building of roads, levees, and so forth without pay. It is, in fact, another form of enslavement.

1866

EDUC. Fisk University in Tennessee is founded on January 6 by the Congregational Church of the American Missionary Association, the Western Freedmen's Aid Commission, and by former Union Army Gen. Clinton D. Fisk of the Freedmen's Bureau. Beginning as a free school that provides primary thorough college education for newly freed blacks, its early days are financially lean as students attended classrooms that are abandoned Union Army barracks.

Rust College in Mississippi and Lincoln University in Missouri are founded.

POLI. The Southern Homestead Act is approved. It provides more than three million acres of land

At the end of the Civil War, 186,107 black soldiers are enlisted in the Union Army, representing some 10 percent to 12 percent of the troops; 8 percent to 25 percent of the Union Navy are black, though none of them are officers. Black officers in the Army number 7,122, mostly chaplains and surgeons. In the last 23 months of the war, black soldiers and sailors participate in 449 engagements, 39 of which are major battles. One-third of all black causalities, 68,178, result in death, of which 2,751 are immediate combat deaths and the rest from wounds and disease. At 14 percent of the population, blacks account for about 20 percent of total Union casualties. Seventeen blacks receive the Medal of Honor.

in Alabama, Arkansas, Florida, Louisiana, and Mississippi to settlers, regardless of race. Poor blacks and whites are generally unable to take advantage of the public land offer due to the land's unsuitability for farming. Eventually, large timber companies are able to benefit from the act.

On February 7, Frederick Douglass and a delegation of blacks meet with President Andrew Johnson during which they urge him to support voting rights for the black population. Their meeting ends in serious disagreement when Johnson refuses to support any move toward black suffrage.

In Memphis throughout the month of March, blacks and whites clash violently in a series of riots than result in the deaths of 44 blacks and 75 seriously injured. Republican newspapers claim the cause is the presence of black soldiers patrolling the streets and not showing deference to whites.

From May 1 to 3, white Democrats and police attack freedmen and white Republicans in Memphis, Tennessee. Forty-six blacks and two white liberals are killed. More than 70 persons are injured and 90 homes, 12 schools, and 4 churches burned.

On April 9, the Freedmen's Bureau Bill and the Civil Rights Act of 1866 are introduced into Congress. The second proposal entitles any person born in the United States to citizenship (except the indigenous population) and entitles them to the rights protected by the United States government. This bill aims to invalidate the southern states' Black Codes. President Andrew Johnson vetoes each bill; however, Congress overrides each of his vetoes.

On June 13, Congress passes the Fourteenth Amendment to the U.S. Constitution, thereby guaranteeing citizenship to anyone born in the United States; citizenship in the state in which they are born; and property rights and due process of law before any citizen can lose their life, liberty, or property.

In July, Radical Republicans, both black and white, react to the passage of Black Codes by the Louisiana legislature and its unwillingness to enfranchise blacks. Twenty-five delegates, along with numerous supporters, attempt to meet on July 30 for a convention at the Mechanics Institute, in New Orleans. That same afternoon, a group of white Democrats led by police, attack the building and the convention's black and white Republicans. At least 40 people, black and white, are killed, and at least 150 are wounded in the violent struggle. Federal troops are summoned to stop the violence but arrived too late. Gen. Phillip Sheridan observes that both "the mayor and the police of the city perpetrated without the shadow of a necessity" on the side of the Democrats.

Edward G. Walker (son of abolitionist David Walker) and Charles L. Mitchell are elected to the Massachusetts Assembly from Boston, making them the first African Americans to sit in that state's legislature in the post–Civil War period.

1867

ASSO. On April 24, the first national meeting of the Ku Klux (Klan) is held at the Maxwell House in Nashville, Tennessee.

CIVI. On April 24, blacks demonstrate in Richmond, Virginia, for the right to sit in streetcars. Troops are mobilized to restore order.

And not this man? Lady Liberty (Columbia) speaking, with hand on shoulder of a Civil War soldier who lost a leg in the war. The illustration appeared in an 1865 *Harper's Weekly* article on black suffrage. Courtesy of Library of Congress.

Peabody amassed a fortune as a merchant and financier in England and the United States. As a result, he not only funds institutes in Baltimore and at Yale and Harvard Universities that bear his name but also establishes an education fund for "the promotion and encouragement of intellectual, moral, or industrial education among the young people of the more destitute portions of the Southern and Southwestern States." Between 1867 and 1914, the fund provides more than $3.5 million for the advancement of education in the South.

In February, Morehouse College is founded in Augusta, Georgia. It is later moved to Atlanta, Georgia.

A number of black colleges and universities are founded throughout the Reconstruction Era: Atlanta University (Atlanta, Georgia), Virginia Union University (Richmond, Virginia) (1865); Fisk University (Nashville, Tennessee), Lincoln University (1866); Talladega College (Talladega, Alabama),

On May 1, the Charleston, South Carolina, City Railway Company adopts a resolution that guarantees the right of all persons to ride in streetcars. Where they are allowed to sit is a different question.

On May 7, black demonstrators staged a sit-in, protesting segregation in New Orleans streetcars. Similar demonstrations occur in Mobile, Alabama.

EDUC. On February 6, the Peabody Fund is established to promote black education. George

Howard University (Washington, D.C.), Morgan State University (Baltimore, Maryland), Morehouse College (Atlanta, Georgia) (1867); Hampton University (Hampton, Virginia) (1868); Clark College (Atlanta, Georgia), Dillard University (New Orleans, Louisiana), Claflin College (Orangeburg, South Carolina) (1869); Allen University (Columbia, South Carolina), Benedict College (Columbia, South Carolina), LeMoyne-Owen College (Memphis, Tennessee) (1870); Alcorn State University (Alcorn, Mississippi) (1872);

Bennett College (Greensboro, North Carolina) (1873); Knoxville College (Knoxville, Tennessee) (1875); Meharry Medical College (Nashville, Tennessee) (1876); and Voorhees College (Denmark, South Carolina) (1897). In this regard, black ministers and their churches become necessary sources of social networking, finance, and labor in support of these schools. Well-known ministers and laymen who support this effort include Frank Quarles, Alonzo Cardozo, James Lynch, and William Jefferson White.

MEDI. On September 1, Robert Tanner Freemen enters Harvard University and becomes the first person of African ancestry to be accepted into an U.S. school of dentistry. Previously, dentists were trained under programs of apprenticeship. This changed in 1840 when the world's first dental school, Baltimore College of Dental Surgery, was established in Maryland. The training of African American dentists increases in the late 1880s with the founding of Howard University's Dental College (Washington, DC) in 1881 and the establishment in 1886 of a dental department at Meharry Medical College in Nashville, Tennessee. These two schools still graduate the largest number of black dentists. A product of this development in medicine is Charles E. Bentley, whose graduation from the Chicago College of Dental Surgery in 1887 launches a career as a clinician, scientist, humanitarian, prolific writer, orator, public health pioneer, and civil rights activist.

OBIT. On August 7, black Shakespearean actor Ira Aldridge dies at the age of 63 in Lodz, Poland.

POLI. On January 6, President Andrew Johnson unsuccessfully attempts to veto legislature that gives suffrage to African Americans.

On March 2, the U.S. Congress passes the first of a succession of Reconstruction acts that divides the country into five military zones under the command of army generals. Military personnel protect the lives of ex-slaves and their new landed status. Delegates from each state at newly formed constitutional conventions are expected to draft a new constitution and submit it to a new constituency

Morehouse College, Atlanta, Georgia. Courtesy of Library of Congress.

of black voters. Maj. Gen. E.R.S. Canby opens the jury system to blacks in South Carolina and North Carolina.

On March 27, blacks demonstrate in Charleston, South Carolina, in an effort to force the desegregation of streetcars.

On May 1, Reconstruction begins with the registering of black and white voters in the South. Gen. Philip H. Sheridan orders that registration begin that day and continue until June 30. Consequently, registration began in Arkansas in May but not until June and even July in other states. By October 31, some 1,363,000 citizens register to vote, including some 700,000 blacks. White proslavery and Confederate sympathizers are very much concerned that black voters constitute the majority in five southern states: Alabama, Florida, Louisiana, Mississippi, and South Carolina.

In early May, the Knights of the White Camellia, a paramilitary organization of white businessmen and political functionaries, is founded in Perry and Monroe Counties, Louisiana. They generally engage in nonviolent psychological terrorism by sending threatening letters and posting warnings to Republican leaders or riding armed along roads frequently used by blacks when they return from Republican political meetings. Law officers and judges belong to this organization; consequently, no jury will or can be summoned in cases relating to the rights of African Americans.

On August 1, blacks in Tennessee vote en masse for the first time in a southern state election, thereby contributing to a sweeping Republican victory.

In September, Gen. E.R.S. Canby orders the South Carolina courts to impanel black jurors.

In October, Monroe Baker, a prosperous black businessman, is named mayor of St. Martin, Louisiana. He is probably the first black to serve as mayor of a U.S. town.

On November 5, the first Reconstruction constitutional convention, consisting of 18 blacks and 90 whites, convenes in Montgomery, Alabama.

On November 23, the Louisiana constitutional convention convenes with 49 black delegates and 49 white delegates. They meet at the Mechanics Institute in New Orleans.

From November 19 to 20, South Carolinians endorse their state's constitutional convention and select delegates. In fulfilling this process,

records indicate that some 66,418 blacks and 2,350 whites vote for holding the convention, and 2,278 whites vote against holding a constitutional convention. Of 71,046 votes cast, not a single black voted against the convention.

On December 3, the Virginia constitutional convention of 25 blacks and 80 whites convenes in Richmond. The constitution is adopted until July 6, 1869.

On December 6, Georgia's constitutional convention convenes in Atlanta with 33 blacks and 137 whites.

WORK. In April, 30 blacks become policemen in Mobile, Alabama.

On July 15, businesswoman and civic leader Maggie Lena Mitchell is born in Richmond, Virginia. Mitchell graduates from normal school in 1883 and teaches primary school. In 1886, she marries Armstead Walker and begins her career as a wife, mother, and civic leader. Active in the Independent Order of St. Luke, an African American mutual aid society, one of many that flourished at that time, Maggie Walker is elected Grand Matron and becomes the Right Worthy Grand Secretary in 1899. When she assumes her duties, the order has $31.61 in funds and 1,080 members. She proves to be an inspirational and dynamic leader who stresses racial solidarity while attacking the lynching of blacks. By the early twentieth century, under Maggie's guidance, the Order of St. Luke has chapters in 22 states. By 1924, the Independent Order of St. Luke has funds totaling $3,480,540. The Order has a newspaper, the *Luke Herald,* and a bank with Maggie Lena Walker as president. She is the first black woman to serve as chief executive of a bank in the United States. The bank subsequently merges with two other banks and is renamed the Consolidated Bank and Trust Company with Walker as president. She is particularly pleased that the bank enables black customers to purchase homes. Walker remains very much concerned with the plight of black women, and she makes certain that the Order employ African American women in significant positions. Financially assisting in the development of Virginia Union University while establishing a number of civic organizations, such as Piedmont Tuberculosis Sanitarium for Negroes, the Virginia Federation of Colored

Women, the Richmond Council for Colored Women, the Council of Women of the Darker Races, she also becomes an active member of the National Association for the Advancement of Colored People (NAACP) in 1912.

1868

CRIM. On June 1, Solomon George Washington Dill, a poor white ally of black Republicans, is assassinated in his home by white terrorists. Dill allegedly made incendiary speeches to South Carolina blacks.

On September 19, white Democrats attack demonstrators marching from Albany to Camilla, Georgia. Nine blacks are killed and several whites wounded.

On September 28 in Opelousas, St. Landry Parish, Louisiana, some 200 to 300 African Americans are killed by roving bands of Klansmen of the Knights of the White Camellia and an allied group of terrorists, the Seymour Knights. The killings begin in the evening when a local teacher of black students receives a warning that his recent article in a local Republican newspaper, the *St. Landry Progress* is politically unsuitable. Refusing to retract any aspect of his article, he is brutally beaten in front of his students. When word of the incident reaches the black community, some blacks arm themselves. Apparently foreseeing this response, armed bands of Klansmen kill and maim any black seen with a gun. Better armed and organized than the local black hamlets, the Klansmen quickly demoralize the black community in St. Landry, to the extent that blacks are forced to vote the Democratic ticket in Seymour and Blair later that fall.

EDUC. On April 1, Hampton Normal and Agriculture Institute is founded in Virginia. Samuel Armstrong, a white missionary with strong southern sympathies, dominates the Institute as its superintendent. The curriculum consists of skills such as shoemaking, carpentry, tailoring, and sewing. Under Armstrong's leadership, the curriculum places little emphasis on critical independent thinking and nurtures southern, white, Christian, middle-class values that caution blacks about involvement in politics. The institute's superintendent personally acquiesces to southern racial segregation codes and hangs pictures of

Andrew Johnson and Confederate Gen. Robert E. Lee throughout the institute.

LAW. In July, Jonathan Jasper Wright is elected as a delegate to South Carolina's constitutional convention. In this role, he helps shape provisions related to the judiciary. In the first election in which freedmen can vote, Wright is elected senator from Beaufort County. Shortly after his election to Congress, he is chosen to be the first African American elected to any appeals court in the nation. As associate justice of the Supreme Court, Wright writes 87 opinions recognized for their clear thinking and solid basis in common law.

On July 9, the U.S. Congress ratifies the Fourteenth Amendment to the U.S. Constitution. Section 1 of this amendment states that anyone born or naturalized in the United States is considered a U.S. citizen and, therefore, cannot be deprived of life, liberty, or property without due process of law. As of this date, people of African heritage become legally Americans of African heritage, or African Americans.

On November 9, Howard University's medical school opens with eight students.

On April 16 and 17, Louisiana voters approve a new constitution and elect the first black lieutenant governor, Oscar J. Dunn, and its first black state treasurer, Antoine DuBuclet (a former slave owner). Article 13 in its new constitution bans segregation in public accommodations.

On May 16, the U.S. Senate fails to impeach President Andrew Johnson. The vote, 34 to 16, is not the needed two-thirds for impeachment.

On June 13, Oscar J. Dunn, is sworn in as lieutenant governor of Louisiana. This is the highest elective office at that time held by an African American.

On June 22, the U.S. Congress agrees to readmit Arkansas to the Union on the condition that it will never change its state constitution to disenfranchise the African American populace.

By July 6, South Carolina has a black majority in its state legislature. More than half of the legislators (87) are African American, and the rest (40) are white. South Carolina is the only state ever to have a black majority and is the first and last U.S. state legislature to have a black majority. White South Carolinians control the state senate and by 1874 also regain control of the state legislature.

Louisiana Gov. Henry C. Warmoth supports a joint state legislature resolution calling for federal military aid as a result of 150 political assassinations in June and July.

On August 11, Thaddeuas Stevens, the architect of the Radical Republican southern Reconstruction program dies in Washington, DC, at the age of 76.

On September 13, the lower house of the Georgia legislature rules that African Americans are ineligible to hold political office. Twenty-eight black legislators are expelled. Ten days later, the state senate expels three blacks. The U.S. Congress refuses to admit Georgia as a state until the black legislators are readmitted.

On November 3, John Willis Menard of Louisiana becomes the first African American to be elected Congress, though Congressman James A. Garfield contests the election, claiming that it is "too early to admit a Negro to the U.S. Congress." Menard, who defeated his white opponent 5,107 votes to 2,833 in Louisiana's Second Congressional District, receives premature congratulations because he is eventually denied a seat in the House of Representatives.

African American voters provide the decisive margin in the presidential election when Ulysses S. Grant becomes the 18th president of the United States.

MUS. Scott Joplin is born in Texarkana, Texas. He is the reputed father of ragtime music.

POLI. On February 10, conservative Republicans, supported by military forces, physically take over the convention hall in Tallahassee, Florida, and draft a new constitution and concentrate political power in the hands of the governor while limiting the political impact of the black populace.

William Edward Burghardt (W.E.B.) Du Bois is born on February 23 in Great Barrington, Massachusetts.

On February 24, the United States House of Representatives votes 126 to 47 to impeach President Andrew Johnson.

From April 14 to 16, South Carolina's voters approved the new state constitution 70,758 to 27,228. Elected state office holders include the first black cabinet officer, Francis L. Cardozo, as secretary of state. Article VIII, Section 2 of the new constitution "Rights of Suffrage," emphasizes "Distinctions on account of race or color, in any case whatever, shall be prohibited, and all classes of citizens shall enjoy equally all common, public, legal and political privileges."

SPOR. On December 11, the color line is drawn in amateur baseball.

WORK. The former slave Elizabeth Keckley authors a best-selling memoir entitled *Behind the Scenes: Or Thirty Years a Slave and Four Years in the White House*. Once a dressmaker for the wife of Jefferson Davis and Mary Todd Lincoln, she has a unique perspective on the wives of these two opposing presidents as well as their husbands' personalities. Both of her sons die as Union soldiers early in the Civil War.

1869

CULT. On June 24, Mary Ellen Pleasant, businesswoman, newspaper publisher, and antislavery ally of Harriett Tubman and John Brown, is officially made the Voodoo Queen of San Francisco.

EDUC. On March 3, the University of South Carolina opens to all races. Two African Americans are voted onto the university's seven-man Board of Directors: B. A. Boseman and Francis L. Cardozo.

LAW. The Fifteenth Amendment to the U.S. Constitution, guaranteeing African Americans (males) the right to vote, is sent to the states for ratification.

On April 12, the North Carolina legislature passes an anti-Klan law.

MILI. In March, Robert B. Elliott is appointed assistant adjutant general of South Carolina, which also makes him the first African American commanding general when he takes over the South Carolina National Guard. In this position, his duties include formation and maintenance of the state guard at a time when the Ku Klux Klan is terrorizing and killing South Carolina citizens who are either black or Republican.

On July 15, A. J. Hayne, a black captain in the Arkansas militia, is assassinated in Marion, Arkansas.

POLI. On January 13, the national convention of black leaders meets in Washington, DC. Frederick Douglass is elected the convention's president.

On February 27, John W. Menard is denied his seat in the U.S. Congress. While appealing to Congress, Menard becomes the first African American to address Congress.

On April 6, Ebenezer Don Carlos Bassett becomes the first official African American diplomat when President Ulysses Grant names him minister to Haiti. He serves as minister for 10 years. Born in Litchfield, Connecticut, of African and Pequot ancestry, Bassett receives his education at the Connecticut Normal School and works for 14 years as a teacher and principal at the Institute for Colored Youth in Philadelphia, Pennsylvania.

On July 6, African American candidate for lieutenant governor, Dr. J. H. Harris, is defeated by a vote of 120,000 to 99,600 in Virginia elections.

On August 6, Tennessee's state elections are marred by assassinations and widespread violence as white conservative and Democratic Party supporters suppress the African American vote.

WORK. The National Black Labor Convention meets on December 6 in Washington, DC. James M. Harris of North Carolina is elected its president.

On February 10, Nat Love, former enslaved African American from Tennessee, goes west to make his fortune. He becomes known as Deadwood Dick, one of the most famous cowboys in U.S. history.

1870

ABOL. On April 9, the American Anti-Slavery Society (AASS) disbands after 37 years.

LAW. On February 1, Jonathan Jasper Wright becomes the first African American to hold a major judicial position when he is elected to the South Carolina Supreme Court.

MILI. Robert Elliot becomes the first African American general when he assumes the position of commanding general for the South Carolina National Guard.

On July 1, James W. Smith of South Carolina is the first African American admitted to the U.S. Military Academy at West Point, New York. He leaves the Academy on June 26, 1874, without receiving a degree.

POLI. On January 20, the Mississippi legislature elects Hiram Rhodes Revels the first African American U.S. senator. He replaces and finishes the unexpired term of Jefferson Davis. Born free in 1822, he is raised in Fayetteville, North Carolina, and attends Knox College in Illinois. Revels becomes Mississippi's secretary of state and near the end of the century abandons the Republican Party and becomes a Democrat while obtaining a large plantation in Mississippi.

On January 26 and February 17, Virginia and Mississippi, respectively, are readmitted to the United States on the condition that their state constitutions never be changed to disenfranchise the African American population.

On February 26, Wyatt Outlaw, an outspoken leader of the Union League and town commissioner of Graham, Alamance County, North Carolina, is dragged from his house at night and lynched from an Oak tree in front of the county courthouse by members of the Ku Klux Klan. No one interferes with Outlaw's murder, and his body is not taken down from the tree until 11:00 A.M. the next day. Dozens of admitted members of the Ku Klux Klan are arrested and confess to their role in the murder. Despite their confessions and complaints by Governor William W. Holden, a federal judge in Salisbury orders their release. Disliked by conservative whites and southern Democrats due to his advocacy of an African American schoolhouse, Outlaw is particularly hated for his active participation in the Republican-inspired political organization the Union League. Originating in 1862 as Confederate military successes seemed unstoppable, the League's ability to inspire southern runaway blacks, liberals, and northern Republican whites in more than 18 northern states was critical to the eventual success of the Union's war efforts. The League raised troops, paid some of their expenses, sent supplies to the field, and distributed political literature to those blacks that could read or knew someone who could. After the Civil War, the League becomes an important arm for Republican and African American Reconstruction efforts in those southern states that have a large if not majority black population, such as South Carolina. Often supplying the ex-slave class the arms to defend themselves against recalcitrant southern whites, the League is viewed by many conservative whites as the enemy, as is Wyatt Outlaw.

On March 7, Governor William Holden of North Carolina declares Alamance County in a state of insurrection due to continued whippings and hanging of blacks and Republicans by terror groups and growing armed resistance by blacks.

On March 30, the Fifteenth Amendment to the U.S. Constitution, giving African Americans the right to vote, is ratified. The amendment becomes a political lighting rod both for former Confederate states desiring white racial hegemony and for southern African Americans striving for political and economic empowerment.

On July 8, Governor Holden of North Carolina declares Casswell County in a state of insurrection. Social and political conditions in Casswell deteriorate to a similar extent, as they do in Alamance County. Governor Holden attempts to fight the Ku Klux Klan rather than look for conciliatory means.

On December 2, Joseph H. Rainey of South Carolina becomes the first black in the House of Representatives.

POPU. African Americans make up 12.7 percent (4,880,009) of the total population of 39,818,449.

1871

INVE. On May 23, L. Bell receives patent no. 115,153 for the locomotive smoke stack.

MUS. On October 6, the Fisk University Jubilee Singers start their first tour throughout the United States and Europe, singing African American spiritual music. Hoping to raise money for Fisk University, they raise $150,000, thereby securing the school's financial future. These funds help purchase the school's campus in North Nashville, Tennessee, and construct the Jubilee Hall, the first permanent building constructed for the education of African Americans. The university becomes a national historic landmark. Each year on October 6, the school celebrates Jubilee Day in honor of the original singers and their contribution to the success of the university.

POLI. James Weldon Johnson is born in Jacksonville, Florida, to parents who had not been slaves. His father is a waiter in a fashionable hotel, and his mother is a schoolteacher.

On February 1, Jefferson Franklin Long becomes the first African American to address the House of Representatives as a congressman.

On March 1, J. Milton Turner is named the first accredited black minister to an African country, Liberia.

On April 20, Congress passes the third Enforcement Act, which defines Ku Klux Klan–inspired acts of violence as a conspiracy against the U.S. government. This act empowers the president to suspend the writ of habeas corpus and declare martial law in rebellious areas.

In June, a series of trials begins in Oxford, Mississippi, known as the Ku Klux Klan trials. White Mississippians from a variety of backgrounds— doctors, lawyers, ministers, and college professors—are arrested and jailed in the state's anti-Klan campaign. Some 930 people are indicted, but only 243 are actually tried and found guilty. South Carolina has a similar program that results in some 1,180 indictments, and North Carolina's program results in 1,849 indictments. Relatively few indictments end in convictions and long jail terms.

On October 17, and after violent attacks by groups of night-riding terrorists against African Americans and Republicans, President Ulysses S. Grant suspends the writ of habeas corpus and declares martial law in nine South Carolina counties affected by Ku Klux Klan–inspired violence.

On November 22, African American Lieutenant Governor Oscar J. Dunn dies suddenly during a bitter political struggle for control of Louisiana's state government. His aides claim that political dissidents, mainly Democratic elements, poisoned him.

On November 28, Ku Klux Klan trials begin in the federal district court in Columbia, South Carolina.

On December 6, P.B.S. Pinchback is elected the president pro tem of the Louisiana Senate and acting lieutenant governor.

1872

EDUC. On February 27, Charlotte Ray graduates from Howard University's law school,

Nineteenth Century **59**

becoming the first African American female lawyer in the United States and the third woman admitted to the bar.

On October 5, a 16-year-old ex-slave from Malden, West Virginia, Booker T. Washington, walks, hitches buggy rides, jumps railroad cars, and without money travels some 300 miles to reach Hampton Institute in Virginia. Once at the institute, the head teacher, Ms. Mackie, informs him that based on his appearance, he is not the kind of student desired at Hampton. Mackie, however, tells Washington that if he agrees to sweep a dirty classroom she will give him some money so that he can at least purchase something to eat. An hour later, Washington not only sweeps the classroom but dusts all the furniture, mops the floors, and washes the walls. Surprised at his enterprise, Mackie hires Washington as the school's maintenance man with the understanding that his salary will go toward his school fees. Three years later, in 1875, Booker T. Washington graduates from Hampton at the top of his class. Returning to West Virginia, Washington finds a teaching position but returns to Hampton to teach until 1881. Hampton Institute's founder, Gen. Samuel Armstrong, a Confederate sympathizer who believes that southern blacks need to be channeled into agriculture, moral training, and practical industrial (vocational) pursuits, recommends Washington as the head of a new institute in Alabama, the Tuskegee Institute.

INVE. On March 19, T. J. Byrd receives a patent (no. 124,790) for a device that detaches a horse from a carriage.

On May 26, Thomas J. Marshall receives a patent (no. 125,063) for the fire extinguisher.

LAW. Charlotte E. Ray becomes the first African American female lawyer when she graduates from the Howard University Law School on February 27. She is admitted to the bar on April 23.

Macon B. Allen becomes the first African American judge on the municipal level.

LIT. On June 27, poet and writer Paul Lawrence Dunbar is born in Dayton, Ohio.

MEDI. Rebecca Cole becomes one of the first African American female physicians to practice in New York and practices there for nine years. Two other women who also become physicians during this period were Susan McKinney, who was graduated from the New York Medical College two years earlier, and Rebecca Lee, who was graduated from the New England Female Medical College in March 1864.

MILI. On September 21, John Henry Conyers becomes the first African American to enter the United States Naval Academy at Annapolis, Maryland. He resigns before completing the required four years of training.

POLI. Louisiana's Lt. Gov. P.B.S. Pinchback serves as governor for one month, from December 1972 to January 1873, after the white governor is removed from office.

African American delegates Robert B. Elliot, Joseph H. Rainey, and John R. Lynch address the Republican National Convention in Philadelphia.

On April 7, civil rights leader and editor of the *Boston Guardian,* William Monroe Trotter, is born in Boston, Massachusetts. Educated at Harvard University, William Trotter becomes an outspoken advocate of African Americans' full participation in U.S. society and of the destruction of the Booker T. Washington philosophy. He is an instrumental leader in the Niagara Movement and attends its first meeting at Niagara Falls, Ontario, Canada, in 1905. Trotter, along with a number of civil rights activists, also becomes a founding member of the National Association for the Advancement of Colored People (NAACP) in 1909. Known as a staunch militant, he attacks black supporters of racial segregation, such as Booker T. Washington, as well as white segregationists like President Woodrow Wilson, who is determined to insure that Washington, DC's, federal facilities and buildings remain segregated because the policy, Wilson argues, is beneficial for blacks. When Trotter and a group of civil rights leaders meet with President Wilson on November 12, 1914, to discuss federal segregationist policies, the president lets it be known that he does not wish to be bothered by such complaints. William Trotter immediately berates Wilson in a face-to-face encounter that the Virginia-born president later recalls as insulting. Wilson then threaten the rest of the group of civil rights advocates that he will no longer meet with them if Trotter remains a member of their group.

In Mississippi and South Carolina, a majority of the representatives running for office are African Americans, and each of these states has two black speakers of the house during the 1870s. Jonathan J. Wright serves seven years as a state supreme court justice, Frank Cardozo serves as secretary of state and then treasurer, and some 112 African Americans are elected state senators and representatives during the entire Reconstruction period. Forty-one black sheriffs, five black mayors, and thirty-one black coroners also are elected. Many of these men are well educated. Of the 1,465 black officeholders, at least 378 are free before the Civil War, 933 are literate, and 195 are illiterate. Data indicates that 64 have some college or professional college education, and 4 were at one time students at Oberlin College in Ohio. Interestingly, black farmers and artisans, such as tailors, carpenters, and barbers, are among those who hold political office. Also represented in the political arena are 237 ministers, 172 teachers, at least 129 who served in the Union Army, and 46 who worked previously for the Freedmen's Bureau. Several of these African American political activists are financially secure, whereas others are poor. For example, Antoine Dubuclet was an owner of more than 100 slaves before the Civil War and has land that was valued at more than $100,000. Ferdinand Havis, however, was a slave before he became a representative in the Arkansas House of Representatives. He eventually owns a saloon, a whiskey business, and 2,000 acres of land near Pine Bluff, where he is known as the Colored Millionaire. Throughout this era, African American men such as Blanche K. Bruce and Robert Smalls serve as major political icons for the black populace. Bruce served in Mississippi as sheriff, tax collector, and superintendent of schools, and Smalls served consecutively in the South Carolina state house, state senate, and the U.S. House of Representatives. Smalls also serves as a member of South Carolina's Constitutional Conventions in 1868 and 1895. As a Republican, he serves as customs collector in Beaufort, South Carolina, from 1889 to 1913.

1873

CRIM. On Easter Sunday, April 13, more than 60 blacks are killed at Colfax, Grant Parish, Louisiana.

EDUC. On November 16, Richard T. Greener, the first African American graduate of Harvard University, is named professor of metaphysics at the University of South Carolina.

Bennett College, Wiley College, and Alabama State College are founded.

FINA. With the financial panic in full effect, many investors in the Freedmen's bank withdraw their accounts. Unsecured bank railroad loans and unwise real estate ventures in the Washington, DC, area become so great a problem that the Freedmen's Savings Bank and Trust Company asks Frederick Douglass to become its president in an attempt to win investors' confidence. Douglass invests $10,000 of his own money to no avail.

LAW. On April 14, the U.S. Supreme Court makes a series of judicial decisions in what is called the Slaughterhouse Cases that signals a more conservative swing in constitutional law. In these cases, the court rules that the Fourteenth Amendment to the Constitution protects federal civil rights not state civil rights.

MILI. On July 1, Henry O. Flipper of Georgia enters the U.S. Military Academy at West Point, New York.

MUS. On November 16, musician and reputed Father of the Blues W. C. Handy is born in Florence, Alabama.

POLI. On January 13, Governor, P.B.S. Pinchback relinquishes his office at the inauguration of the new governor of Louisiana.

On November 16, African Americans win three state offices in Mississippi: Alexander K. Davis, lieutenant governor; James Hill, secretary of state; and T. W. Cardozo, superintendent of education. Blacks also win 55 of the 115 seats in the house and 9 of the 37 seats in the senate, 42 percent of the total number.

On December 1, the 43rd Congress (1873–75) convenes with the youngest African American representative, John R. Lynch of Mississippi. He is 26 years old.

1874

BUSI. On August 1, businessman Charles Clinton Spaulding is born.

CRIM. On January 17, armed white Democrats seize the Texas government and ended Radical Reconstruction in Texas.

On April, 27, the White League, a paramilitary white supremacist organization, is formed in Opelousas, Louisiana.

On August 26, 16 African Americans are lynched in Tennessee.

On August 30, white Democrats kill more than 60 blacks and whites in Coushatta, Louisiana.

On September 14, white Democrats seize the statehouse in Louisiana in a coup d'état. President Ulysses S. Grant orders the rebels to disperse but only after 27 people are killed (16 whites and 11 blacks) in battles between Democrats and Republicans.

On December 7, white Democrats kill 75 Republicans in a massacre at Vicksburg, Mississippi.

EDUC. Edward Alexander Bouchet becomes the first African American to be inducted into Phi Beta Kappa honor society.

On July 31, Patrick Francis Healy, SJ, becomes the first African American to be inaugurated as head of a predominately white university, Georgetown University, the oldest Catholic university in the United States.

FINA. On March 11, Frederick Douglass is named president of the financially troubled Freedmen's Bank. The Freedmen's Savings Bank and Trust Company continues to lose money as African Americans in general lose about $3 million throughout the southern States. When the bank closes in June, nearly half of its depositors received three-fifths of the value of their accounts.

On June 28, the Freedmen's Savings Bank and Trust Company closes. African Americans have deposited about $3 million in the bank that has imposing headquarters in Washington, DC, and branches throughout various southern states. Commenting on the bank's failure, Frederick Douglass opines that the bank has been "the black man's cow and the white man's milk."

MIGR. On November 3, James Theodore Holly, an African American who advocated emigration from the United States to Haiti during the latter part of the 1850s as a means to develop a strong African nationalism base in the Western Hemisphere, is elected bishop of Haiti. He is consecrated in a ceremony in New York's Grace Church on November 8.

1875

CRIM. On January 5, President Ulysses S. Grant sends federal troops to maintain racial order in Vicksburg, Mississippi.

On July 4, white Democrats kill several blacks in terrorist attacks in Vicksburg, Mississippi.

On September 1, white Democrats attack Republicans at Yazoo City, Mississippi. One white and three blacks are killed.

From September 4 to 6, 20 to 30 African Americans are killed in racial clashes in Clinton, Mississippi. Two days later, the governor of Mississippi requests soldiers from the federal government for the protection of African Americans seeking to exercise their constitutional right to vote. The attorney general of the United States rejects the request, citing, "The whole public is tired of these annual autumnal outbreaks in the south."

EDUC. On July 10, Mary McLeod Bethune, educator and civil rights leader, is born in Mayesville, South Carolina.

On December 19, historian Carter G. Woodson is born in New Canton, Buckingham County, Virginia. Woodson founds the Association for the Study of Negro Life and History and publishes the fist edition of the *Journal of Negro History* on January 1, 1916.

On December 25, Alabama A&M College, Knoxville College, and Lane College are founded.

INVE. On June 1, A. P. Ashebourne receives a patent (no. 163,962) for a machine that refines coconut, thereby making coconut oil available for domestic use. Contemporary use of soap, cooking oil, margarine, and lotion made from refined and processed coconut is credited to Ashebourne. He also invents the biscuit cutter.

LAW. On March 1, the U.S. Congress passes the weakened Civil Rights Act of 1875, which essentially bans racial discrimination in public accommodations and facilities and insures equal rights in public conveyances, theaters, and other places of public use. The House of Representatives deletes clauses that ban racial discrimination in churches, cemeteries, and schools.

RELI. On June 10, James Patrick Francis Healy is elected the first African American Roman Catholic bishop. He presides over a diocese in Portland, Maine.

SPOR. Oliver Lewis, a thoroughbred jockey, rides in the first Kentucky Derby on the winning horse, Aristides. Thirteen of the fourteen jockeys in the first race are black. Later in the year, Lewis riding Aristides takes second place in the Belmont Stakes, now the third race in the Triple Crown. In the southern part of the United States, only a decade after the Civil War, African Americans are the predominate working class in horse racing, including jockeys and trainers.

1876

ARTS. On July 4, E. M. Bannister, an African painter, exhibits "Under the Oaks" at the Centennial Exposition in Philadelphia, Pennsylvania, and is awarded the gold medal.

EDUC. Edward Alexander Bouchet is graduated from Yale University with a doctorate in physics. He is the first African American to receive such a degree.

Meharry Medical College is established in Nashville, Tennessee, as the first all–African American medical college. Originally part of Central Tennessee College, Meharry Medical College is founded by five white men, the Meharry brothers, who had been befriended earlier in their lives by a group of African Americans and who furnish the resources for a four story-story building that provides the basis for the medical facility.

Today, only three all-black medical colleges exist in the United States. Meharry Medical College graduates nearly 40 percent of African American medical doctors and dentists.

1877

EDUC. Robert Tanner becomes the first black man to graduate from a U.S. school of dentistry, Harvard University.

In October, all-black Jackson College in Mississippi is established.

MIGR. W. R. Hill, an African American real estate promoter from Kentucky, is successful in establishing the all-black town of Nicodemus, Kansas. Quickly thereafter, other all-black towns such as Boley, Liberty, and Langston are founded in what is called Indian Territory. This territory later becomes the state of Oklahoma.

MILI. On June 15, Henry Ossian Flipper becomes the first African American to graduate from the U.S. Military Academy at West Point, New York. Henry Flipper, the oldest of five brothers was born in rural Georgia. His father, a shoemaker, was able to save enough money to purchase his wife's and children's freedom before the Civil War. At the end of the war, Flipper's father moved the family to Atlanta, Georgia, where he began a successful shoemaking business that was patronized by both blacks and whites. As a result of his economic success, the senior Flipper sent his sons to prestigious schools in Atlanta, the Storrs Grammar School and Atlanta University, both of which were established by missionary and Reconstruction northerners after the war to help facilitate a class of educated elites.

When Henry Flipper entered the Academy in 1873 he was the seventh African American cadet to do so. The six previous black cadets were eliminated in a process that included both extreme racist tactics and a code of debilitating silence both from fellow cadets and from instructors. Flipper's arrival at West Point was unusually tinged with notoriety when it was reported in the newspapers throughout the country that he had refused a $5,000 offer from a white man who was attempting to get his son into the Academy as a replacement for Flipper. Once at the Academy, Flipper's fellow cadets began to ostracize and insult him to a degree beyond the acceptable level for new cadets. In his own response to the fact that "terrorism reigned supreme" and his own awareness that if he "lost the use of language" he would lose the fight to graduate, Flipper sought respite elsewhere, such as with the Academy's bugler, barber, and commissary clerk. It was in his second year, 1875, however, that an incident gave him special encouragement to continue. While on a weekend furlough to New York City, he was walking with a young lady along Sixth Avenue in the heart of the black community at that time. As they passed a one-legged black Civil War veteran, Flipper notice that the veteran immediately stopped what he was doing, came to attention, raised his right crutch to present arms, and saluted Flipper. Deeply touched by this gesture and fully understanding the immediate impact and value of this moment in his own life, he also raised his cap to the veteran. Flipper is graduated two years later on June 15, 1877.

POLI. On February 26, Republican candidate Rutherford B. Hayes agrees to withdraw all federal troops from southern states if elected president of the United States over Democratic candidate Samuel J. Tilden. At a conference held at the Wormley Hotel in Washington, DC, representatives of the South negotiate a complex political agreement, known as the Compromise of 1877, that in effect paves the way for Hayes's election with the assurance that once elected he will not support Republican influence throughout the southern states. In 1876, Samuel Tilden won the popular vote with 4,288,546 to Hayes's 4,034,311, and Tilden received 53 electoral college votes to Hayes's 47, with 20 uncommitted electoral votes in Louisiana, Florida, and South Carolina. This all-important balance leads to the compromise whereby the Democratic Party agrees to commit those 20 electoral votes to Republican Rutherford Hayes if he agrees to withdraw federal troops from southern states and terminate major aspects of the Reconstruction Act of 1867. For the first time since 1867, black and white Republicans no longer hold political control of the former Confederate states.

On March 18, President Rutherford B. Hayes appoints Frederick Douglass as marshal of the District of Columbia.

On April 10, as a result of an earlier political compromise between the Republican and Democratic parties, federal troops withdraw from Columbia, South Carolina.

On April 20, Democrats assume control over federal and public buildings in New Orleans as Republican political elements withdraw.

On June 15, John Mercer Langston becomes United States minister to Haiti.

SPOR. Bud Fowler becomes the first African American to play professional baseball for a previously all-white team in New Castle, Pennsylvania.

1878

ARTS. On May 25, dancer and entertainer Bill "Bojangles" Robinson is born in Richmond, Virginia. At the age of six, Robinson begins dancing for a living at local beer gardens as a hoofer or song-and-dance man. By 1905, he gains success

---

Henry Flipper, the first African American to graduate from the United States Military Academy at West Point, New York, comments on his experience:

I believe that all my success at West Point is due not so much to my perseverance and general conduct there as to the early moral and mental training I received at the hands of those philanthropic men and women who left their pleasant homes in the North to educated and elevate the black portion of American citizens. How they have borne the sneers of the Southern press, the ostracism from society … the dangers of Kuklux [*sic*] … to raise up a down trodden race, not for personal aggrandizement, but for the building up and glory of His Kingdom who is no respecter of persons, is surely worth of our deepest gratitude. (Henry Ossian Flipper, *The Colored Cadet at West Point*. Salem, NH: Ayer, 1986; reprint 1878, pp. 37, 165)

as a nightclub comedy performer with a vaude-ville team. Before the age of 50, all of his performances are in front of black audiences. With a growing success with white audiences, his income increases to $3,500 per week by the 1940s. His famous stair dance, which he claims he invented on the spur of the moment when receiving an award from the king of England, is considered to be his trademark. He performs in numerous films and plays throughout the 1930s and 1940s and is considered the greatest tap dancer of his time.

INVE. Lewis Latimer draws the blueprints for Alexander Graham Bell's telephone in preparation for its patent.

SPOR. On March 31, Jack Johnson, the first African American heavyweight boxing champion is born.

World champion cyclist Marshall "Major" Taylor is born on November 21, in Indianapolis, Indiana. Taylor is encouraged to begin a career as a cyclist while working as a youth in a bicycle plant. He wins his first amateur race in Lexington, Kentucky, at age 13. Within a few years, he competes internationally in Canada, Europe, Australia, and New Zealand. In 1899, he wins the world title and becomes the first African American world champion cyclist. In 16 years of competition, Taylor wins numerous titles, including the American Sprint Championship title in 1898, 1899, and 1900, and establishes several records. In his career, he races in 168 events in which he finishes first in 117 and second in 32. Marshall Taylor is inducted into the United States Bicycling Hall of Fame in 1989. In honor of his accomplishments, one of the world's renowned cycling venues, the Major Taylor Velodrome in Indianapolis, and is named in his honor.

1879

MEDI. In 1878 Mary Eliza Mahoney, at age 33, was admitted as a student into New England's Hospital for Women and Children's Nursing Program, established by Dr. Marie Zakrzewska. Having worked previously at the same hospital, first as a cook, washerwoman, and unofficial nurse's assistant, Mahoney is one of only four to complete the rigorous training, out of 42 who started, because all of the students are required to begin as

maids. Graduating in 1879, she works primarily as a private-duty nurse for the next 30 years throughout the eastern United States. She is thought to be the first African American woman in Boston to register to vote after the passage of the Nineteenth Amendment, which grants women the right to vote. In 1896, Mahoney is an original member of the predominately white Nurses Associated Alumnae of the United States and Canada, which is renamed the American Nurses Association (ANA) in 1911. In 1908, she cofounds of the National Association of Colored Graduate Nurses (NACGN) and serves as the association's national chaplain. The NACGN establishes the Mary Mahoney Award in her honor in 1936, and after the NACGN merges with the ANA in 1951, the Association continues the award.

MIGR. In February, Benjamin "Pap" Singleton, an ex-slave from Tennessee, leads several thousand African Americans in an exodus from Tennessee to Kansas. Fleeing southern racial and economic terrorism such as peonage, the abuse of African American women, inadequate educational facilities, and political intimidation, these migrants settle among earlier black migrants in towns such as Nicodemus, Kansas; and Boley, Liberty, and Langston, Oklahoma. Though the exact numbers of migrants are not known, there is little doubt that the numbers exceed several hundreds of thousands. Many of these migrants must confront and face down white patrols attempting to stop them from leaving areas that are critical to the southern economy. Violent clashes are frequent and bloody.

On April 15, emigrants on the ship *Azor*, leave Charleston, South Carolina, bound for the Republic of Liberia. Formed by several black men, the Liberian Exodus Joint Stock Steamship Company becomes the principal organizer of this venture. They raise $6,000 to hire the *Azor*, which leaves Charleston with 206 emigrants. Some 175 are left behind due to lack of room. Though the ship has insufficient medical supplies and food, which causes the deaths of 23 migrants, it arrives in Liberia on June 30. Once settled in Liberia, these migrants prosper quickly. Samuel Hill establishes a 700-acre coffee plantation, and another migrant becomes the chief justice of the

Liberian Supreme Court. Eventually, the emigration company experiences financial difficulties and goes out of business.

In May, African American delegates from 14 states hold a convention in Nashville, Tennessee, to discuss the viability of black migration from southern states. Presided by Representative John R. Lynch of Mississippi, the delegates resolve, "colored people should emigrate to those States and Territories where they can enjoy all the rights which are guaranteed by the laws and Constitution of the United States." Similarly, the convention requests that $500,000 be appropriated from the U.S. Congress to support this migration.

TERR. White terrorists led by former Confederate Gen. James R. Chalmers, who became infamous for his part in the killing of black prisoners at Fort Pillow during the Civil War, close the Mississippi River to black migrants leaving Mississippi. He threatens to sink any boats used by migrants.

1880

ARTS. Composer and violinist Clarence C. White is born in Clarksville, Tennessee. White studies at the Oberlin Conservatory in Ohio and also in Europe. From 1912 to 1923, he teaches violin in Boston and New York City. He later becomes director of music at West Virginia State College (1924–30) and Hampton Institute (1932–35). His compositions for the violin include "Bandanna Sketches" and arrangements of spirituals. He also writes an opera, *Owanga* (1932), based on Haitian history.

CENS. The population of the United States is 50,155,783, of which 6,580,793 (13.1%) are African Americans.

1881

CIVI. Tennessee enacts the first of a series of Jim Crow laws that enforce racial segregation in almost every sector of society (see 1896). A major Jim Crow law requires segregation on railroad cars as a result of the U.S. Supreme Court's decision in *Plessy v. Ferguson* (1896). Though a number of explanations for the origin of the term *Jim Crow* exist, the most popular is that it derives

from a popular 1828 minstrel song "Jump Jim Crow." Played by an English actor, Thomas Dartmouth "Daddy" Rice, in blackface (by using charcoal), the fictitious character Jim Crow was depicted as a shabbily dressed rural black whose buffoonish presence, while entertaining, was unacceptable as a social equal to whites. This character also was associated with another blackface minstrel depiction of African Americans, Zip Coon, who wore flamboyant attire in an attempt to imitate and associate with white American culture. By 1837, the term *Jim Crow* was used to proclaim racial segregation. By 1870, Tennessee enacted anti-interracial marriage laws. Other southern states followed the same practice: Florida (1887); Mississippi (1888); Texas (1889); Louisiana (1890); Alabama, Kentucky, Arkansas, and Georgia (1891); South Carolina (1898); North Carolina (1899); Virginia (1900); Maryland (1904); and Oklahoma (1907).

EDUC. On July 4, Booker T. Washington founds the Tuskegee Institute in Tuskegee, Alabama.

Spelman College and Morris Brown College are founded in Atlanta, Georgia.

INVE. On September 13, Lewis H. Latimer, with his assistant Joseph V. Nichols, receives a patent (no. 247,097) for the commonly used light bulb (electric light) used today. Before Latimer's invention, the electric lamp was problematic due to its limited ability to provide light. Latimer's light bulb utilizes a new method of manufacturing carbon filaments that provide illumination for useful periods of time. As a result, he is asked to write a manual for, as well as supervise, the installation of incandescent light plants around the world. In 1884, Latimer becomes a member of Thomas Edison's small team of engineers, the Edison Pioneers.

MIGR. Between December 24 and 31, approximately 5,000 African Americans from Edgefield County, South Carolina, protesting racial bias and violence, migrate in a mass exodus to Arkansas.

POLI. On May 17, Frederick Douglass is appointed recorder of deeds for the District of Columbia.

On June 30, Henry Highland Garnet, a former antislavery leader who once advocated slave resistance and rebellion, is named minister to Liberia.

SPOR. In spring, Moses Fleetwood Walker becomes the first African American to play varsity college baseball when he joins the Oberlin College team, the school's first intercollegiate team. A bare-handed catcher, Walker signs with the Toledo, Ohio, team of the Northwestern League in 1883.

1882

CRIM. The federal government reports that during the year, approximately 50 African Americans are lynched in the United States.

EDUC. In April, Virginia State College is established.

LAW. On July 16, V. A. Johnson is born. Johnson becomes the first female to argue before the U.S. Supreme Court.

LIT. George Washington Williams publishes the first major historical text on African Americans, entitled *History of the Negro Race in America, 1619–1880*. This work is followed by *A History of Negro Troops in the War of Rebellion* in 1888.

OBIT. On February 13, Henry Highland Garnet, minister to Liberia, dies in Monrovia, Liberia.

SCIE. Lewis Latimer develops the carbon filament of electric lamps.

1883

CRIM. The federal government reports that approximately 53 African Americans are lynched by mobs during the year.

INVE. On March 20, Jan Ernst Matzeliger receives a patent (no. 274,207) for a shoe lasting machine. While working in shoe factories in Massachusetts, Matzeliger studies and experiments with machines that hold the shoe in place, stretch the leather, and automatically tack on the sole of the shoe. After perfecting his device, he receives a patent. His invention revolutionizes the shoe industry in the United States and makes Lynn, Massachusetts, the shoe capital of the world.

On August 14, W. Washington receives a patent (no. 283,173) for a corn husking machine.

LAW. The U.S. Supreme Court declares that the Civil Rights Act of 1875 is unconstitutional. The majority opinion is written by Justice Joseph Bradley and claims that the Fourteenth Amendment to the U.S. Constitution protects African Americans against encroachment of their rights by states, not by individual citizens or private businesses.

MUS. On February 7, Eubie Blake is born in Baltimore, Maryland. He becomes a major jazz pianist.

OBIT. On November 26, Sojourner Truth dies in Battle Creek, Michigan.

SCIE. Dr. Ernest Everett Just is born on August 14 in Charleston, South Carolina. At an early age he demonstrates a talent for academic research. In 1907, he is the only person to graduate magna cum laude from Dartmouth College with a degree in zoology, special honors in botany and history, and honors in sociology. He teaches at Howard University, where he serves as head of the Department of Zoology in 1912. He also serves as a professor in the medical school and head of the Department of Physiology until his death in 1941. In 1915, he receives the first Spingarn Medal for his accomplishment as a pure scientist (see 1915). He receives international acclaim for his research conducted during summers from 1909 to 1930 at the Marine Biological Laboratory in Woods Hole, Massachusetts, on the fertilization of marine mammal cells. In 1922, he successfully challenges Jacques Loeb's theory of artificial parthenogenesis. From this research, Just publishes the book *Basic Methods of the Cell Surface* as well as a number of papers related to cell cytoplasm. Just dies on October 27, 1941, in Washington, DC.

1884

CRIM. The federal government reports that approximately 51 African Americans are lynched by mobs during the year.

INVE. On June 3, G. T. Woods receives a patent (no. 299,894) for the steam boiler furnace.

On December 2, G. T. Woods receives a patent (no. 308,816) for a telephone transmitter.

JOUR. Ida Wells-Barnett is removed from a segregated first class railroad car in Memphis, Tennessee. She sues the railroad and wins a settlement of $500 dollars. A higher court reverses that decision. Wells, one of eight children, was born in Holly Springs, Mississippi, in 1862. After the Civil War, she and her mother learned to read and write at the same time while attending a school for former slaves. When her parents died in 1878 as a result of a yellow fever epidemic, 16-year-old Ida became the significant adult for her siblings. She eventually was able to attend Shaw College (now Rust College) and taught school in Mississippi and Tennessee. After her racial bias incident on the railroad, Wells-Barnett decides to write a column for a Memphis journal, the *Living Way*, as a way to express her growing concerns about an increasing violent antiblack southern political atmosphere. By 1889, she purchases a one-third interest in the Memphis journal *Free Speech and Headlight*, in which she writes about racial issues, particularly the poor quality of education for blacks. Highly critical of black educators and the quality of black schools, she becomes well known for her outspoken nature within and outside the African American community.

On November 22, T. Thomas Fortune starts the *New York Freeman* newspaper, which becomes the *New York Age*.

In November, Christopher J. Perry founds the *Philadelphia Tribune* newspaper.

POLI. On June 3, John R. Lynch, former congressman from Mississippi, is elected temporary chairman of the Republican convention and becomes the first African American to preside at a national political party's deliberations.

On November 15, an international conference of European powers and the United States meets in Berlin, Germany, to formally organize the colonization of Africa. The conference continues until February 16, 1885.

George Washington Williams is extremely interested in the plight of the Congolese under Belgian rule in Africa. He meets with King Leopold II of Belgium, who abhors Williams's planned visit to examine health conditions in the African colony. Upon his return from the Congo, Williams writes a detailed description of Belgium's greed and cruelty toward the Congolese population. At the end of his administration, President Chester A. Arthur appoints Williams as minister to Haiti. The new president, Grover Cleveland, cancels William's political appointment.

SPOR. The first jockey to win the Kentucky Derby three times is African American Isaac Murphy, who is victorious this year, in 1890, and in 1891.

1885

CRIM. The federal government reports that 74 African Americans are lynched during the year.

OBIT. On January 24, Martin R. Delany, politician, soldier, and African nationalist, dies at the age of 72 in Wilberforce, Ohio.

POLI. On December 7, two African American congressmen are present at the opening of the 49th Congress: James O'Hara of North Carolina and Robert Smalls of South Carolina.

RELI. On June 24, Samuel David Ferguson is consecrated bishop of the Protestant Episcopal Church and named bishop of Liberia. He is the first African American with full membership in the House of Bishops.

SPOR. The Cuban Giants become the first African American professional baseball team.

1886

CRIM. On March 17, a racial riot in Carrollton, Mississippi, results in the death of 20 African Americans.

The federal government reports that as in the previous year, 74 African Americans are lynched during the year.

EDUC. Kentucky State College is founded.

MILI. On March 26, Hugh N. Mulzac, the first African American captain of a U.S. merchant marine ship (*S.S. Booker T. Washington*), is born in the West Indies.

The Knights of Labor, a farmers' craft and factory workers' union reaches its peak membership of 700,000, of which some 60,000 to 90,000 are African Americans. The organization plays a major role in the struggle for an eight-hour work day.

1887

CRIM. The federal government reports that 70 African Americans are lynched during the year.

EDUC. Florida A&M University and Central State College are established.

INVE. On October 11, A. Miles receives a patent (no. 371,207) for the elevator.

POLI. On March 28, Democratic President Grover Cleveland names James M. Trotter, from Boston, recorder of deeds.

1888

CRIM. The federal government reports that 69 African Americans are lynched during the year.

FINA. The Bank of the Order of True Believers is chartered on October 17 in Richmond, Virginia.

On October 17, Capital Savings Bank opens in Washington, DC.

POLI. On June 23, former slave, abolitionist leader, and ambassador Frederick Douglass receives one vote from the Kentucky delegation at the Republican convention in Chicago, essentially making him the first African American candidate nominated for U.S. president.

1889

CIVI. On April 18, labor leader and civil rights organizer Asa Philip Randolph is born in Crescent City, Florida.

CRIM. The federal government reports that 94 African Americans are lynched during the year.

FINA. On April 3, the Savings Bank of the Order of True Believers opens in Richmond, Virginia.

INVE. On June 18, W. H. Richardson receives a patent (no. 405,599) for a children's carriage.

MILI. In June, Charles D. Young graduates from the United States Military Academy at West Point, New York.

POLI. On March 4, the 51st U.S. Congress convenes with three African American congressmen present. They are Henry P. Cheatham of North Carolina, Thomas E. Miller of South Carolina, and John M. Langston of Virginia.

On July 1, Frederick Douglass is named minister to Haiti.

1890

CIVI. On January 25, the National Afro-American League is formed. A pioneer black protest organization, it is established in Chicago by Joseph C. Price, president of Livingston College. He becomes the League's first president.

On August 12, the Mississippi Constitutional Congress conceives a systematic plan to exclude and eliminate African Americans from Mississippi's voter rolls. Known as the Mississippi Plan, it requires blacks to take literacy and understanding tests that are rigged so that the blacks fail the necessary requirements to vote. This plan is later adopted with unique embellishments by seven other southern states: South Carolina (1895), Louisiana (1898), North Carolina (1900), Alabama (1901), Virginia (1901), Georgia (1908), and Oklahoma (1910). Later, southern states use white-only primaries to exclude the black vote.

CRIM. The federal government reports that 85 African Americans are lynched during the year.

EDUC. Savannah State College is established.

EXPO. In May, William Henry Shepard, at the age of 24, departs for the Belgian Congo with Samuel Lapsley, a southern white who is the son of a well-known Alabama plantation owner and judge. Lapsley soon dies of fever, but Shepard spends 20 years in the Congo, running a mission center staffed by African Americans.

FINA. On October 15, the Alabama Penny Savings Bank is organized in Birmingham, Alabama.

HHC. On February 27, Mabel K. Staupers is born in Barbados, British West Indies. Her family immigrates to New York in 1903, and Mabel becomes a naturalized citizen in 1917. She receives her RN diploma from the Freedmen's Hospital School of Nursing in Washington, DC. She works as a private-duty nurse in Washington, DC, and in New York City and organizes and serves as superintendent of the Booker T. Washington Sanatorium (an inpatient clinic for African Americans with tuberculosis) from 1920 to 1922. The sanatorium is one of the few health care institutions to allow black physicians to treat their patients when they are hospitalized. Most other hospitals deny blacks in the medical profession attending or staff privileges and positions of responsibility. Staupers serves as executive of the Harlem Committee of the New York Tuberculosis and Health Association from 1922 to 1934. In 1935, she joins Mary McLeod Bethune to found the National Council of Negro Women. She reconstitutes the National Association of Colored Graduate Nurses (NACGN) and becomes its first executive director in 1934 and serves until 1949, when she becomes its president. Under her leadership, the NACGN dissolves in 1951, and black nurses gain membership, though problematic, in the American Nursing Association. During World War II, she mobilizes efforts to get black nurses into the Armed Forces Nurse Corps. Although the army eventually accepts 56 African American nurses, the Navy refuses to accept any. In 1945, President Franklin Roosevelt announces that the government will draft black nurses. This, Staupers argues, is ridiculous, considering black nurses were eager to join the military earlier. In 1961, she writes about this fight with the military to integrate black nurses in a book entitled *No Time for Prejudice: A Story of the Integration of Negroes in Nursing in the United States*. In recognition of her efforts in the struggle against racism and discrimination, she receives the Spingarn Medal in 1951.

INVE. On January 7, inventor, W. B. Purvis receives a patent (#419,065) for the fountain pen.

MED. On August 13, the first issue of the *Baltimore Afro-American* newspaper is published.

MEDI. Dr. Daniel Hale Williams establishes the Provident Hospital and Training Institute in Chicago's south side. It is the first hospital operated solely by African Americans.

Ida Gray Nelson Rollins graduates from the University of Michigan Dental School and becomes the first African American woman to earn a dental degree in the United States.

POLI. On March 20, New Hampshire Senator Henry W. Blair's bill to provide federal financial support for education, particularly in the reduction of illiteracy among former slaves, is defeated in the U.S. Senate, 37 to 31.

POPU. The population of the United States is 62,947,714, of which 7,488,676 (11.9%) are African Americans.

SPOR. On June 27, George Dixon wins the bantamweight boxing title by defeating Nunc Wallace in the 18th round, and thereby becomes the first African American world champion boxer.

1891

CRIM. The federal government reports that 113 African Americans are lynched during the year.

EDUC. North Carolina A&T College, Delaware State College, and West Virginia State College are established.

INVE. On July 14, J. Standard receives a patent (no. 455,891) for a refrigerator.

On September 21, F. W. Leslie receives a patent (no. 590,325) for the envelope seal.

On October 27, P. B. Downing receives a patent (no. 462,093) for the mailbox (letter box) and a patent (no. 462,096) for the street mailbox.

MEDI. On January 23, Chicago's Provident Hospital is incorporated along with its school for African American nurses.

On July 23, physician Louis Tompkins Wright is born in La Grange, Georgia. Wright is the son of a trained doctor. His father dies when Louis is four years old. With little money, Wright's mother obtains a job as a matron in a dormitory at Clark University. When Louis is eight years old, his mother remarries Dr. William Fletcher Penn, the first African American to receive a degree from Yale Medical School. He inspires Louis to study medicine. During World War I, Wright serves in the U.S. Army Medical Corps. He introduces a special method of smallpox vaccination used for soldiers. He heads a base hospital located in France and at that time is the youngest surgeon with that responsibility. After the war, he is discharged as a captain and is awarded the Purple Heart. After the war, he marries and begins work in 1919 as a clinical assistant, the lowest job available at Harlem Hospital. As a result of his appointment as the first black man on staff at any city hospital, four white doctors resign in protest. In 1920, he receives a permanent job on the surgical staff. Twenty-three years later, he becomes the director of surgery, and five years later, president of the hospital's medical board. Wright's specialty is surgery dealing with fractures and head injuries. He designs a neck brace still in use today and a special blade plate used to treat fractures around the knee joint. In 1934, as a result of his surgical skills, he becomes part of the American College of Surgeons. Though Wright's specialty is surgery, he is also an authority on the antibiotics Aureomycin and Terramycin and founds the Cancer Research Foundation at Harlem Hospital. In 1940, the National Association for the Advancement of Colored People (NAACP) honors him for his surgical work.

POLI. On January 22, Senator Henry Cabot Lodge's bill calling for federal supervision of U.S. elections is abandoned in the U.S. Senate after a southern filibuster.

On December 2, the 52nd U.S. Congress convenes. Only one African American congressman is present, Henry P. Cheatham of North Carolina.

WORK. The Texas People's Party, which is interracial and radical, is founded in Dallas in summer. Their intraparty political debates capture the issues of the day. For example, a black delegate, active in the Knights of Labor, is dissatisfied with vague statements about equality and states, "If we were equal, why does not the sheriff summon Negroes on juries? And why hang up the sign "Negro," in passenger cars. I want to tell my people what the People Party's is going to do. I want to tell them if it is going to work a black and white horse in the same field." The reality is that blacks are mostly hired field hands and whites are

the owners of farms and local stores. When the Colored Alliance declares a strike in the cotton fields during summer, the White Farmers Alliance denounces it as hurting the farmers who have to pay increased wages. In Arkansas, a 30-year-old black cotton worker named Ben Patterson leads a strike of cotton workers by traveling from plantation to plantation organizing support. Paterson's band of supporters becomes involved in gun battles with white posses, resulting in the killing of a plantation owner and the destruction of a cotton gin. Paterson and his band are eventually caught, and all 15 of them are shot to death.

1892

CRIM. The federal government reports that 160 African Americans are lynched during the year.

INVE. On July 5, Andrew Beard is issued a patent (no. 478,271) for the rotary engine (see 1897).

MED. On August 13, the Baltimore *Afro-American* newspaper is founded.

POLI. On January 11, William D. McCoy of Indiana is appointed minister to Liberia.

On June 8, Homer Adolph Plessy refuses to sit in a segregated railroad car in New Orleans, Louisiana. His actions cause him to be jailed. He goes to court and argues in *Plessy v. State of Louisiana*, that his constitutional Thirteenth and Fourteenth Amendment rights have been violated. The state supreme court argues, however, that Louisiana has the right to regulate railroad companies within the state as it sees fit, particularly if such actions reduce racial conflict. Plessy then appeals to the U.S. Supreme Court and again loses in *Plessy v. Ferguson*.

SPOR. On December 27, the first African American college football game is played between Biddle University (now Johnson C. Smith University) and Livingstone College in North Carolina in the middle of a snowstorm two days after Christmas. An edition of a 1930s Livingstone College newspaper states that team members purchase a regulation football and uniforms, and the players equip their street shoes with cleats, which they then remove after practice. The young women of the school's industrial department make their uniforms for the first game. The teams play two 45-minute halves on Livingstone College's front lawn. W. J. Trent scores Livingstone's only touchdown on a fumble recovery. By then, the snow covers the field's markings, and Biddle argues that the fumble is recovered out of bounds. The officials rule in Biddle's favor, allowing them to keep their 5–0 lead and giving the visitors the victory.

WORK. On April 11, African American longshoremen strike for higher wages in St. Louis, Missouri.

1893

ARTS. The renowned African American painter Henry Ossawa Tanner, who attended the Pennsylvania Academy of Fine Arts, produces the award-winner painting *The Banjo Lesson*. Tanner, who once stated that "he could not fight prejudice and paint at the same time," leaves the United States in 1891 to live and paint in France until his death in 1937.

CRIM. The federal government reports that 118 African Americans are lynched during the year.

EDUC. On November 22, educator and historian Alrutheus A. Taylor is born.

On November 23, J. L. Love receives a patent (no. 594,114) for a pencil sharpener.

Nella Marion Larson, who is the first African American woman to receive a Guggenheim Fellowship in creative writing, is born. Her highly acclaimed novels are *Quicksand* (1928) and *Passing* (1929). Both of these creative works focus on the tragic mulatto theme. Larson's style of writing on this theme grants her the title of being the foremother of African American novelists.

MEDI. On July 9, Daniel Hale Williams performs the world's first successful heart operation and founds the nation's first hospital to employ an interracial staff. Williams saves the life of James Cornish, who had been stabbed in the heart. Williams opens Cornish's chest and sutures the wound. The patient recovers completely, and the operation makes Williams famous throughout the country.

POLI. On August 7, the 53rd U.S. Congress convene with one African American representative in-attendance, George W. Murray of South Carolina.

SPOR. On October 31, noted sportswriter Caspar Whitney names football player William Henry Lewis of Harvard University to the All American Team for a second consecutive year. The first African American to receive this honor, Lewis, in his final game, is voted acting captain. He leads the Crimson to victory against the University of Pennsylvania. Later in life, he serves as an assistant attorney general of the United States under President William Howard Taft (then the highest federal position ever held by an African American) and afterward becomes a criminal defense attorney, heading one of the most successful practices in Boston.

WORK. On January 26, pilot Bessie Coleman is born in Texas. She is one of the first African Americans to earn a pilot license and one of the first women in the country to do so.

1894

ARTS. On April 15, Bessie Smith is born in Chattanooga, Tennessee. Coming from a background of extreme poverty, she suffers the death of both parents and two older brothers while still a child. She sings on street corners in Chattanooga to earn money for the rest of her siblings. In 1912, she tours briefly with Gertrude "Ma" Rainey, and in 1913, she works in Atlanta, Georgia, for $10 per week plus tips. By the early 1920s, her fame brings her to Philadelphia and Atlantic City. In 1923, she records so-called race records, or records produced by white companies for African American audiences. Among her earliest songs are "Downhearted Blues" and "Gulf Coast Blues." Her song "Tain't Nobody's Business if I Do" sells 780,000 records within months. By 1925, she records "St. Louis Blues" and "Careless Love" with Louis Armstrong and then begins touring cities such as Pittsburgh, Cleveland, and Chicago in a private railroad car as huge crowds show up at her appearances. Bessie Smith is not a delicate woman. She weighs more than 200 pounds, and she outeats, outdrinks, and fights anyone who crosses her path, yet many see her as a sweet and caring person. She likes to hang out in some of the roughest nightclubs of the time. Undoubtedly, some of her inspiration comes from places where she admits, "The funk was flying.' Her last recording before dying in a car accident is entitled "Nobody Knows When You're Down and Out."

EDUC. On September 24, educator and sociologist E. Franklin Frazier is born in Baltimore, Maryland. The son of a bank messenger, Frazier is graduated from Howard University and teaches mathematics at Tuskegee Institute (1916–17), modern languages at St. Paul Industrial School (1917–18), and history at Baltimore High School (1918–19). He obtains a master's degree in sociology from Clark University and a PhD from Atlanta University. His 1932 doctoral dissertation, *The Negro Family in Chicago,* is considered the most important work on African Americans since W.E.B. Du Bois's *The Philadelphia Negro* in 1899 (see 1899). In 1939, Frazier publishes what is considered his most important work, *The Negro Family in the United States.* This work analyzes the African American since the eighteenth century and issues such as slavery, segregation, racial discrimination, and migration. Franklin Frazier's most controversial work, *Black Bourgeoisie,* is critical of the black middle class.

MILI. The first African American fighter pilot, Eugene Jacques Bullard, is born in Columbus, Georgia.

SCIE. On June 20, Dr. Lloyd A. Hall is born in Illinois. Hall is a major pioneer in food chemistry.

1895

ASSO. On July 29, the First National Convention of Black Women is held in Boston, Massachusetts.

CRIM. The federal government reports that 113 African Americans are lynched during the year.

EDUC. In June, W.E.B. Du Bois earns a doctorate from Harvard University. Harvard Historical Studies publishes his dissertation, *Suppression of the African Slave Trade.*

LAW. On September 3, Charles Hamilton Houston is born in Washington, DC. Houston becomes the first African American lawyer to win a U.S. Supreme Court case for the National Association for the Advancement of Colored People (NAACP). A magna cum laude graduate from Amherst College in Massachusetts, he earns his LLB from Harvard Law School in 1922 and his doctorate a year later. He is the first African American editor of the *Harvard Law Review.* He teaches at Howard University for the next 12 years and becomes special counsel for the NAACP and takes a number of cases relating to discrimination in public education before state and federal courts. Houston establishes a strategy to overturn the 1896 *Plessy v. Ferguson* "separate but equal" decision that allows legal segregation throughout society and to attack segregation on the state level to establish a series of precedent decisions against *Plessy.* His success in this regard is noted in a series of cases relating to black teachers' salaries in South Carolina, integration of graduate and law schools throughout the South, and equal pay scales for black workers in the railroad industry, all of which eventually lead to 1954's *Brown v. Board of*

Portrait of Bessie Smith holding feathers. Courtesy of Library of Congress.

Education. Houston, however, does not live to see the fulfillment of his efforts, though his prodigy, Thurgood Marshall, successfully pursues these efforts and gives full credit to Houston.

MEDI. In October, the National Medical Association of Physicians, Dentist and Pharmacists (NMA) is founded in Atlanta, Georgia, with Robert F. Boyd, MD, DDS, as its first president. The goals of the group are: (1) to create a national program for postgraduate education for black physicians and meaningful experiences in the medical specialties, (2) to combat racial discrimination and exclusion in hospital care and functions, and (3) to represent allied health practitioners in actions to eliminate inequities in health care services. These points aim to elevate the quality of health care for African Americans.

MIGR. On March 18, 200 African Americans emigrate from Savannah, Georgia, to Liberia.

OBIT. On February 20, Frederick Douglass dies in Anacostia Heights, Washington, DC. Douglass was a leading political abolitionist, lecturer, writer, and statesmen for almost 50 years.

On February 21, the North Carolina legislature, dominated by African American Republican and white populists, recesses in honor of Frederick Douglass's legacy.

POLI. On September 18, Booker T. Washington delivers a controversial presentation to the Cotton States Exposition in Atlanta, Georgia. Remembered as the "Atlanta Compromise" speech, Washington proclaims: "No race can prosper till it learns that there is as much dignity in tilling a field as in writing a poem. It is at the bottom of life we must begin, and not at the top." His message receives much support from southern and northern political leaders and philanthropists concerned about African American economic thrust into skilled northern jobs essentially filled by European migrants. He also appeals to blacks not to emigrate from the South but to cast down their buckets and draw subsistence from the southern agricultural resources. Many African American political activists receive his message as an appeal to withdraw or concede political control of society to white Americans.

On December 2, the 54th U.S. Congress (1895–97) convenes. One African American is in attendance, George W. Murray of South Carolina.

RELI. On September 28, three Baptist groups—the Foreign Mission Convention of the United States, the American National Baptist Convention, and the Baptist National Education Convention—merge to establish the National Baptist Convention in Atlanta, Georgia.

1896

ASSO. On July 21, under the leadership of Mary Church Terrell, the National Federation of Afro-American Women and the Colored Women's League merge to form the National Association of Colored Women in Washington, DC. Terrell is elected president of the Association during a meeting at the Nineteenth Street Baptist Church.

CRIM. The federal government reports that 78 African American are lynched during the year.

EDUC. On April 15, Booker T. Washington receives an honorary degree from Harvard University.

South Carolina State College is founded.

ENTE. John W. Isham's *Oriental America* becomes the first New York Broadway show with an all–African American cast.

LAW. On May 18, the U.S. Supreme Court renders a decision in *Plessy v. Ferguson* that upholds the doctrine of "separate but equal" as practiced in Louisiana since 1890. Though *Plessy* is essentially a transportation case, it applies to every other aspect of U.S. society and signals the beginning of institutional racial segregation and the Jim Crow era. The case sets the precedent that separate facilities for blacks and whites are constitutional as long as they are equal. This doctrine is quickly applied to many areas of public life, such as restaurants, theaters, restrooms, and public schools. Not until 1954 is this decision successfully challenged and overturned.

Poster for John W. Isham's *Oriental America,* the first Broadway show with an all–African American cast. Courtesy of Library of Congress.

1897

ASSO. On March 5, Episcopal priest Alexander Crummel and 16 other black men found the American Negro Academy in Washington, DC. The Academy members are men of African descent who assemble to discuss published works on history, literature, religion, and science. The organization also concerns itself with issues pertaining to woman suffrage, though no women are invited to join the Academy. Among those who attended its initial meeting are W.E.B. Du Bois,

Paul Lawrence Dunbar, Kelly Miller, and Francis Grimke.

CRIM. The federal government reports that 123 African Americans are lynched during the year.

EDUC. Langston University and Voorhees College are established.

INVE. On November 23, Andrew J. Beard receives patent no. 594,059 for his invention of an automatic linkage (car coupler) that makes it possible for railroad cars to join and lock with no human assistance. This invention is inspired by the need to reduce loss of life when men are killed or lose limbs while attempting to separate railroad cars manually. Beard receives $50,000 for an invention that remains a standard feature on railroad cars throughout the world.

OBIT. On November 15, John Mercer Langston, age 67, dies in Washington, DC.

POLI. On March 15, the 55th U.S. Congress (1898–99) convenes with one African American in attendance, George H. White of North Carolina, On June 17, William Frank Powell, a New Jersey educator, is named minister to Haiti.

1898

BUSI. On October 20, John Merrick and associates in Durham, North Carolina, form the North Carolina Mutual and Provident Insurance Company.

On November 10, Samuel W. Rutherford establishes in Washington, DC, the National Benefit Life Insurance Company. It is the largest African American–owned insurance company for several years.

CIVI. On April 9, political activist, athlete, actor, and singer Paul Robeson is born in Princeton, New Jersey. His father, a former slave, leaves Princeton when his wife dies and resettles in Westfield, New Jersey, where he is named pastor of the St. Thomas AME Zion Church. While attending Somerville High School, Paul Robeson excels in sports, drama, singing, academics, and debate. Upon graduating in 1915, he receives a four-year academic scholarship to Rutgers

University. Despite the blatant racist attitudes of some of the students and faculty, Robeson becomes a star athlete, graduates in 1919 a Phi Beta Kappa scholar, belongs to the Cap and Skull Honor Society, and is valedictorian of his class. He graduates from Columbia Law School in 1923, and meets a schoolmate at Columbia, Eslanda Cardozo Goode, the first black woman to head a pathology laboratory. He acquires a job at a New York law firm but soon leaves when the white secretary refuses to take dictation from him. Turning to his love of the arts, he stars in Eugene O'Neill's *All God's Chillun Got Wings* in 1924 and later stars in O'Neill's *Emperor Jones.* Robeson also receives recognition for his roles in musicals such as *Showboat,* in which he changes the lines of he song "Old Man River." His 11 films include *Body and Soul, Jericho,* and *Proud Valley.* Traveling the world as an artist and political spokesperson for the oppressed and exploited, Robeson becomes a citizen of the world and crosses a number of political boundaries. He finds the Soviet Union before World War II more tolerant than many states in his own country, and he protests the Cold War as a political dividing line between people. During this postwar era, protests such as his were viewed as pro–Soviet Union or Communist and anti-American. By 1947, with the advent of the House Committee on Un-American Activities (HUAC), he is viewed as an enemy of the state. The government revokes his passport, thereby curtailing his livelihood as an international artist and branding him as anti-American.

On May 12, the state of Louisiana adopts a new constitution with a grandfather clause designed to eliminate African American voters.

CRIM. On February 22, an African American postmaster is lynched, and his wife and three daughters are shot and maimed by racists in Lack City, South Carolina.

On November 10, a race riot in Wilmington, North Carolina, results in the deaths of eight African Americans.

The federal government reports that 101 African Americans are lynched during the year.

EDUC. On May 27, educator Victoria E. Matthews is born.

ENTE. The first African American musical comedy, *A Trip to Coon Town,* is produced by Bob Cole and directed and managed by African Americans. It plays for three consecutive seasons in New York City.

WAR. On February 15, the battleship USS *Maine* sinks in the harbor of Havana, Cuba, after a horrific explosion that kills 260 sailors and soldiers. Preliminary accusations blame the Cubans for planting a bomb under the ship. Investigations years later note that the explosion was probably caused by a boiler defect.

On April 21, the 113-day Spanish-American War begins. African American soldiers stationed in western states and territories fighting Native Americans are quickly transferred by train and wagon eastward to Tampa, Florida, where they board troopships heading to Cuba. Elements of the Seventh through Tenth Colored Cavalries and the Twenty-Fourth and Twenty-Fifth Colored Infantries are among the first troops to arrive in Cuba. Thirty-four-year-old 1st Lt. Charles Young, Ninth Cavalry, West Point class of 1889, is the only black officer in the regular army to lead troops in combat. A military instructor at Wilberforce University, Young writes to the War Department asking to rejoin his regiment when it is called to active service, but his request is refused. West Point graduate or not, black officers are not allowed to lead troops in combat. However, in the wake of the Spanish-American War, Captain Young was sent to the Philippines, where he led U.S. troops against insurgents in the jungles of Samar, Bianca Aurora, Tobaco, and Rosano for 18 months, earning the nickname "follow me." When the all-black units (with exception of their officers) arrive in Cuba, their combat experience fighting Native Americans in small-unit warfare proves to be invaluable experience.

On June 21, the Tenth Cavalry and other U.S. troops distinguish themselves at Las Guasimas, Cuba, by driving Spanish soldiers from entrenched positions.

On July 1, elements of the Twenty-Fourth and Twenty-Fifth Colored Infantries attack Spanish positions at El Caney, Cuba, and in doing so save from annihilation a unit of entrapped Rough Riders under the command of Theodore Roosevelt.

At the battle for San Juan Hill, one reporter for the *New York Mail and Express* in honor of the Ninth and Tenth Cavalries writes:

> No more striking example of bravery and coolness has been shown since the destruction of the Maine than by the colored veterans of the Tenth Calvary during the attack upon San Juan…. Firing as they marched, their aim was splendid, their coolness was superb, and their courage aroused the admiration of their comrades. Their advance was greeted with wild cheers from the white regiments, and with answering shouts they pressed onward over the trenches they had taken close in pursuit of the retreating enemy. The war has not shown greater heroism. The men whose own freedom was baptized in blood have proved themselves capable of giving up their lives that others may be free.

Five Tenth Calvary troopers receive the Medal of Honor during the Spanish-American War: Privates Dennis Bell, Fritz Lee, William H. Thompkins, and George Wanton and Sgt. Maj. Edward L. Baker.

The commander in chief of the Cuban Army compliments the African American troops by stating, "If you will be as brave in the future to your country as you have proved yourself to-day, it will not be very long before you will have generals in the army of the United States."

WORK. In August, African American longshoremen strike for higher wages and better working conditions in Galveston, Texas.

1899

ARTS. On May 26, painter Aaron Douglas is born in Topeka, Kansas, to Aaron and Elizabeth Douglas. He discovers his ability to draw at an early age and later recalls how his parents hang his drawings and paintings.

On April 4, musician and composer Edward Kennedy (Duke) Ellington is born in Washington, DC.

On July 1, Thomas Dorsey, the reputed father of gospel music, is born in Villa Rica, Georgia.

Musician Deford Bailey Sr. is born in Tennessee.

Scott Joplin, the innovator of a style of piano compositions known as ragtime, produces his most famous tune, "Maple Leaf Rag," named after a social club (brothel) in Sedalia, Missouri. This one tune sells one million copies. Joplin learned to play on the piano as a child when his mother purchased one from money she earned as a maid. He quickly improvised American and European classical music into his own unique renditions, producing more than 40 ragtime tunes. Invited to play at the Columbia Exposition in 1893, he astounded the audience with a style of music that earned him a place as an accomplished musician. Though the popularity of ragtime music fades by the 1920s, Joplin's reputation and compositions continue into the 1970s and are resurrected for the soundtracks of films such as *The Sting* and *The Entertainer*. In 1976, Joplin is posthumously awarded a Pulitzer Prize for music.

ASSO. On June 10, the Improved Benevolent and Protective Order of Elks is established in Cincinnati, Ohio.

BUSI. Under the leadership of Charles Clinton Spaulding, the North Carolina Mutual Life Insurance Company in Durham, North Carolina, is founded. Spaulding starts the company with two partners, John Merrick, a former slave and leading realtor and owner of a chain of six barber shops (three for blacks and three for whites), and Dr. Aaron McDuffie Moore, Spaulding's uncle and Durham's only black physician. Utilizing Booker T. Washington's philosophy of thrift, hard work, and self-help, the company survives a number of national economic crises.

CIVI. On June 2, the National Afro-American Council calls for a day of fasting to protest the lynching and racial massacres of blacks.

CRIM. The federal government reports that 85 African Americans are lynched during the year.

INVE. On October 10, I. R. Johnson receives a patent (no. 634,823) for the bicycle frame.

On December 19, G. T. Woods receives a patent (no. 639,692) for the roller coaster amusement apparatus.

POLI. On December 4, the 56th U.S. Congress convenes with one African American in attendance, George H. White of North Carolina.

SCIE. On April 11, chemist Percy Lavon Julian is born. Julian is graduated with honors from DePauw University in Greencastle, Indiana, and he teaches at Fisk University, West Virginia State College, and Howard University before attending Harvard University and the University of Vienna. His research is used to treat glaucoma and helps create the precursors of cortisone, used for the treatment of arthritis. During his lifetime, Julian owns more than 100 chemical patents. He heads the soybean research department of Glidden Company. In 1953, Julian founds his own pharmaceutical company, Julian Laboratories, and soon manufactures a synthetic hormone derived from the soybean that is used in the treatment of cancer. He receives the Spingarn Medal in 1947 and 1968. (The Spingarn Medal is instituted in 1914 by J. E. Spingarn, who is the chairman of the board of he National Association for the Advancement of Colored People. The award is presented annually for the highest achievement by an African American in any field of endeavor.) Julian also receives the Chemical Pioneer Award from the American Institute of Chemists.

TWENTIETH CENTURY

1900

ARTS. On July 4, Daniel Louis "Satchmo" Armstrong is born in New Orleans, Louisiana.

ASSO. On August 23 and 24, Booker T. Washington forms the National Negro Business League (NNBL) in Boston, Massachusetts, and is elected its president. The NNBL seeks to promote the "commercial, agricultural, educational, and industrial advancement" of African Americans. Its aims are much broader than the legalistic orientations of the National Association for the Advancement of Colored People (NAACP). Although Booker T. Washington's critics attack his philosophy as accommodation in the face of institutionalized and personal white racism, close scrutiny of NNBL records suggests that the core membership is cognizant of the price paid for any economic developmental program by African Americans within the hostile environment of the South. For example, many NNBL leaders believe that black businesses cannot thrive for long unless their prosperity is spread through the community. Hence, there is a pronounced communitarian ethic within the movement, not unlike later African American political movements, that functions under a more radical political rhetoric. The NNBL avidly recruits businesswomen, who, in turn, activate social networks that aid black business development and understanding of the importance of demographic details for any form of community economic development.

CENS. The population of the United States is 75,994,575, of which 8,833,994 (11.6%) are African Americans.

CRIM. In November, the federal government reports that 106 African Americans are lynched during the year.

INVE. On February 20, J. F. Pickering receives a patent (no. 643,975) for his airship.

LIT. In November, James Weldon Johnson writes the poem "Lift Every Voice and Sing," which, with the assistance of J. Rosamond Johnson, becomes an unofficial national anthem for African Americans.

OBIT. On August 5, African American Roman Catholic Bishop James Augustine Healy dies at age 70 in Portland, Maine.

POLI. From July 24 to 27, the first Pan-African Congress meets in London. Among the leaders to attend are H. Sylvester Williams, a West Indian lawyer with a practice in London, England, W.E.B. Du Bois, and Bishop Alexander Walters. Du Bois chairs the Committee on the Address to the Nations of the World. He calls for the creation of "a great central Negro state of the world"; however, he does not insist European colonial powers withdraw immediately from Africa, but "as soon as practicable the rights of responsible self-government to the black colonies of African and the West Indies" should be established.

1901

ARTS. On March 18, creative artist and teacher William H. Johnson is born in Florence, South Carolina. His creative art depicting African Americans is exhibited at museums and art galleries throughout the world. From 1921 to 1926 he is associated with the National Academy of Design in New York City. Johnson leaves the United States for Paris in 1926 then lives and paints in Tunisia in 1932. Returning to the United States in 1939, he teaches art at the Harlem Community of Arts Center that is associated with the Works Progress Administration (WPA) until 1943. One of his more noted exhibitions, entitled "Homecoming," is presented at Washington, DC's, National Museum of American Art in 1991, 21 years after his death.

CRIM. The federal government reports that 105 African Americans are lynched during the year.

CIVI. On August 30, Roy Wilkins is born in St. Louis, Missouri. While attending the University of Minnesota, he majors in sociology and graduates in 1923. He works as a journalist for the *Minnesota Daily* and the *Kansas City Call* and eventually becomes editor of the *St. Paul Appeal*, an African American weekly. He rises fast within the National Association for the Advancement of Colored People (NAACP) and from 1931 to 1934, he is assistant secretary under the organization's executive director, Walter Francis White. When W.E.B. Du Bois is forced out of the NAACP, Wilkins takes over his position as editor of the *Crisis* magazine. Following the death of Walter White in 1955, Wilkins becomes the second executive director of the organization. In the following years, he becomes directly involved in the civil rights movement and on more than one occasion comes in direct conflict with some of the more militant elements of the civil and human rights movement of the 1950s and 1960s. Wilkins stands philosophically and politically against the use of violence in self-defense and disapproves of the term *Black Power*. He categorically rejects students' demands for all-black university departments, describing that possibility as a "return to segregation and Jim Crow." He dies on September 9, 1981.

Roy Wilkins as executive director of the NAACP, 1958. Courtesy of Library of Congress.

EDUC. In November, Grambling State University is founded.

MED. On November 9, William Monroe Trotter founds the Boston *Guardian* newspaper.

On October 11, Bert Williams and George Walker are probably the first African American recording artists when they cut several songs for the Victor Talking Machine Company in New York City.

POLI. On March 4, at noon, the term of the last post-Reconstruction congressman, George H. White of North Carolina, ends.

On October 16, Booker T. Washington dines at the White House with President Theodore Roosevelt. Many white southerners berate Roosevelt for disgracing the White House with Washington's presence. Two days later, Washington and Roosevelt dine again at Yale University, where Washington uses his considerable influence to secure the political appointment of a number of African Americans to public office.

On November 11, Alabama adopts a new state constitution with a grandfather clause designed to eliminate African American voters.

1902

ARTS. On February 27, noted opera singer Marian Anderson is born in South Philadelphia, Pennsylvania. Marian began singing in the nearby Union Baptist Church Choir; however, the demands of the choir have the contralto singing high soprano and low baritone. By 1925, Marian has a strong enough voice to enter a contest with 300 other singers for the Lewisohn Stadium Concert Award in New York City. The prize, which she wins, gives her an opportunity to sing with the New York Philharmonic Orchestra on August 26, 1925. After singing, she receives a Rosenwald Foundation fellowship and an opportunity to travel to England and Germany. Marian Anderson is received throughout Europe as an accomplished if not great opera singer.

Jazz pianist Jelly Roll Morton begins performances in the Storyville district of New Orleans, Louisiana.

LIT. On February 1, African American poet laureate, author, and social activist James Langston Mercer Hughes is born in Joplin, Missouri.

SPOR. On May 12, lightweight champion Joe Gans (Joseph Gaines) becomes the first African American to win a world crown in boxing by knocking out Frank Erne in the fist round at Fort Erie, Ontario.

1903

CRIM. The federal government reports that 84 African Americans are lynched during the year.

LAW. On April 27, the U.S. Supreme Court upholds the grandfather clause in Alabama's state constitution that eliminates African American voter rights in Alabama.

LIT. In April, W.E.B. Du Bois publishes *The Soul of Black Folk*. In this autobiography, Du Bois reveals his own discovery of self as a younger man and student at Fisk University in Tennessee. Du Bois also challenges Booker T. Washington's philosophy of racial accommodation and subordination of African American political rights to southern racist.

On March 30, noted poet Countee Cullen is generally considered to have been in born New York City though there is little evidence to say that this is an unquestionable fact. Langston Hughes, Cullen's transcript from New York University, and others in the know state that Louisville, Kentucky, is his birthplace. Though his literary fame occurs during the Harlem Renaissance period of the 1920s, Cullen's marriage to W.E.B. Du Bois's daughter on April 9, 1928, is of the most lavish weddings in African American history. The wedding is organized in a manner that symbolizes the union of an elite African American intellectual family and a new breed of younger African American responsible for the Renaissance itself. Though the marriage ends quickly in a flurry of innuendo, his poems still excite the imaginations of the public. In 1929, he publishes *The Black Christ and other Poems,* which is not well received by critics. In the 1930s, he teaches French at Frederick Douglass Junior High School, where his most famous student is the writer James Baldwin. His 1934 novel *One Way to Heaven* is judged to be one his best works and is regarded by critics as one of the better black satires and is one of three important fictional retrospectives of the Harlem Renaissance. At the time of his death on January 9, 1946, he is working on a musical with writer Arna Bontemps called *St. Louis Woman.*

Zora Neale Hurston is born in Notasulga, Alabama, and raised in the all-black town of Eatonville, Florida. She attends Morgan State College in Maryland and Howard University but is graduated with a degree in anthropology from Barnard University in New York City. An avid student of African Caribbean culture and folklore, Hurston writes novels that reflect those interests. Her most important novel, *Their Eyes Are Watching God,* is published in 1936 and is followed by *Moses, Man of the Mountain* (1939) and *Seraph on the Suwanee* (1948). Her books that directly reflect her cultural folkloric interest are *Mules and Men* (1935) and *Tell My Horse* (1937). Her 1942 autobiographical work, *Dust Tracks on a Road,* is an extremely revealing look at this highly complex and creative artist.

1904

ARTS. Vaudeville singer Ma Rainey, known as the Mother of the Blues, begins her national tour.

Zora Neale Hurston, 1935. Courtesy of Library of Congress.

BUSI. On June 6, James C. Napier is the founder and cashier (manager) of the One Cent (now Citizens) Savings Bank. This Nashville bank is the first such institution founded by African Americans in Tennessee. As a result, Napier becomes Nashville's most powerful politician and its most influential citizen. His reputation is built upon years as a member of Nashville's City Council, over which he once presided. He is also instrumental in the hiring of black teachers for the colored black schools during the 1870s as well as the hiring of black detectives and black fire-engine companies during the 1880s. His highest political accomplishment is his service as President William H. Taft's registrar of the United States Treasury from 1911 to 1913.

CRIM. In October, the federal government reports that 76 African Americans are lynched during the year.

EDUC. On October 3, Mary McLeod Bethune opens the Daytona Normal and Industrial School in Daytona Beach, Florida.

INVE. On June 10, Granville T. Woods receives a patent (no. 701,981) for the automatic air brake.

MEDI. Charles Drew, the oldest of five siblings, is born to Richard and Nora Drew on June 3 in Washington, DC. Excelling in both academics and sports, Drew attends graduate school at Amherst College in Massachusetts and receives his medical degree with honors from McGill University in Montreal, Quebec. While researching blood plasma and transfusions at Columbia University, he makes a number of discoveries related to the preservation of blood. He discovers that by separating the red blood cells from the plasma and freezing the two separately, blood can be preserved and reconstituted at a later date. This ability to store blood plasma leads to the establishment of blood banks. Dr. Drew also establishes the American Red Cross Blood Bank, for which he becomes its first director. During World War II, blood banks become a major factor in saving Allied lives on the battlefield. Among U.S. soldiers, however, institutionalized racial segregation in the military demands that so-called Negro blood be kept separate from "white" blood. In 1944, Dr. Drew receives the Spingarn Medal for the development of blood plasma and other related medical achievements. After the war, Dr. Drew becomes chairmen of surgery at Howard University. Unfortunately, in 1950 at the age of 46, Drew dies from injuries suffered in an automobile accident in North Carolina. Speculation surrounding his demise suggests that after the accident he is taken to a white's only hospital and is refused medical care, and while being transported to the colored hospital, he dies.

SPOR. George Page is the first African American to compete in the Olympic Games held in St. Louis. Page, who is associated with the Milwaukee Athletic club, runs in the 400 meters and the 400-meter hurdles.

1905

ASSO. From July 11 to 13, African American intellectuals and activists meet and structure the Niagara movement. Twenty-nine delegates from fourteen states, led by W.E.B. Du Bois and William Monroe Trotter, come together at

Niagara Falls, New York, to demand the abolition of social and political distinctions based on race. The Niagara movement eventually attracts some 400 supporters and remains active with Du Bois as its ideological leader. Its immediate counterbalance is Booker T. Washington's well-financed Tuskegee Institute. Reportedly, the editor of the black newspaper the *Washington Bee,* W. Calvin Chase, who years earlier attacked Washington's Atlanta Compromise Speech, is now paid to attack the Niagara movement. Booker T. Washington supposedly sends spies to Niagara Falls to bring back information. Washington then lets it be known that African American federal employees might lose their jobs if they join or continue to support the Niagara movement.

BUSI. On September 6, A. F. Herdon establishes the Atlanta Life Insurance Company in Atlanta, Georgia.

CRIM. In November, the federal government reports that 57 African Americans are lynched during the year.

FAMI. On April 1, child care advocate and founder of Hale House Clara McBride Hale is born.

MED. On May 5, Robert S. Abbott publishes the first issue of the *Chicago Defender.* The *Defender* becomes a major newspaper for African Americans in the areas of current affairs and opinion making. By 1929, it reaches a national circulation of 250,000.

MEDI. On April 6, W. Warwick Cardozo, physician and pioneering researcher in sickle cell anemia, is born in Washington, DC.

POLI. On November 23, Henry Watson Furness, an Indiana physician, is named minister to Haiti. He is the last African American minister to Haiti for many years. U.S. President Woodrow Wilson, who promotes segregation in federal employment, appoints a white minister to Haiti in 1913.

1906

ARTS. On October 22, 3,000 African Americans demonstrate forcibly in Philadelphia, Pennsylvania,

Newsboy selling the *Chicago Defender,* still a leading Negro newspaper in 1942. Courtesy of Library of Congress.

to protest a theatrical presentation of Thomas Dixon's *The Clansman.*

ASSO. On December 4, the first African American Greek fraternity is founded.

BUSI. Madame C. J. Walker (born Sarah Breedlove) establishes her first black hair-care business in Detroit, Michigan, and becomes the first African American female millionaire.

CRIM. The federal government reports that 62 African Americans are lynched during the past year.

EDUC. On June 9, John Hope is named the first African American president of Morehouse College in Atlanta, Georgia.

MILI. In August, three companies of the all-black Twenty-Fifth regiment stationed in Brownsville, Texas, are involved in racial conflict with local white townspeople over the mistreatment and physical abuse of one of the black troopers. When it is over, one white citizen is killed and another is wounded along with the police chief. White citizens claim that the black troopers had "shot up the town," and as a result, racial hostility is at a fever pitch. Only the firmness of the base commander prevents a more devastating attack by the incensed black troopers on local white provocateurs.

In November, President Theodore Roosevelt receives an inspector's report that faults the African American troopers with causing the murder and wounding of local whites in Brownsville, Texas. Roosevelt dishonorably discharges an entire battalion of black troopers, 167 soldiers, and makes it a condition that they are never able to obtain a civil service job. Even conservative Senator Tillman notes that President Roosevelt's actions appear to be an "executive lynching."

OBIT. On February 9, poet and writer Paul Lawrence Dunbar dies in Dayton, Ohio. Through his relatively short life, Paul Dunbar writes several novels, including *The Uncalled* (1898) and *The Love of Landry* (1900). It is for his poetry, however, that he is best remembered. Frederick Douglass once described him as "the most promising black man of his time." Dunbar's poems *Oak and Ivy* (1893), *Majors and Minors* (1896), and *Lyrics of Lowly Life* (1896) cause many critics to refer to him as the poet laureate of the Negro race. By the year of his death, he is considered one of the most important men of letters in the United States.

POLI. From September 22 to 26, a major racial riot occurs in Atlanta, Georgia. Twenty-five African Americans and two whites are officially listed as killed, and marshal law is proclaimed. The race riot occurs after a white male jumps on a

box on Decatur Street in downtown Atlanta and waves a newspaper with the headline "THIRD ASSAULT." He yells, "Are white men going to stand for this?" The crowd roars back, "No! Save our women!" "Kill the niggers," thereby commencing five days of bloodshed. Thousands of whites roam the streets looking for black people to assault, and those blacks that are armed attempt to defend themselves.

SPOR. Well-known and respected Negro Baseball League and the American League baseball pitcher Leroy Robert "Satchel" Paige is born in Mobile, Alabama.

1907

EDUC. Alain L. Locke becomes the first African American to become a Rhodes scholar. The second African American Rhodes scholar is not selected until 1960.

MEDI. On April 13, Harlem Hospital in New York City opens.

1908

ASSO. On January 29, Alpha Phi Alpha fraternity is incorporated at Cornell University.

BUSI. On June 30, Allen Allensworth founds the town of Allensworth, California. Allensworth, a former soldier, and William Payne, a teacher, create the California colony and the Home Promoting Association with offices in the San Fernando Building on Main Street in downtown Los Angeles. They soon interest John Palmer, a miner, William Peck, a minister, and Harry A. Mitchell, a real estate agent, in the idea of establishing an

The September 1906 Atlanta race riots so motivate conservative African Americans such as W.E.B. Du Bois that he proclaims, "I waited on my front porch with a shotgun for a mob that never came, but had they, I would without hesitation have sprayed their guts over the grass." Similarly, T. Thomas Fortune, once the secretary for Booker T. Washington, states, "I cannot believe that the policy of non-resistance in a situation like that of Atlanta can result in anything by contempt and massacre of the race." Yet, Booker T. Washington seeks a middle perspective when he notes, "While there is disorder in one community, there is peace and harmony in thousands of others."

all–African American town. They find land in Solito, a rural area in Tulare County, 30 miles north of Bakersfield, California. Naming the soon-to-be-constructed town Allensworth, it is close to a depot station on the main Santa Fe Railroad line from Los Angeles to San Francisco. The soil is rich, water seemingly abundant, and the available acreage is reasonably priced. By 1915, Allensworth is a thriving community, the *New York Age* chronicles its growth, and the *Washington Bee* congratulates all involved in its development. The *California Eagle* notes, "there is not a single white person having anything to do with the affairs of the colony." The *Oakland Sunshine,* a leading San Francisco Bay Area black newspaper claims that the citizens of Allensworth generate nearly $5,000 per month in their business ventures. Allen Allensworth becomes politically involved in the town as a county school district member, a member of the regional library system, and a supporter of the first African American justice of the peace in post-Mexican California. In 1915, the *California Eagle* reports that the town of Allensworth's 900 acres is worth more than $112,500. After World War II, the town youth begin to migrate to Oakland, San Francisco, and Los Angeles for jobs. Though the town shrinks in size, its future is assured by the development of a nearby state park on October 6, 1976.

CRIM. From August 14 to 19, racial rioting in Springfield, Illinois, Abraham Lincoln's home town, forces the governor to call out troops to restore order. The sheer cruelty of this violence is important in the forming of the National Association for the Advancement of Colored People (NAACP).

In December, the federal government reports that 89 African Americans are lynched during the year.

HHC. On August 25, 1908, Martha Minerva founds the National Association of Colored Graduate Nurses (NACGN). The organization is dedicated to promoting the standards and welfare of African American nurses and the breaking down of racial barriers within the profession, particularly in the American Nurses Association (ANA), which does not welcome black nurses. Primary for the NACGN is to get blacks into nursing schools,

nursing jobs, and nursing organizations. In 1934, Estelle Massey Riddle Osborne (the first black person to obtain a master's degree in nursing) is elected president of the NACGN. She hires Mabel K. Staupers as a paid executive director, and the two begin a campaign to force the integration of the black nurses into every aspect of the profession. For 12 years, they lobby the ANA for recognition as a bona fide nursing association. In 1933, the NACGN has 175 members; however, by 1949, their membership grows to 947. One major achievement is the integration of the Cadet Nurse Corps during World War II. After the war, the ANA invites the NACGN to become apart of their organization, thereby integrating the ANA. An element of the reorganization involves the ANA agreeing to continue awarding the Mary Mahoney Medal to the person or group contributing the most to intergroup relations.

LAW. On July 2, the first African American U.S. Supreme Court justice, Thurgood Marshall, is born in Baltimore, Maryland.

POLI. On November 29, minister and political and civil rights activist Rev. Adam Clayton Powell Jr. is born in New Haven, Connecticut.

SPOR. On December 26, Jack Johnson defeats Tommy Burns at Sydney, Australia, for the heavyweight championship of the world.

1909

ARTS. On June 22, dancer and choreographer Katherine Dunham is born in Chicago; she is raised in Joliet, Illinois.

ASSO. On February 12, the National Association for the Advancement of Colored People (NAACP) is founded. Occurring 100 years after the birth of Abraham Lincoln, a group of African Americans and white liberals and social activists meets to form an organization to address the increasing racial, ethnic, and religious violence that consumes much of the southern and midsouthern states. Specific goals of the NAACP are to work for the abolition of segregation, equal education for black and white children, complete enfranchisement for African Americans, and the enforcement of the Fourteenth and Fifteenth Amendments to the

U.S. Constitution. The initial group consists of 6 blacks and 47 whites. Many radical blacks such as Monroe Trotter do not attend because of suspicions about whites' intentions for the organization, though publisher and social activist Ida B. Wells, W.E.B. Du Bois, and Mary Church Terrell attend. Du Bois is eventually asked to be director of publicity for the NAACP and, as such, founds the organization's journal, *The Crisis,* in 1910.

On May 31, approximately 300 African Americans and whites meet at the United Charities Building in New York City for the first NAACP two-day conference.

CRIM. In December, the federal government reports that 69 African Americans are lynched during the year.

EDUC. In December, Tennessee State A&I University is founded.

EXPO. On April 6, Cdr. Robert E. Perry reaches the North Pole with his African American assistant, Matthew Henson. There is some disagreement as to whether Perry or Henson is the person to reach the point of the North Pole.

MED. On December 4, James H. Anderson founds the *New York Amsterdam* newspaper.

SPOR. Lincoln University, Virginia Union University, Hampton University, and Wilberforce University field the first African American college basketball teams.

WORK. On May 17, white firemen working for the Georgia Railroad Company start a strike against the employment of African Americans. In the past, the position of train fireman is a generally lowly position on steam engine trains due to the strenuous work required to stoke the boiler with coal. With the introduction of diesel engines, however, whites fight to replace blacks in this now-enhanced occupation.

1910

ARTS. Bert Williams, the first major African American male theater star, becomes the first black man to appear in the otherwise all-white Ziegfeld Follies on Broadway.

ASSO. On March 23, the National Urban League is founded in New York City.

From May 12 to 14, the second National Association for the Advancement of Colored People (NAACP) conference is held in New York City. The purpose is to create a permanent national structure.

CENS. The population of the United States is 93,402,151, of which 9,828,763 (10.7%) are African Americans.

CIVI. On March 17, civil rights leader and pacifist ideologue Bayard Rustin is born in West Chester, Pennsylvania. He begins his political career as a member of the Young Communist League, associates himself with the Fellowship of Reconciliation, and experiments with Gandhian techniques of nonviolent resistance and their possible application within a U.S. political context. In 1942, he becomes an active and founding member of the Congress of Racial Equality (CORE) along with James Farmer. Refusing to be drafted in World War II, he is convicted of violating the Selective Service Act and serves three years in a federal penitentiary in Ashland, Kentucky. Once released from jail, he organizes a committee within the A. Philip Randolph's Committee against Discrimination to fight discrimination in the armed forces. In the 1950s, he is an important advisor to Rev. Dr. Martin Luther King Jr. as a strategist. In the 1960s, he organizes CORE's Freedom Rides, which test the application of the decision in *Brown v. Board of Education of Topeka, Kansas,* the Fourteenth Amendment, and the federal guidelines that outlaw discriminatory practice in interstate travel and accommodations. His value to the civil rights movement is tested by the development of radical youth organizations within the urban centers of the United States and the growing militant antiwar movement. His growing ineffectiveness against direct action by armed groups is beyond his ability to comprehend or agree with. During the urban disturbances from 1963 to 1968, he is totally rejected by younger, more militant advocates for social change. By the 1980s, social and civil rights issues concerning alternative lifestyles such as lesbianism, gay rights, and homophobia become another part of Rustin's fight. For some, Rustin's own gay lifestyle becomes a criticism of his value during the civil rights movement.

While in prison, civil rights leader Bayard Rustin develops his philosophy for social action: "There are three ways in which one can deal with an injustice, (a) One can accept it without protest. (b) One seek to avoid it. (c) One can resist the injustice nonviolently. To accept it is to perpetuate it. To avoid it is impossible. To resist by intelligent means, and with an attitude of mutual responsibility and respect, is much the better course."

CRIM. In December, the federal government reports that 67 African Americans are lynched during the year.

ECON. On March 25, the United States Liberian Commission recommends that financial aid be given to Liberia as well as the establishment of a U.S. Navy coal station in the West African country.

MED. On November 1, W.E.B. Du Bois publishes the first issue of the National Association for the Advancement of Colored People (NAACP) journal, *The Crisis*. In this journal, Du Bois denounces racism and racial violence and more dramatically advocates that the African American "agitate, then brother; protest, reveal the truth and refuse to be silenced." Du Bois's views contradict Booker T. Washington's more compliant public stance. *The Crisis* also presents a more middle-class, upwardly mobile view of African American communities throughout the country and attempts to offset a more victimized version that is more popular in the South.

In December, the Norfolk *Journal and Guide* is established under the leadership of P. B. Young Sr.

In December, the *Pittsburgh Courier* is founded.

POLI. On June 13, William D. Crum, a physician from South Carolina, is appointed minister to Liberia.

On December 19, Baltimore, Maryland's City Council passes the first urban ordinance requiring blacks and whites to reside in segregated residential areas. Similar laws are passed in Norfolk, Richmond, and Roanoke, Virginia; Greensboro, North Carolina; St. Louis, Missouri; Oklahoma City, Oklahoma; Louisville, Kentucky; and Dallas, Texas.

SPOR. On July 4, Jack Johnson, the first African American heavyweight champion, retains his title by knocking out Jim "the Great White Hope" Jeffries, who comes out of retirement "to win back the title for the white race."

1911

ARTS. Mahalia Jackson is born on October 11 in New Orleans, Louisiana. Jackson grows up singing gospel at the Plymouth Rock Baptist Church, where her father preaches. At 16, she moves to Chicago and supports herself my doing housework and odd jobs, but she also sings in her local church.

ASSO. On May 15, the African American fraternity Kappa Alpha Psi is incorporated at Indiana University.

On June 20, the National Association for the Advancement of Colored People (NAACP) is incorporated in New York City.

On October 20, three organizations—the Committee for Improving the Industrial Conditions of Negroes in New York, the Committee on Urban Conditions, and the National League for the Protection of Colored Women—merge to form a larger, all-encompassing organization: the National Urban League. Under the leadership of Dr. George E. Hayne and Eugene Kinckle Jones, the League attempts to gain the financial support of individuals such as philanthropist Julius Rosenwald and Mrs. Baldwin as well as sponsors such as Booker T. Washington and Kelly Miller.

CRIM. In October, the federal government reports that 60 African Americans are lynched during the year.

EDUC. On July 11, the foremost scholar on contemporary and ancient African and African American history, Frank Snowden, is born in York County, Virginia.

POLI. On March 26, William H. Lewis is appointed assistant attorney general of the United States.

WORK. On March 9, white railroad firemen from the Cincinnati, New Orleans, and Texas Pacific Railroad strike to protest the hiring of African American firemen.

On June 28, Samuel J. Battle becomes the first African American police officer in New York City.

1912

ARTS. On September 27, the first published blues composition, W. C. Handy's *Memphis Blues,* goes on sale in Memphis, Tennessee.

Pioneer filmmaker Bill Foster directs a comedy, *The Railroad Porter,* the first African American film production.

ASSO. On January 1, the National Association for the Advancement of Colored People (NAACP) reports that its total receipts from May to December for the previous year are $10,317.43. The Association has local chapters in Chicago, Boston, and New York.

CRIM. In November, the federal government reports that 61 African Americans are lynched during the year.

EDUC. On June 19, Tennessee University opens as Tennessee A&L State College.

MED. In November, the *St. Louis Argus* newspaper is founded in Missouri.

1913

ASSO. On January 29, Alpha Kappa Alpha sorority at Howard University in Washington, DC, is incorporated.

Throughout January, African Americans celebrate the 50th anniversary of the Emancipation Proclamation.

CIVI. On April 11, U.S. President Woodrow Wilson and his cabinet begin discussions on the relationships of blacks and whites in government agencies. Shortly afterward, the Wilson administration imposes a segregation policy that separates working areas, lavatories, and luncheon rooms in many government departments throughout Washington, DC.

On February 4, civil rights activist and symbol of the modern civil rights movement Rosa Parks (Rosa McCauley) is born in Tuskegee, Alabama, to James McCauley, a carpenter, and Leona McCauley, a teacher. Raised in a southern environment premised upon fear and terror, Parks recalls that previous to the Montgomery bus boycott in 1955, which is stimulated by her refusal on December 1, 1955, to give up her seat to a white man, she and her husband, Raymond Parks, decide to join the National Association for the Advancement of Colored People (NAACP) to work toward improving the lifestyle of African Americans.

CRIM. In September, the federal government reports that 51 African Americans are lynched during the year.

MED. In September, the *Cleveland Call & Post* newspaper is founded in Cleveland, Ohio.

MEDI. On November 13, Dr. Daniel Hale Williams, pioneering African American surgeon, becomes a member of the American College of Surgeons.

OBIT. On March 10, Harriet Tubman, engineer of the Underground Railroad, supporter of John Brown's efforts at Harpers Ferry, Virginia, Union

---

Of her work with the NAACP, Rosa Parks recalls, "I worked on numerous cases … but we did not get the publicity. There were cases of flogging, peonage, murder, and rape. We didn't seem to have too many successes. It was more a matter of trying to challenge the powers that be, and to let it be known that we did not wish to continue being second-class citizens."

guerrilla fighter against the Confederacy, and agent for the U.S. Secret Service during the Civil War, dies in Auburn, New York.

SPOR. Jesse Owens is born on a sharecropper's farm in Alabama.

1914

ARTS. On July 8, musician and singer Billy Eckstine is born.

ASSO. On January 10, Phi Beta Sigma fraternity is founded at Howard University in Washington, DC.

On October 28, Omega Psi Phi fraternity is incorporated at Howard University in Washington, DC.

EDUC. On March 9, the "New" Southern University campus opens in Scotlandville, near Baton Rouge, Louisiana, with 9 professors and 47 students.

LIT. Noted author Ralph Waldo Ellison is born on March 1, in Oklahoma City, Oklahoma.

MED. Sam Lucas becomes the first African American actor to star in a full-length Hollywood film when he portrays Uncle Tom in an adaptation of Harriet Beecher Stowe's *Uncle Tom's Cabin*.

The first African American film company, Lincoln Motion Production Company, is founded in Los Angeles.

SPOR. On May 20, Heavyweight Champion of the World Joe Louis is born in Lafayette, Alabama, but the family moves to Detroit, Michigan, when Joe is 12 years old, and the parents have high aspirations for their children. One of his sisters becomes a school principal, and his mother attempts to interest young Louis in ballet dancing. More attracted to the bruising sport of boxing, Louis becomes a Golden Glove boxer and by 1932 defeats all comers in Detroit and Chicago. By 1934, he is boxing professionally and in three years defeats James Braddock to become the world's heavyweight champion. Louis's major challenge and accomplishment as a fighter occurs in the latter part of the 1930s when he fights and loses the heavyweight championship in 1936 to Max Schmeling, a reluctant representative of Nazi Germany's philosophy of Aryan racial superiority. In a return match two years later at Yankee Stadium on June 22, 1938, Louis knocks out Schmeling in the first round. There never is a third fight. During World War II, Joe Louis is drafted into the segregated U.S. Army and spends two years touring military bases to build the morale of soldiers, black and white, by sparring local fighters. He becomes both a symbol of African American support for the war and a symbol for African Americans in their struggle against racism at home and abroad. The Double V, as understood by most black organizations, clarifies the duplicity of African Americans fighting against both Nazi Germany and U.S. institutional racism. Joe Louis defends his title 25 times between 1937 and 1949, when he retires. Financial problems due to a mishandling of his money force him into serious difficulties with the Internal Revenue Service. Joe Louis is best remembered as the Brown Bomber, whose character and fighting style epitomize the best in boxing.

WAR. Eugene Jacques Bullard, born in Columbus, Georgia, ran away from home in 1902 at the age of eight as his father hid from a white lynch mob. As an African American expatriate who joins the French army, Bullard sees more combat than most Americans during World War I. Bullard serves in both the French army and their air corps and is the first African American fighter pilot in the world. His extraordinary life is chronicled in *The Black Swallow of Death* (1972) by P. J. Carisella and James W. Ryan.

1915

ARTS. On April 7, Eleanora Fagan (Billie Holiday) is born to teenagers Sadie Fagan and Clarence Holiday. She sings and performs with big band leaders such as Lester Young, Louis Armstrong, who is her mentor, and Duke Ellington, and she develops a reputation and singing style that influences other singers, such as Lena Horne, Sarah Vaughan, and Carmen McRae. Billie Holiday's established reputation as one of the greatest jazz soloists is reinforced by her rendition of the song "Strange Fruit," which is written by a white schoolteacher, Abel

Merpol, that captures the essence and pain of being an African American during the early period of the twentieth century when the lynching of southern blacks by whites is an expected occurrence.

By the 1940s, Holiday's addiction to drugs begins to affect her career. Treatments in a number of clinics prove unsuccessful, and she spends nine months in a federal reformatory for women at Alderson, West Virginia. Throughout the difficult periods in her life, she manages to sing in nightclubs, give concerts, and make international tours. A year before her death on July 17, 1959, her most popular album, *A Lady in Satin,* is released.

ASSO. On May 17, the National Black Baptist Convention is chartered.

On September 9, the Association for the Study of Negro Life and History is organized in Chicago, Illinois, by Carter G. Woodson. The Association publishes *The Journal of Negro History* (now *The Journal of African American History*). Today, the association is as the Association for the Study of Afro-American Life and History.

On December 4, the second appearance of the Ku Klux Klan as a national organization occurs when the group receives a charter from Fulton County, Georgia's, superior court. This reconstituted version of the nineteenth-century, post–Civil War Ku Klux Klan expands primarily, but not exclusively, throughout the southern states and reaches an estimated membership of four million members by the mid-1920s. In 1924, the organization is strong in nontraditional southern states such as Oklahoma, Indiana, California, Oregon, and Ohio.

CIVI. On June 21, the U.S. Supreme Court rules in *Guinn v. United States* that the grandfather clauses in the Oklahoma and Maryland constitutions violate the Fifteenth Amendment to the U.S. Constitution.

CRIM. In December, the federal government reports that 56 African Americans are lynched during the year.

EDUC. On September 22, Xavier University, the first African American Catholic university, opens in New Orleans, Louisiana.

LIT. On January 2, historian, writer, and presidential advisor John Hope Franklin is born.

On July 7, writer and poet Margaret Walker is born. In 1942, she publishes *For My People,* an important collection of poetry derived from her experiences in the Chicago Renaissance.

MED. In December, the National Association for the Advancement of Colored People (NAACP) leads a protest against the film *Birth of a Nation,* in which African Americans are depicted as the cause of the Civil War and as lazy, shiftless men seeking to assault white women.

The first African American film production company, the Lincoln Motion Picture Company, is founded in Los Angeles, California, by two African American actors, Clarence Brooks and Noble Johnson, a druggist, James T. Smith, and a white cameraman, Harry Grant.

MIGR. Beginning in December and lasting over the next two decades, approximately two million southern African Americans migrate northward to urban industrial centers such as Philadelphia, Chicago, Washington, DC, and New York. They generally find work in industrial plants that suffer a lack of manpower as white males fight in World War I. The migration differs from the previous post–Civil War migration primarily in volume. In the 40-year period between 1870 and 1910, the number of southern-born African Americans in the North increases from 146,490 to 415,533, a decennial increase of 54,000. From 1910 to 1920, however, there is an increase of 311,910 that is more than the aggregate increase of the preceding 40 years and six times the previous average decennial increase.

POLI. On July 28, United States Marines invade Haiti and force the country to become a de facto protectorate of the United States.

OBIT. On February 23, Civil War hero and Reconstruction Congressman Robert Small dies at age 75 in Beaufort, South Carolina.

On May 8, the first African American chaplain in the U.S. Army and bishop in the African Methodist Church, Henry McNeal Turner, dies.

On November 14, educator, entrepreneur, organizer, politician, and founder of the Tuskegee

Institute Booker T. Washington dies at age 59 in Tuskegee, Alabama.

SCIE. The first Spingarn Medal for the achievements in science is given to Ernest E. Just for his pioneering research on fertilization and cell division. Dr. Just is the chairman of the department of physiology at Howard University in Washington, DC.

1916

ASSO. On March 22, Black Nationalist Marcus Mosiah Garvey arrives in the United States from Jamaica. Hoping to meet his philosophical mentor, Booker T. Washington, Garvey, upon hearing of Washington's death, founds the Universal Negro Improvement Association (UNIA) in Harlem, New York.

CRIM. The federal government reports that 50 African Americans are lynched during the year.

MED. On January 1, the first issue of *The Journal of Negro History* is published in Washington, DC, by Dr. Carter G. Woodson. A teacher, historian, and publisher, Dr. Woodson is responsible more than any other person for founding an association that establishes the idea of Negro History Week, later African American Month.

MILI. Col. Charles Young of the U.S. Army receives the National Association for the Advancement of Colored People (NAACP) Spingarn Medal on November 7 for his organization of the Liberian constabulary and the establishment of order on the frontiers of Liberia.

1917

ARTS. On April 25, singer Ella Fitzgerald is born in Virginia, but she is raised in New York City. Known as the First Lady of Song, Fitzgerald begins her singing career at the age of 16 when she intends to dance at amateur night at the Harlem Opera House but loses her nerve once she is onstage. The master of ceremonies tells her to do something, so she sings "Object of My Affection" and "Judy" and wins first place. Winning $25 for her efforts, she soon signs with noted bandleader Chick Webb and makes her fame singing "A-Tisket, A-Tasket." Years later, Ella Fitzgerald is celebrated for her scat singing style developed when she is with the Dizzie Gillespie band. Scatting is a vocal attempt to imitate the various sounds from Dizzies big band horns.

On March 17, Nathaniel Adams "King" Cole is born in Montgomery, Alabama.

On June 30, actress, vocalist, and social activist Lena Horne is born in Brooklyn, New York. At the age of 16, she is hired as a dancer in the chorus at the Cotton Club in Harlem, New York. While performing at the Cotton Club, she meets other jazz performers such as Billy Holiday, Cab Calloway, Duke Ellington, and songwriter Harold Arlen, who writes her biggest hit, "Stormy Weather." During the 1930s, she plays bit parts in two movies, *Cabin in the Sky* and *Stormy Weather;* however, most of her singing roles are cut before the movies show in the South. By the mid-1940s, however, Lena Horne is the highest paid African American actor in the country. During World War II, she is a pinup star for many black servicemen. After World War II, she and her close friend Paul Robeson are blacklisted as Communist sympathizers because of their intense civil rights activities. As a result, neither is able to work in Hollywood or in the entertainment industry for approximately seven years. Lena Horne, however, works a few clubs and in 1957 records some of her best songs in the album *Lena Horne at the Waldorf Astoria*. By the 1960s, she is involved in a number of civil right protest movements and performs at several rallies for the National Council for Negro Women. Tragedy comes into her life when her father, son, and husband die within a 12-month period during the 1970s. She does not recover from these events until 1981, when she returns to the entertainment business in a one-person Broadway show entitled *Lena Horne: The Lady and Her Music*. This show runs for 14 months and becomes the standard for such performances.

On August 22, blues singer and guitarist John Lee Hooker is born near Clarksdale, Mississippi, to a sharecropping family. His earliest musical influence is his stepfather, Will Moore. By the 1940s, Hooker moves to Detroit by way of Memphis, Tennessee, and Cincinnati, Ohio. Playing at house parties, he is discovered by record store owner Elmer Barbee, who introduces Hooker to Bernard Besman, a record producer, distributor, and owner of Sensation Records. Hooker's earliest hit, "Boogie Chillen," is played on jukeboxes and sells five million records. "I'm in the Mood," an even bigger hit, follows, as do other classic recordings such as "Crawling King-snake" and "Hobo Blues." By the 1960s, Hooker's fame as a so-called blood-bucket blues singer captures the musical imaginations of young bohemian audiences in Europe as well as the United States, particularly when he combines his talents with other blues singers, such as B. B. King, Branford Marsalis, and Van Morrison. In 1991, Hooker is inducted into the Rock and Roll Hall of Fame. At the age of 80, Hooker receives his third Grammy Award for the best traditional blues recording, "Don't Look Back."

In December, jazz musician Joe Oliver leaves New Orleans for Chicago, where he begins his career.

In December, the National Association for the Advancement of Colored People (NAACP) awards its Spingarn Medal to music composer and singer Harry T. Burleigh for excellence in the field of music.

CIVI. Civil rights activist Fannie Lou Hamer, the youngest of 19 siblings, is born on October 6 in Montgomery County, Mississippi. The grand-daughter of slaves, she and her sharecropping family have a socioeconomic status not too different from slavery.

CRIM. Racial tensions become violent from July 1 to 3 in the segregated town of East St. Louis, Illinois, after a series of incidents bring competing racial economic interests between blacks and whites to an explosive level. In February, some 470 African American workers are hired to replace white members of the American Federation of Labor on strike against the Aluminum Ore Company. On July 1, several whites attempting to frighten blacks drive through a black community firing guns into homes. Soon after, two plain-clothes police officers drive through the same community and are immediately fired upon. Both officers are shot and killed by black residents who believe that the officers are apart of the earlier

group of shooters. Armed white mobs seeking revenge rampage through black neighborhoods, shooting and killing any blacks caught in their path. Interestingly, in one incident, white National Guardsmen who participated in the killing think otherwise when an armed African American confronts them. Reportedly, the guardsmen turn to the mob and say, "He's armed boys. You can have him. A white man's life is worth the lives of a thousand Negroes." Some 312 buildings and 44 railroad freight cars and their contents are destroyed by fire. As a result of the fires throughout the city, it is impossible to accurately determine the number of deaths, black or white. When some semblance of peace is restored, white officials claim that 39 people are killed. A federal inquiry is stifled by President Woodrow Wilson. In the ensuing trials, however, African American defendants are punished more harshly than their white counterparts. W.E.B. Du Bois heads a team of investigators to report on what is called the Massacre at East St. Louis. Later, the NAACP organizes a silent march in New York City to protest the lawlessness and murder of African Americans.

On July 28, thousands of African Americans organized by the NAACP march silently down Fifth Avenue in New York City to protest the slaughter of 35 blacks and the maiming and wounding of others in East St. Louis, the complicity of the Illinois National Guard in this action, and the ongoing wave of lynching throughout the United States.

On August 23, a violent racial conflict occurs between black soldiers stationed at Camp Logan near Houston, Texas, and local white and Hispanic residents. The Third Battalion of the Twenty-Fourth Colored Infantry was transferred to Camp Logan from Wyoming and California and was not used to enforce the Jim Crow policies of the South. Similarly, they did not accept the habit of both whites and Hispanics to refer to them as "niggers." On this day, a black soldier attempts to stop a white policeman, Lee Sparks, from beating a black woman. Sparks clubs the soldier and hauls him off to jail. Hearing about this incident, Cpl. Charles W. Baltimore goes to the local police station to inquire about the jailed soldier, and he, too, is beaten and jailed.

Rumors circulate that Sparks is killed. Incensed by these reports, approximately 100 armed soldiers from Camp Logan mount a two-hour assault on the town's jail. When it is over, 16 white and Hispanic residents, including 5 policemen, 4 black soldiers, and 2 African American citizens are killed. The U.S. Army charges 63 soldiers with mutiny, and the NAACP retains the son of legendary Sam Houston to defend the soldiers. He is unsuccessful, however, and 19 black soldiers are hanged, including Corporal Baltimore. Sixty-seven are sentenced to prison. Police Officer Lee Sparks remains on the force and kills two black people later that year.

On December 11, 13 African American soldiers are hanged for their participation in the August 23 violence in Houston, Texas.

In December, the federal government reports that 36 African Americans are lynched during the year.

LAW. On November 5, the U.S. Supreme Court in *Buchanan v. Warley* strikes down a Louisville, Kentucky, ordinance that mandates blacks and whites to live in separate residential areas.

LIT. On June 7, Gwendolyn Brooks, a poet and the first African American to receive a Pulitzer Prize, is born in Topeka, Kansas. Brooks is graduated from Wilson Junior College in 1936 and becomes publicity director for the NAACP in Chicago. Having taught in many schools in Illinois and having written numerous poems, short stories, and books, Brooks replaces Carl Sandburg as poet laureate of Illinois in 1968. Her verse narrative *Annie Allen,* written in 1949, receives a Pulitzer Prize and makes her the first African American woman to win this award in 1950. Some of her later writings include *Riot* (1970), *Disembark* (1981), and *Blacks* (1991). Brooks dies in 2000.

MILI. The federal government reports that some 370,000 (13%) of all draftees in World War I are African Americans.

POLI. On January 17, Denmark relinquishes its sovereignty over the Caribbean Virgin Islands (St. Thomas, St. John, and St. Croix) to the United States. This makes the predominant African descendant population African Americans.

SPOR. Tally Holmes and Lucy Stone become the first African Americans to win the American Tennis Association Championship Title in the men's and women's categories.

1918

CRIM. From July 25 to 28, a race riot occurs in Chester, Pennsylvania. Three African Americans and two whites are killed and scores of people injured.

From July 25 to 29, a race riot occurs in Philadelphia, Pennsylvania. Three whites and one African American are killed.

In December, the federal government reports that 60 African Americans are lynched during the year.

LIT. In December, the National Association for the Advancement of Colored People (NAACP) awards its Spingarn Medal to poet, literary critic, and editor William Stanley Braithwaite for his distinguished achievements in literature.

MED. On January 19, publisher John H. Johnson is born. Johnson is responsible for the first commercially successful African American general magazine, *Negro Digest,* first published on November 1, 1943. In November, Johnson publishes *Ebony* magazine, the largest black-owned magazine in the world. He also produces the highly popular *Jet* magazine, which becomes known for its centerfolds of female bathing-suit models.

The first full-length African American film, *Birthright,* produced and directed by pioneer filmmaker Oscar Micheaux, is released.

MILI. On September 3, five African American soldiers are hanged for their alleged participation in the Houston, Texas, riot of 1917.

OBIT. The last post-Reconstruction congressmen, George H. White of North Carolina, dies at age 66 in Philadelphia, Pennsylvania.

POLI. Cyril Briggs founds the African Blood Brotherhood, a radical Black Nationalist organization.

WAR. On August 17, Gen. John J. Pershing issues a policy directive to the French Military Mission stationed with the U.S. Army in France. This directive establishes, from the U.S. Army's perspective, how racial relationships between allied forces will be conducted. The French army and government for the most part ignore the following directive:

> Secret information concerning Black American Troops:
>
> It is important for French officers who have been called upon to exercise command over black American troops, or to live in close contact with them, to have an exact idea of the position occupied by Negroes in the United States.... Although a citizen of the United States, the black man is regarded by the white American as an inferior being with whom relations of business or service only are possible. The black is constantly being censured for his want of intelligence and discretion, his lack of civic and professional conscience, and for his tendency toward undue familiarity. The vices of the Negro are a constant menace to the American who has to repress them sternly.... We must prevent the rise of any pronounced degree of intimacy between French officers and black officers. We may be courteous and amiable with these last, but we cannot deal with them on the same plane as with white American officers without deeply offending the latter. We must not eat with them, must not shake hands or seek to talk or meet with them outside the requirements of military service. We must not commend too highly the black American troops, particularly in the presence of Americans.... Make a point of keeping the native cantonment population from "spoiling" the Negroes. Americans become greatly incensed at any public expression of intimacy between white women with black men.... Familiarity on the part of white women with black men is furthermore a source of profound regret to our experienced colonials, who see in it an overwhelming menace to the prestige of the white race.

On November 11, an armistice is signed, ending World War I. Official records indicate that some 370,000 African American soldiers, of whom 1,400 are officers, serve in the conflict. Three black infantry regiments, the 369th, 371st, and 372nd, receive the Croix de Guerre, France's highest military award for valor. The 369th is especially cited as the first U.S. military unit to reach the Rhine River that separates France from Germany. Similarly, the first soldier's in the U.S. Army to be decorated for bravery in France with the Croix de Guerre are Henry Johnson and Needham Roberts, both of whom are from the 369th Regiment. Although Johnson and Roberts are cited by U.S. Gen. John J. "Black Jack" Pershing and French Gen. Ferdinand Foch, neither soldier receives any military recognition or honors from the United States. U.S. racism and segregation of its military forces are a constant irritant for black soldiers throughout the war.

1919

ASSO. From February 19 to 21, W.E.B. Du Bois is the prime organizer of the second Pan-African Congress that meets at the Grand Hotel in Paris, France. Sent to France by the National Association for the Advancement of Colored People (NAACP) to pull together a Pan-African Congress, Du Bois and the association hope to put the question of African colonialism on the agenda at the post–World War I Paris Peace Conference. Not receiving much encouragement from European Allies, Du Bois pulls together 57 delegates of African heritage; 16 come from the United States, 20 from the West Indies, and 12 from colonized African from countries (data on the other 9 is unconfirmed). Blaise Diagne, a respected member of the French Chamber of Deputies from Senegal, is elected president, and Du Bois is named secretary of the conference. Though the meeting occurs at the same time as the European Peace Conference at Versailles, the Paris Pan-African Congress passes resolutions that call attention to the demands of oppressed indigenous colonial African people and lays the basis for a more militant anticolonial struggle 30 years later. The idea of the Congress is a dream of Du Bois's since the 1900 Paris Conference, at which he and West

Indian lawyer Harold Williams petitioned England's Queen Victoria for a Pan-African conference.

Oscar Micheaux becomes the first African American independent filmmaker when he releases the film *The Homesteaders.*

BUSI. On June 3, Liberty Life Insurance Company of Chicago is incorporated as the first African American old-line reserve company in the North.

CRIM. On May 10, a race riot in Charleston, South Carolina, ends with two African Americans killed.

On July 13, a race riot is so severe in Longview and Gregg Counties, Texas, that martial law is declared. Usually, when martial law is declared, it implies that the black population is to some extent successfully defending itself. Twenty-six major riots break out in the United States during the summer months, and the period is known as the Red Summer.

From July 19 to 23, raids by white soldiers on the African American residential community in Washington, DC, trigger a race riot as blacks defend themselves. Six persons are killed, and more than 100 people are wounded.

On Sunday, July 27, in Chicago, Illinois, one day after African American soldiers are welcomed home from World War I with a parade down Michigan Avenue, a black man, Eugene Williams, crosses the invisible boundary that separates black and white beach and swimming areas in Lake Michigan. He is stoned and drowned by white bathers. The only person arrested after this murder is an African American who complains about the attack. Williams's death sets off a week of intense fighting between African Americans and whites. Police join the white mobs as they attempt to invade black neighborhoods and attack blacks. Recently returned black soldiers, however, organize to prevent the total annihilation of the black communities. Forming a barrier along State Street, they stop the advance of white gangs from the stockyard district. Eventually, the governor brings in three regiments of Illinois National Guard troops to quell the fighting, but that is not until August 1. The give-and-take between the races is indicative of a fighting spirit among African Americans to resist racial brutality. One report in the *Chicago Defender* notes, "In the early [Tuesday] morning a thirteen-year-old lad standing on his porch at 51st and Wabash Avenue was shot to death by a white man who, in an attempt to get away, encountered a [black] mob and his existence became history. A mounted [white] policeman unknown fatally wounded a small boy in the block of Dearborn Street and was shot to death by some unknown rioter." Official reports note that 23 African Americans and 15 whites are killed, with more than 500 of both races wounded.

From October 1 to 3, a race riot erupts in Elaine, Phillips County, Arkansas. The riot starts when African American sharecroppers attempt to organize a union and withhold cotton from the market until they receive a better price for their crop. White deputy sheriffs try to break up a union meeting held in a church. In the ensuing struggle, a deputy is shot and killed along with four other whites. In retaliation, white mobs kill dozens of blacks. No whites are prosecuted for the killings; however, 12 blacks are prosecuted for the killing of the deputy. The 12 black defendants are sentenced to death, and 67 are sentenced to 20 years in jail. Many are tortured and badly beaten while in prison. After appeals and publicity generated by Ida Wells-Barnett and the NAACP and the efforts of attorney Moorfield Storey, the Supreme Court in 1923 overturns the convictions.

The federal government reports that 76 African Americans are lynched during 1919.

INVE. On December 23, Alice Parker patents an improved version of the heating furnace (patent no. 1,325,905).

MED. In October, Chester Arthur Franklin founds the *Kansas City Call* newspaper.

OBIT. On May 25, wealthy cosmetics manufacturer Madame C. J. Walker dies at home in Irvington-on-the-Hudson, New York, at the age of 52.

POLI. In October, the NAACP awards its Spingarn Medal to Archibald Grimke, president of the American Negro Academy and former U.S. consul to Santo Domingo.

SPOR. On March 20, middleweight boxing champion Sugar Ray Robinson is born.

On May 2, the Indianapolis ABCs defeat the Chicago American Giants 4 to 2 in the first game of the National Negro Baseball League.

Fritz Pollard becomes the first African American professional football player when he begins playing for the Akron, Ohio, Indians of the American Professional Football League. Pollard also acts as the team's coach and, as such, leads the team to the world professional championship in 1920.

1920

ARTS. On November 3, Charles Gilpin stars in the play *Emperor Jones* at the Provincetown Theater.

On June 11, classical pianist and singer Hazel Dorothy Scott is born in Trinidad. Though she obtains her early training in classical music at the Juilliard School of Music in New York City, she learns her jazz piano techniques from musicians Art Tatum and Teddy Wilson. From the moment she stars at the opening of Barney Josephson's Cafe Society Uptown in October 1940, her fame as a singer and pianist becomes international in scope. Hazel Scott appears in a number of movies that feature her piano skills, as in *Something to Shout About, I DooD It, Broadway Melody, The Heat's On,* and *Rhapsody in Blue.* She becomes the wife of noted African American congressmen from Harlem, New York, Adam Clayton Powell Jr.

On August 29, Charlie Parker, one of the most influential African American musician, is born in Kansas City, Kansas. In 1927, his family moves across the state line to Missouri. This does not prohibit him from traveling back and forth to Kansas City and learning much about music in the local nightclubs. By 1939, as an accomplished alto saxophonist, he travels to New York City and begins playing at Harlem clubs, such as Monroe's and Minton's. Throughout this period, he continues to enrich his playing style by traveling back and forth to Kansas, Nebraska, and New Orleans, Louisiana. Known as Bird, Charlie Parker reflects upon the various playing styles. Musicians such as "Little" Benny Harris, Bennie Green, and Wardell Gray and vocalists Billy Eckstine and Sarah

Vaughan push him and foster in him a new and innovative style of playing that is uniquely Bird's. By 1944, Bird joins the first bebop band, formed by Billy Eckstine. The band also includes other bebop greats such as Art Blakey, John Gillespie, and Bidd Johnson. In 1945, Gillespie and Parker record their first commercial record. Soon, younger musicians such as Miles Davis, Dexter Gordon, and others join the band. In 1947, Parker forms his own classic quintet with trumpeter Miles Davis, drummer Max Roach, pianist Duke Jordan, and bassist Tommy Potter. With this group on the Savoy label, Parker's reputation reaches new heights in musical explorations. By the 1950s, Bird is very ill as a result of years of heroin use and addiction. He dies on March 12, 1955, in New York City. In his honor, a New York City nightclub is named after him, Birdland.

On October 20, vocalist William Warfield is born.

ASSO. On January 31, Phi Beta Sigma fraternity is incorporated at Howard University in Washington, DC.

On August 1, the national convention of the Universal Negro Improvement Association, under the leadership of Marcus Mosiah Garvey, opens in Liberty Hall in Harlem, New York. The following night, Garvey addresses 25,000 people in Madison Square Garden in Manhattan.

On November 6, James Weldon Johnson becomes the first African American executive secretary of the National Association for the Advancement of Colored People (NAACP). This position requires him to monitor the day-to-day activities of the organization. Johnson is a well-known intellect before he assumes this new position; he is an editorial writer for the *New York Age,* author of the *Autobiography of an Ex-Colored Man* (1912), organizer of the July 17, 1917, protest march against the East St. Louis riot, and documenter in *The Nation* of the U.S. occupation troops' abuse of Haitian civilians. In 1900, to celebrate Abraham Lincoln's birthday, Johnson pens the lyrics of a song entitled "Lift Every Voice and Sing," for which his younger brother, John Rosamond Johnson, composes the music. The song is published in 1921, and the NAACP embraces it as the so-called Negro national anthem. As late as 1998, the *New Yorker* magazine suggests that it replace the "Star Spangled Banner" as the U.S. national anthem.

CENS. The federal government reports that the United States population is 105,710,620, of which 10,463,131 (9.9%) are African Americans.

CRIM. The federal government reports that 53 African Americans are lynched during the year.

CULT. Throughout the decade of the 1920s, artists, writers, musicians, and performers proliferate to such an extent, particularly in Harlem, that this era is known as the Harlem Renaissance. Among the artists who contribute to this era are Jamaican-born writer Claude McKay, who in 1922 writes *Harlem Shadows;* Jean Toomer, who in 1923 writes *Cane;* Alaine Locke, who in 1925 writes *The New Negro;* Langston Hughes, who in 1926 writes *Weary Blues;* Countee Cullen, who in 1925 writes *Color;* and Zora Neale Hurston, who arrives in Harlem in 1925 and immediately pens a number of articles for the popular journal *Opportunity* and the *New Negro.* Though the notion of the Harlem Renaissance is centered around African American creativity in the arts, it is to a degree supported, and in some cases dependent upon, recognition from white cultural institutions and patronage. This leads to some bitter conflicts between some artists, such as Zora Neale Hurston and Langston Hughes, who view white patronage differently.

POLI. In November, W.E.B. Du Bois receives the NAACP's Spingarn Medal for "founding and calling of the Pan African Congress."

SPOR. On January 4, Andrew "Rube" Foster organizes the first African American baseball league, the Negro National League.

1921

ARTS. On May 23, *Shuffle Along,* written by Eubie Blake, becomes the first of a succession of popular musicals featuring African American performers when it opens at the Sixty-Third Street Musical Hall in New York City.

In December, the National Association for the Advancement of Colored People (NAACP) awards the Spingarn Medal to actor Charles S. Gilpin for his performance in the title role of *Emperor Jones.*

ASSO. From August 28 to September 6, the second Pan-African Congress meets in London, Brussels, and Paris. Of the 113 delegates, 39 are from Africa and 36 are from the United States.

CIVI. On July 31, Whitney Young, an executive director of the National Urban League, is born.

CRIM. From May 31 to June 1, a major race riot erupts in Tulsa, Oklahoma, when the first reported bombing of Americans by Americans occurs as white men flying airplanes bomb the African American community of Greenwood, Oklahoma, killing as many as 300 people. The impetus of this riot occurs when an African American, Dick Rowland, is falsely accused of raping a white female elevator operator in Tulsa. Rowland is taken to a local courthouse surrounded by both black and white crowds. Hostile words between the two groups lead to shootings and killings in both groups. African American men return to their homes in Greenwood to retrieve additional guns and ammunition to protect their families. On the morning of June 1, approximately 500 well-armed whites confront approximately 1,000 armed blacks outside Greenwood, with only a railroad track separating the two groups. Shooting begins, and both sides fight bitterly until airplanes drop incendiary devices on Greenwood, reducing approximately 40 square blocks to rubble in an intense firestorm. More than 1,000 homes, stores, schools, businesses, and churches go up in flames. Though the charge of rape is used as the catalyst for whites to attack blacks, a poor plausible factor exists. The African American community is economically more advanced than the neighboring white community. This reality bodes ill for African Americans as the country's most racist and conservative political elements experience a rebirth amid a wave of anti–African American, anti-Italian, anti-Catholic, anti-Jewish, and anti-immigrant sentiment.

In December, the federal government reports that 59 African Americans are lynched during the year.

LIT. On August 11, writer Alexander Murray Palmer Haley, the oldest of three male siblings, is born in Ithaca, New York. Soon after his birth, his parents return to Henning, Tennessee, to raise their family. At 15, Haley is graduated from high school then attends college for two years, and in 1939, he joins the U.S. Coast Guard as a mess boy. While in the Coast Guard, he writes short stories and, 13 years later, becomes a chief journalist for the Coast Guard. Retiring in 1959 with 20 years of military service, Haley becomes an assignment writer for *Reader's Digest* magazine and later is associated with *Playboy* magazine. With *Playboy*, he conducts his historic interviews with Malcolm X, which lead to his first award-winning book, *Autobiography of Malcolm X: As Told to Alex Haley* (1965). In 1976, Haley's second award-wining book, *Roots: Saga of an American Family*, is published. Though he calls this literary work *faction*, meaning a combination of fact and fiction, its impact upon African Americans as well as the African diaspora and European Americans is, for many, unexpected and clearly unprecedented. *Roots* sells 1.6 million copies in its first six months of publication; it is translated into 37 languages and serialized in a number of newspapers around the world. When *Roots* is filmed as an eight-segment television miniseries in 1977, it exceeds the audience record previously set by the Civil War film *Gone with the Wind* by more than 130 million viewers. In 1977, *Roots* receives the National Book Award and the Pulitzer Prize for literature as well as the Spingarn Medal for literature. In 1989, Alex Haley becomes the first person to receive an honorary degree from the U.S. Coast Guard Academy. Haley's boyhood homestead, a 10-room bungalow in Henning, Tennessee, is the first state-owned historic site devoted to African Americans in Tennessee and is placed on the National Register of Historic Places on December 14, 1978. Alex Haley dies on February 10, 1992, at the age of 70.

OBIT. On December 21, Reconstruction-era politician P.B.S. Pinchback dies at the age of 84 in Washington, DC.

SCIE. Plant scientist Dr. George Washington Carver revolutionizes southern agriculture by publishing his research on peanuts and sweet potatoes, thereby saving farmers their entire crop productions as a result of pest and exhausted soil. Carver presents some of his findings before the U.S. Congress.

SPOR. On May 3, Walker Smith, better known as "Sugar" Ray Robinson, is born in Ailey, Georgia. He is discovered by boxing coach George Gainford, who watches his early fights and says that his fluid motions are as "smooth

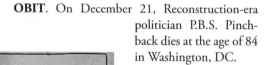

George Washington Carver, one of America's great scientists. Courtesy of the National Archives and Records Administration.

as sugar," and Gainford helps him polish his fighting technique. At 19, Sugar Ray turns professional and begins a career that includes 91 fights without a loss. In 1946, he wins the welterweight championship, holds it for five years, and wins the world middleweight title. When he retires, his record is 128 victories, 1 defeat, and 2 ties. *Ring* magazine hails "Sugar" Ray Robinson as, pound for pound, the best boxer of all time. In 1999, the Associated Press hails him as the greatest welterweight and middleweight boxer of the century.

1922

ASSO. Lucy Diggs Stowe cofounds the African American sorority Alpha Kappa Alpha. Stowe also serves as dean of women students at Howard University in Washington, DC.

CRIM. In November, the federal government reports that 51 African Americans are lynched during the year.

CULT. On August 12, Frederick Douglass's home in Washington, DC, is declared a national shrine.

OBIT. On January 8, Col. Charles D. Young, the first African American to achieve the rank of colonel in the U.S. Army, dies at the age of 58 in Lagos, Nigeria, while on furlough. Colonel Young, a graduate of the U.S. Military Academy at West Point, New York, served in Cuba, the Philippines, Haiti, and Mexico; however, he was not permitted to command troops in World War I. At the termination of the war, he returned to military service and served in Liberia to help train the country's military.

Vaudeville actor and minstrel Bert Williams dies in New York City at the age of 46.

POLI. After Leonidas Dyer, a white St. Louis, Missouri, congressmen, forces passage of an antilynching law in the U.S. House of Representatives by a vote of 230 to 119, the bill fails in the conservative Democrat-controlled Senate.

In November, the Spingarn Medal is awarded to former president of the National Association of Colored Women, Mary B. Talbert, for service to black women and for her restorative work on

Frederick Douglass's home in near Washington, DC.

1923

ARTS. On February 16, noted blues singer Bessie Smith records the southern blues song "Down Heart Blues," which sells 800,000 copies.

ASSO. On March 30, Zeta Phi Beta sorority, originally founded at Howard University in Washington, DC, is incorporated.

On November 7 and 8, the third Pan-African Congress convenes in Lisbon, Portugal, and is considered successful in delineating the problems of colonialism on the African continent. Efforts to hold this conference on the African continent are frustrated by European colonial powers that fear it will further encourage nascent anticolonial movements.

CRIM. On September 15, Oklahoma's governor declares that the state is in a "state of virtual rebellion and insurrection" due to Ku Klux Klan activities. Martial law is declared.

In November, the federal government reports that 29 African Americans are lynched during the year.

EDUC. Mary McLeod Bethune's Daytona Normal and Industrial School in Daytona Beach, Florida, merges with Cookman Institute and becomes Bethune-Cookman College.

INVE. On November 20, Garrett T. Morgan patents (# 77180) the traffic signal.

MIGR. On October 24, the U.S. Department of Labor reports that 500,000 African Americans emigrated from the South during the last year.

OBIT. On September 17, Nancy Green, the world's first living trademark (Aunt Jemima), is struck and killed in an automobile accident.

POLI. On June 21, Marcus Mosiah Garvey is sentenced to five years in prison after his conviction for mail fraud. Garvey, who claims that the charges are motivated by political intrigues from both American and European colonial interests, is also cognizant of a number of African American leaders who distrust his efforts through the Universal Negro Improvement Association (UNIA). Chief among these critics is W.E.B. Du Bois. An essential aspect of the downfall of the UNIA and Marcus Garvey are the efforts of J. Edgar Hoover of the Bureau of Investigations, a predecessor of the Federal Bureau of Investigation, who employs black agents to infiltrate the UNIA and compile information about what they consider his dangerous ideas and practices, which can be used to deport Garvey. Garvey sees the National Association for the Advancement of Colored People (NAACP) and Du Bois supporters as more representative of white American interests than those of people of African heritage. Even black labor leader A. Philip Randolph, the copublisher of the labor journal the *Messenger,* and the chief organizers of the Brotherhood of Sleeping Car Porters and Maids attack Garvey two years later in 1925. At the core of the attacks against Garvey are his organizing abilities among the black disenfranchised population that most laboring whites see as their major competitors for jobs not only in the United States but throughout the colonized world, where chapters (*divisions* as the call them) of UNIA are organizing prounion, anticolonial political agendas. Similarly, Garvey believes that, unlike most civil rights organizations of the time, racial separation and self-development are directly associated to separate racial destinies and asserts that interracial cooperation is fraught with dangers.

SCIE. In November, the NAACP awards the Spingarn Medal to Dr. George Washington Carver, who chairs the department of research at Tuskegee Institute and provided the basis for pioneer work in agricultural chemistry.

1924

ARTS. On October 24, Florence Mills stars in *Dixie to Broadway,* the first real African American revue, which opens at the Broadhurst Theater in New York City.

In November, Fletcher Henderson, the first African American musician to make a name with a big jazz band, opens at the Roseland Ballroom on Broadway.

In November, Roland Hayes receives the National Association for the Advancement of Colored People (NAACP) Spingarn Medal for his achievements as a singer and representative of the race in Europe and the United States.

LIT. On August 2, noted author James Baldwin is born in Harlem, New York.

POLI. The United States Immigration Act restricts the number of persons of African ancestry or decent, mainly from the West Indies, while allowing and encouraging an increased number of European immigrants to enter the country.

SPOR. DeHart Hubbard becomes the first African American to win an Olympic gold medal in the long jump at the Paris Olympic Games.

1925

ARTS. African American dancer and singer Josephine Baker begins her performance in *La Revue Nègre* at the Théâtre des Champs-Elysées in Paris, France. Baker fashions a career as a popular and provocative cabaret star.

New Orleans jazz great Louis Armstrong makes the first "Hot Five" and "Hot Seven" recordings that influence the direction of jazz.

ASSO. On August 25, the Brotherhood of Sleeping Car Porters and Maids is organized at a mass meeting at the Elk Hall in Harlem. A. Philip Randolph is elected its president. Dissatisfied with their treatment by the Chicago-based Pullman Company, Randolph and others organize their own union in New York City. The union assigns Milton Webster with the task of organizing in Chicago, the home of some 15,000 porters. During this era, a Pullman car porter receives higher wages due to the tips they receive from white riders, and African Americans dominate this service position. Other opportunities on the railroad are prohibited to them, and the servile nature of the job supports the notion of their racial inferiority. The maid component of the union is important and often ignored; however, their position, in conjunction with the wives of porters, strengthens the economic and social power of the union. More than half of Chicago's so-called Inside Committee are women. As an organization, the Brotherhood involves itself in allied functions, as when they distribute the *Chicago Defender* newspaper, which is prohibited in many southern cities, when traveling from city to city.

CRIM. On September 8, Ossian Sweet, a prominent Detroit physician, is arrested on murder charges stemming from shots fired into a mob in front of his home in a previously all-white neighborhood. Sweet is defended by the well-known attorney Clarence Darrow, who wins an acquittal after a second trial.

EDUC. In November, Xavier University in New Orleans is founded.

POLI. On February 8, Marcus Garvey enters the federal prison in Atlanta, Georgia.

On May 19, political activist, Muslim leader, and outspoken orator on human rights Malcolm Little (Malcolm X), also known as El Hajj Malik El Shabazz, is born in Omaha, Nebraska. Two major factors in his young life form much of Malcolm's personality. His father is a militant member of nationalist leader Marcus Garvey's Universal Negro Improvement Association (UNIA), and his antiracist, pro-African nationalist stance surely provokes hostility from local white racist elements in Omaha, Nebraska. Unfortunately, the elder Little is killed under mysterious circumstances when he is placed in the path of a streetcar that runs over his body. When Malcolm is 12 years old, his mother, who is emotionally devastated by her husband's murder, falls into an emotional depression that causes her to be committed to a mental hospital. Malcolm, forced to live in a series of foster homes, is sent to Boston, Massachusetts, to live with his aunt. By 1946, he is involved in a number of criminal activities, is sent to prison, and while incarcerated is introduced to Islam by an older brother, Raymond, who is a member of the Nation of Islam (NOI), commonly known as the Black Muslims. Adopting the letter *X* to symbolize his unknown African ancestry, Malcolm quickly becomes an effective and well-known minister for the Nation of Islam. His several trips to Africa and his rising popularity often place him in opposition to Elijah Muhammad, the founder and head of the NOI. Malcolm's increasing disagreement with the civil rights movement's tactics and what he describes as the passivity of its leaders, along with his criticism of Elijah Muhammad, forces him out of the NOI. His attempts to establish his own organizational base make Malcolm an easy target, and on February 21, 1965, he is assassinated at the Audubon Casino in New York City. In 1965, writer Alex Haley, in the *Autobiography of Malcolm X,* captures Malcolm's legacy and its importance on the civil and human rights movements of the twentieth century.

1926

ASSO. From August 21 to 24, the fourth Pan-African Congress meets in New York City. Delegates from around the United States attend with a large representation from the Caribbean and Latin America. Marcus Garvey's efforts as a Pan-Africanist are aimed at the lower economic strata of the black community. Du Bois's efforts in this regard are aimed at an aspiring middle-class intellectual segment of the population and are therefore limited in number and scope.

EDUC. On June 20, Mordecai W. Johnson becomes the first African American president of Howard University in Washington, DC. Reportedly, Howard University at the end of the nineteenth century is not noted for intellectual or academic prowess. Johnson is determined to change this reputation. Upon assuming the presidency, Johnson fires those whom he considers incompetent and hires younger, outspoken African American scholars such as E. Franklin Frazier in sociology, Ralph Bunche in political science, Charles Drew in medicine, and John Hope Franklin and Rayford W. Logan in history. He hires Charles H. Huston, a brilliant attorney, as dean of Howard's law school. Houston uses Howard's law school as a training ground for those attorneys, such as Thurgood Marshall, who will successfully challenge institutional racism and defeat the 1896 *Plessy v. Ferguson* separate but equal doctrine by winning the *Brown v. Board of Education of Topeka, Kansas,* in 1954. President Mordecai Johnson raises faculty salaries and academic standards, toughens admission requirements, and ensures that Howard's graduate and professional schools are accredited and nationally respected.

In July, Carter G. Woodson receives the National Association for the Advancement of Colored People (NAACP) Spingarn Medal.

Arthur Schomburg donates his personal collection of African diaspora literature to the New York Public Library's division on Negro literature. Known as the Schomburg Collection on Black Culture, it is considered one of the foremost repositories of African diaspora literary artifacts in the world.

LAW. On July 26, the National Bar Association is founded.

POLI. In February, Carter G. Woodson establishes the first Negro History Week celebration during the second week of February so that it includes the birthday of Abraham Lincoln and the generally accepted birth date of Frederick Douglass.

SPOR. The first African American middleweight champion is Theodore "Tiger" (the Georgia Deacon) Flowers, who wins the title in New York City on February 26 by defeating Harry Greb in 15 rounds.

1927

ARTS. On December 4, Duke Ellington opens at the Cotton Club in Harlem.

On February 3, internationally acclaimed opera singer Leontyne Price is born in Laurel, Mississippi.

BUSI. In December, the National Association for the Advancement of Colored People (NAACP) awards the Spingarn Medal to Anthony Overton, who made a name for himself as a publisher, insurance executive, and cosmetics manufacturer and for his overall achievements as a businessman.

CIVI. On March 7, the U.S. Supreme Court in *Nixon v. Herndon* overturns a Texas law that prohibits African Americans from voting in a so-called white primary.

On April 27, civil rights activist (and wife of Rev. Dr. Martin Luther King Jr.) Coretta Scott King is born. After her husband's assassination in 1968, Mrs. King establishes a number of educational memorials in Atlanta, Georgia, and throughout the United States in memory of Dr. King's nonviolent approach to human and civil rights.

CRIM. On November 26, Marcus Mosiah Garvey is released from the federal prison in Atlanta, Georgia, and is immediately deported to Jamaica.

OBIT. On November 1, dancer and singer Florence Mills dies in New York City at the age of 32.

POLI. On December 4, U.S. President Calvin Coolidge commutes Marcus Garvey's sentence. Garvey is taken to New Orleans and deported to his native Jamaica, where he receives a hero's welcome.

1928

LIT. In November, novelist Charles W. Chesnutt receives the National Association for the Advancement of Colored People (NAACP) Spingarn Medal for his widespread recognition as a creative literary artist.

MED. In November, W. A. Scott Jr. founds the *Atlanta Daily World*. The paper becomes a daily in 1933.

POLI. On November 6, Oscar DePriest is elected to the 71st Congress from Illinois. Representing the Chicago's First Congressional District, he is the first African American congressmen elected since the departure of George H. White of North Carolina in 1901.

WORK. On April 15, pioneer African American architect and fellow of the American Institute of Architects Norma Merrick-Sklarerk is born in New York City. She is the first licensed woman architect in the United States.

1929

BUSI. On October 29, the U.S. stock market collapses and the beginning of the Great Depression begins. By 1937, 26 percent of the African American male population is unemployed. By 1934, the federal government notes that although 17 percent of the white population cannot support themselves, 38 percent of the African American population cannot do so. In Chicago, African American unemployment is 40 percent, in Pittsburgh it is 48 percent, in Harlem it is 50 percent, in Philadelphia it is 56 percent, and in

Detroit it is 60 percent. The Depression destroys many successful black enterprises such as the Binga Bank in Chicago. The Binga Bank is the first black-owned and operated financial institution in Chicago. The bank was founded in 1908, and its president, Jesse Binga, who was once a barber and Pullman porter, purchased real estate that helped provide the financial capital for the bank. By 1930, Binga Bank is valued at $1.5 million, and Jesse Binga announces that he owns more footage on State Street than anyone else in Chicago. He is a prime example of successful African American capitalism. When the crash of 1929 occurs, however, Binga finds his bank too deeply leveraged in real estate and not cash. Many of his mortgages are to churches and fraternal societies whose members, out of work, cannot make their bank payments. Binga refuses to lay claim or seize these properties, and this and other financial improprieties lead to the bank's closing. On July 31, Illinois state bank auditors padlock the institution and file a federal misuse of funds against the once-proud financier. Sent to prison in 1932, he is pardoned by President Franklin Delano Roosevelt a year later. He never rebuilds his bank or financial position.

EDUC. On April 1, Morehouse College, Spelman College, and Atlanta University are officially affiliated to create the new Atlanta University. John Hope is named president.

In December, Mordecai W. Johnson receives the National Association for the Advancement of Colored People (NAACP) Spingarn Medal for his work as the first African American president of Howard University.

MED. The first full-length African American Hollywood films produced this year are *Hearts in Dixie,* a production that some critics argue is "the first real talking picture," and *Hallelujah,* a movie starring Daniel Haynes and Nina Mae McKinney.

POLI. On January 15, Martin Luther King Jr. is born in Atlanta, Georgia.

1930

ARTS. On February 26, the play *The Green Pastures* opens at the Mansfield Theater in New York City. In this production, Richard B. Harrison portrays "the Lawd."

ASSO. On December 19, James Weldon Johnson resigns as executive secretary of the National Association for the Advancement of Colored People (NAACP) due to personal health concerns.

In December, Delta Sigma Theta sorority is incorporated at Howard University.

CENS. The federal government reports that the United States population is 122,775,046, of which 11,891,143 (9.7%) are African Americans.

OBIT. On August 16, Robert Johnson, a major southern blues guitarist, dies in Greenwood, Mississippi.

LAW. On March 30, U.S. President Herbert Hoover nominates Judge J. Parker of North Carolina for a seat on the U.S. Supreme Court. Parker is an avowed racist who openly embraces white supremacy. The NAACP forms a coalition with the American Federation of Labor to wage a national campaign and lobbying effort against Parker's nomination. As a result, the Senate rejects Parker's nomination.

1931

ARTS. Jazz singer and symbol of a racial struggle Billie Holiday receives her first singing job at a Harlem club. Two years later she records her first song.

In August, the National Association for the Advancement of Colored People (NAACP) awards the Spingarn Medal to Richard B. Harrison for his portrayal of "de Lawd" in *The Green Pastures.*

Jazz composer and innovator Duke Ellington composes "Creole Rhapsody," marking the beginning of his experimentation with new jazz forms.

Famed dancer, choreographer, social anthropologist, and writer Katherine Dunham founds the Negro Dance Group in Chicago. While in Chicago, she studies with Lulmilla Speranzena and Mark Turbyfil and dances her first leading role in Ruth Page's ballet *La Guiablesse* in 1933. She attends the University of Chicago on a scholarship and receives a BA in social anthropology and in the process inspires anthropologists Robert Redfield and Melville Herskovits to understand the importance of African culture and ritual retentions in the Western world. While in college, Dunham teaches and gives recitals in a Chicago storefront on African culture and dance that she names "Ballet Negre." Awarded a Rosenfeld Travel Fellowship in 1936, she departs for the Caribbean and conducts field research in Jamaica, Trinidad, Cuba, Haiti, and Martinique, thereby consolidating her passion for dance with African Caribbean rituals. By 1943, Dunham moves to New York City and opens the Katherine Dunham School of Arts and Research that trains artists in world dance, theater, and literature. From the 1940s until the early 1990s, Dunham combines her interest in African culture and politics, as witnessed by her 47-day fast in 1992 at her home in East St. Louis, Illinois, to protest the U.S. government's treatment of Haitian refugees. She agrees to stop her fast only after president-elect Jean-Bertrand Aristide, the democratically elected Haitian president overthrown by the military, appeals to her to stop the fast.

ASSO. On December 9, Walter F. White is named NAACP executive secretary.

CRIM. On March 25, nine African American migrant youths are arrested in Paint Rock, Alabama. They are falsely accused of raping two migrant white women on a freight train traveling westward through Alabama. They are transferred to Scottsboro, Alabama, and the youths become known internationally at the Scottsboro Boys.

LAW. On April 6, the first trial of the Scottsboro rape case begins in Scottsboro, Alabama. Within a half-day, they are found guilty of rape. This case becomes a cause célèbre.

OBIT. On March 25, noted publisher, writer, and human rights advocate Ida B. Wells-Barnett dies at the age of 75 in Chicago, Illinois.

1933

MED. Leon H. Washington founds the *Los Angeles Sentinel.*

ARTS. Caterina Jarboro becomes the first African American to perform with a major U.S. opera company when she is featured in a Chicago opera

company production of Verdi's *Aida* at the New York Hippodrome on July 22. She also sings the title role of the opera in Milan, Italy, in May 1930.

WORK. President Franklin D. Roosevelt's 1933 New Deal program to overcome the effects of the Great Depression and invigorate the economy and Americans in general provides an opportunity for many African Americans to benefit from federal assistance programs, but only after Roosevelt's second term begins in 1936. The Works Program Administration (WPA), for example, in 1936 administers more fairly and explicitly rejects racial discrimination traditions and practices that plagued the first New Deal. As a consequence, anthropologist and writer Zora Neale Hurston, for example, is able to collect valuable folklore data and study a number of ethnic groups as part of the Historical Records Survey project created in 1937. The WPA's other four arts programs—the federal Art Project, the federal Music Project, the federal Theatre Project, and the federal Writer's Project—employ thousands of African American musicians, intellectuals, writers, and artist.

1934

ARTS. Harlem's Apollo Theater hosts its first Amateur Night. These productions become important in the budding careers of many African American entertainers.

ASSO. On June 26, W.E.B. Du Bois resigns from his position in the National Association for the Advancement of Colored People (NAACP) in a disagreement over policy and racial strategy. Du Bois's criticism of the NAACP's overemphasis on integration as opposed to a political strategy moving toward self-determination leads to his forced withdrawal from the *Crisis* journal as its editor and from the association itself. The African American intellectual community quickly attacks Du Bois, as witnessed by fellow sociologist E. Franklin Frazier, who claims that Du Bois's idea that black businesses can exist within a segregated society is a fantasy and a dangerous social myth.

CIVI. On October 26, representatives of the NAACP and the American Fund for Public

Service plan a legal campaign against racial segregation and discrimination. As a result, Charles Hamilton Hughes, vice dean of Howard University's law school is named the NAACP's director of its legal campaign.

OBIT. On April 7, Pan-African leader, and collaborator with W.E.B. Du Bois, William Monroe Trotter dies at the age of 62 in Boston, Massachusetts.

1935

ARTS. In December, Langston Hughes's play *The Mulatto* begins a long performance run on Broadway in New York City.

The era of the big band begins as swing becomes a major commercial success. Bandleaders such as Chick Webb, Andy Kirk, Cab Calloway, Count Basie, Jimmie Lunceford, and Duke Ellington become icons for the era.

CIVI. On November 5, Donald Murray is admitted to the University of Maryland after the Maryland Court of Appeals concludes that his Fourteenth Amendment rights have been abridged and that his rights are "Personal, Present and Immediate."

On December 5, the National Council of Negro Women is founded in New York City. The group elects Mary McLeod Bethune as its president.

EDUC. In December, Mary McLeod Bethune is awarded the Spingarn Medal for her work as founder and president of Bethune-Cookman College in Daytona, Florida, as well as for her national leadership on a number of civil rights issues.

SCIE. Dr. George Washington Carver serves in the U.S. Department of Agriculture.

SPOR. On June 25, Joe Louis defeats Primo Carnera at Yankee Stadium to retain his heavyweight boxing championship title. For many African Americans, Louis's defeat of Carnera is a symbolic victory over Italian fascism at home and abroad. By September, Joe Louis is the first African American boxer to draw a million-dollar gate.

WAR. From October 2 to 4, Italy invades Ethiopia. In the United States, African Americans

hold a mass meeting of protest and raise funds for the Ethiopian army. In Chicago, despite a protest ban by Mayor Edward Kelly and threats by the Chicago Police Department's Red Squad, Harry Haywood's Southside Communists organize a huge Ethiopian demonstration. Denied a street permit, Haywood moves the demonstrations to rooftops and from there addresses the crowds.

1936

ASSO. From February 14 to 16, 817 delegates representing 500 organizations attend the National Negro Congress in Chicago. Asa Phillip Randolph of the Brotherhood of Sleeping Car Porters and Maids is elected president of the new organization.

CIVI. On December 8, the National Association for the Advancement of Colored People (NAACP) files suit to equalize salaries of black and white teachers in *Gibbs v. Board of Education* in Montgomery County, Maryland. It is the first of a succession of suits that eliminates salary differentials between African American and white teachers.

POLI. African American voting results during the presidential elections indicate a break with the Republican Party. Franklin D. Roosevelt and the Democratic Party receive overwhelming support from black voters.

SPOR. Jesse Owens wins four track and field gold medals at the Olympic Games in Berlin, Germany. In doing so, Owens debunks the Nazi myth of Aryan racial superiority. Though Adolf Hitler leaves the stadium to avoid congratulating Owens, African Americans are ecstatic over the victory.

WORK. On June 24, Mary McLeod Bethune, founder and president of Bethune-Cookman College, is named director of Negro affairs of the National Youth Administration. She is the first African American to receive such a major federal appointment. She holds this position until January 1, 1944.

1937

ARTS. Opera singer and star Grace Bumbry is born on January 4.

Dr. Mary McLeod Bethune listening to a chorus sing the Lord's Prayer during Sunday chapel services at Bethune-Cookman College, 1943. Courtesy of Library of Congress.

On July 12, entertainer, actor, and social critic William "Bill" Cosby is born in Philadelphia, Pennsylvania.

On December 26, La Julia Rhea sings the role of *Aida* in a major production of the opera in Chicago. Also featured in the performance is William Franklin.

CIVI. In October, the National Association for the Advancement of Colored People (NAACP) awards the Spingarn Medal to Walter White of the NAACP for his leadership and work in anti-lynching campaigns throughout the United States.

LIT. Zora Neale Hurston's novel *Their Eyes Are Watching God* is published.

OBIT. On September 26, singer Bessie Smith dies from injuries sustained in an automobile accident near Clarksdale, Mississippi, at the age of 43.

On May 25, noted painter of *The Banjo Lesson*, Henry Ossawa Tanner, dies at the age of 76 in Paris, France.

POLI. On March 26, William H. Hastie is confirmed as judge of the federal district court in the U.S. Virgin Islands and becomes the first African American federal judge.

SPOR. On June 26, Joe Louis defeats James J. Braddock for the heavyweight boxing championship.

WORK. On September 1, the Pullman Company officially recognizes the Brotherhood of Sleeping Car Porters and Maids in Chicago as the official union representative body for African American porters and maids on their railroad cars.

1938

EDUC. On February 17, Mary Frances Berry, the first African American and the first woman to

Jesse Owens at the start of his record-breaking 200-meter race, Berlin Olympic Games, 1936. Courtesy of Library of Congress.

serve as chancellor of a major research institution, the University of Colorado, is born in Nashville, Tennessee.

LAW. On December 12, the U.S. Supreme Court rules in *Missouri v. Gaines* that a state must provide equal educational facilities for African Americans in its borders. The state of Missouri instead wants to send and pay the expenses of Donald Gaines to go to a college that borders Missouri. Under the legal leadership of Charles H. Houston, the National Association for the Advancement of Colored People (NAACP) argues that Gaines's Fourteenth Amendment rights that render him equal protection under the law are violated. The court agrees and then mandates that the state must find an equal educational institution and experience for Murray within the state of Missouri.

OBIT. On April 10, pioneer jazz star Joe "King" Oliver dies in Savannah, Georgia.

On June 26, James Weldon Johnson dies of injuries sustained in an automobile accident near his home in Wiscasset, Maine.

POLI. Crystal Bird Fauset of Philadelphia is elected the first African American legislator in the Pennsylvania legislature on November 8.

1939

ARTS. World-renowned opera singer Marian Anderson is invited to give a concert in Constitution Hall in Washington, DC. The Daughters of the American Revolution (DAR), who own the hall, refuse to let her perform there because she is an African American. Hearing about this decision by the DAR, First Lady Eleanor Roosevelt, who is a member of the DAR, immediately resigns from the association and helps Anderson give the concert outdoors at the Lincoln Memorial on Easter Sunday before an audience of 75,000. Although this is an important statement against U.S. segregation policy, African Americans at the concert are segregated behind a barrier marked "Colored Only."

Marian Anderson, noted contralto, sings "The Star Spangled Banner" at the dedication of a mural commemorating her free public concert on the steps of the Lincoln Memorial, 1939. Courtesy of Library of Congress.

On March 19, writer and poet Langston Hughes founds the New Negro Theater in Los Angeles, California. Its first performance is his play *Don't You Want to Be Free?*

In October, Marian Anderson receives the National Association for the Advancement of Colored People (NAACP) Spingarn Medal as "one of our greatest singers of our time" and "for her special achievement in the field of Music."

LAW. On July 22, Jane Matilda Bolin becomes the first African American female judge. Mayor Fiorello LaGuardia appoints her to the Court of Domestic Relationships in New York City.

On October 11, Thurgood Marshall becomes the director of the separate and newly incorporated NAACP Legal Defense and Educational Fund.

1940

ARTS. Actress Hattie McDaniel becomes the first African American to receive an Academy Award in her controversial role as Mammy in *Gone with the Wind*.

On June 5, the American Negro Theatre is organized and founded by Frederick O'Neal and Abram Hill.

ASSO. In October, the African American National Newspaper Publishers Association is founded.

CENS. The federal government reports that the United States population is 131,669,275, of which 12,865,518 (9.8%) are African Americans.

CRIM. According to the *New York Times,* May 10 marks the first 12-month period since 1882 without a lynching in the South.

EDUC. On August 1, "the greatest schoolmaster of his generation," Benjamin Mays, is named

president of Morehouse College in Atlanta, Georgia. His persona has a strong influence upon his most notable student, Martin Luther King Jr.

LIT. In February, Richard Wright publishes *Native Son,* the first of many important novels by African American novelists after the Great Depression. Hailed as the new American tragedy novel, *Native Son* reflects the twisted and confusing frustrations of interpersonal racial interactions that often lead to tragic consequences as a result of social mores and fears.

MEDI. Dr. Charles Drew develops a method of processing and storing plasma that becomes crucial in conducting blood transfusions. His discovery has an immediate impact on saving the lives of soldiers wounded in combat. Dr. Drew is also instrumental in developing the concept of blood banks.

In October, the National Association for the Advancement of Colored People (NAACP) awards its Spingarn Medal Dr. Louis T. Wright for his civil rights leadership and his contributions as a surgeon.

MILI. On October 9, the Franklin D. Roosevelt White House releases a statement prohibiting interracial military regiments.

On October 16, Benjamin Davis Sr. becomes the first African American general in the regular, but segregated, U.S. Army.

OBIT. On June 10, Pan-African editor, founder of the Universal Negro Improvement Association (UNIA), and orator Marcus Mosiah Garvey dies at the age of 52 in London, England.

1941

CIVI. In April, bus companies in New York City agree to hire African American bus drivers and

---

In a courtroom scene of Richard Wright's *Native Son,* an attorney warns of the destructive potential of suppressed black rage: "The hate and fear which we have inspired in him, woven by our civilization into the very structure of his consciousness and into his blood and bones, into the hourly functioning of his personality, have become the justification of his existence…. Kill him and swell the tide of pent up lava that will some day break loose, not in a single, blundering crime, but in a wild cataract of emotion that will brook no control."

mechanics. This agreement ends a four-week city-wide boycott of the bus system by blacks.

On April 18, Dr. Robert Weaver is named director of office of production management charged with integrating African Americans into the national defense programs and industries.

On April 28, the U.S. Supreme Court rules in a Jim Crow railroad case brought by the first elected African American Democratic congressman, Arthur Mitchell, that separate facilities must be substantially equal.

On May 1, Asa Philip Randolph issues a call for 100,000 African Americans to march on Washington, DC, to protest racial discrimination in the armed forces and war industries. Emerging from this campaign is the Double V: victory against racism abroad and at home. The idea comes from an African American reader who writes the Pittsburgh *Courier* and suggests this as a campaign slogan. It symbolizes the struggle during the war and after for African Americans.

On June 18, President Franklin D. Roosevelt meets with A. Philip Randolph and the leaders of the march on Washington and urges them to call off a scheduled demonstration. Randolph refuses to do so.

On June 25, President Roosevelt issues Executive Order No. 8802, which forbids racial and religious discrimination in war industries, government training programs, and government industries. As a result of this order, Randolph calls off the march. The executive order instructs all agencies to train workers without discrimination and to insure that guidelines are adhered to as established by the Fair Employment Practices Committee (FEPC). The FEPC also has the authority and power to investigate charges of discrimination.

On July 19, President Roosevelt appoints an oversight FEP Committee.

In December, Lester Granger is named the executive director of the National Urban League.

CRIM. On August 6, an African American soldier and a white military policeman are shot to death on a bus in North Carolina during a fight between black and white soldiers. This is one of many ongoing confrontations between black and white U.S. soldiers inside the country as well as overseas that ends in shootings and death.

LIT. In December, novelist Richard Wright receives the National Association for the Advancement of Colored People (NAACP) Spingarn Medal for "his powerful depiction in his books, 'Uncle Tom's Children,' and 'Native Son,' of the effect of proscription, segregation and denial of opportunities to the American Negro."

MEDI. Dr. Charles Drew becomes the first director of a new project charged with the responsibility of setting up donor stations to collect blood plasma for the U.S. military. The American Red Cross, which is the oversight agency in this effort, segregates blood based on race.

MILI. On January 15, Howard University student Yancey Williams appeals to a federal court as the plaintiff in a suit to order the U.S. Secretary of War and other government officials to consider his application for enlistment in the Army Air Corps Squadron as a flying cadet.

On January 16, the U.S. War Department announces the formation of the first Army Air Corps Pursuit Squadron for African American cadets. The training program is established at Tuskegee Army Air Field, Alabama. Unlike other black units in the army, the Ninety-Ninth Squadron and the 332nd Group—made up of the 100th, 301st, and 302nd Squadrons—have black officers.

OBIT. On July 10, pioneer and legendary jazz pianist Ferdinand "Jelly Roll" Morton dies at the age of 56 in Los Angeles, California.

WAR. On December 7, Japanese naval airplanes attack the United States Navy at Pearl Harbor, Hawaii. Reportedly, the first U.S. hero of World War II is Dorie Miller, a 22-year-old messman and the son of a Texas sharecropper on the USS *West Virginia*, who carries the ship's mortally wounded captain to safety then mans an antiaircraft gun to shoot down what witnesses say are four Japanese planes (officially listed as two). Miller was never taught how to fire the antiaircraft gun due to naval regulations that prohibit blacks from learning this skill. After the attack on Pearl Harbor, the Navy requires all hands, including messmen and stewards, to receive antiaircraft training. Dorie Miller is killed on Thanksgiving

Day 1943 when his ship, the aircraft carrier *Liscome Bay,* is torpedoed and all hands go down with the ship.

1942

ASSO. In November, black and white advocates for direct nonviolent action against racism organize the Congress of Racial Equality (CORE) in Chicago. An interracial organization, CORE brings together civil rights activist who favor the tactics of Indian leader Mohandas Gandhi, who advocates massive direct social action of a nonviolent nature. CORE's leadership concludes that in those areas of society in which blacks' numerical superiority is critical, they can create enough social action to change social policy in favor of social and economic integration. This theory is successfully tested in a staged sit-in demonstration at Stoner's Restaurant in Chicago's downtown Loop. Activists Bayard Rustin and James Farmer are instrumental in starting the organization.

CIVI. In November, Asa Philip Randolph is awarded the National Association for the Advancement of Colored People (NAACP) Spingarn Medal.

MED. On November 1, John H. Johnson publishes the first issue of *Negro Digest.*

MILI. On March 7, the first African American cadets are graduated from the Army Air Corps Squadron's flying school at Tuskegee, Alabama.

On June 18, Harvard medical student Bernard W. Robinson is graduated as an ensign from the U.S. Naval Reserve and becomes the first African American to receive a commission.

On September 29, the *Booker T. Washington,* the first U.S. merchant ship commanded by an African American captain, Hugh Mulzac, is launched at Wilmington, Delaware. Born in the British West Indies, Hugh Mulzac first becomes interested in the sea after high school by sailing on British vessels. Attending the Nautical School in Swansea, England, he eventually earns a mate's license. He sails as a ship's officer in World War I and afterward comes to the United States to become a citizen. By 1920, he passes the examination to become a U.S. shipmaster;

however, because of U.S. racism and segregation policies, there are no berths available for a black captain. For the next 20 years, he works in the stewards department of various shipping lines. He eventually becomes an expert in this field. With the outbreak of World War II, and at the age of 56, Mulzac recognizes an opportunity to use his license to receive command of a vessel and is named captain of the new Liberty Ship *Booker T. Washington.* He argues for a racially mixed rather than an all-black crew. The U.S. Maritime Commission relents, and the *Booker T. Washington* makes 22 round-trip voyages with Mulzac as captain. After the war, due to his prewar involvement with labor unions that are now the target for the Communist-seeking House Committee on Un-American Activities, chaired by Wisconsin Senator Joseph McCarthy, Mulzac can no longer find work in the maritime service. Only in 1960 can he again find work as a maritime officer.

SPOR. Negro Baseball League pitcher Satchel Paige leads the Kansas City Monarchs to their fourth consecutive Negro American League Championship.

1943

ARTS. The play *Porgy and Bess* opens on February 28 on Broadway in New York City with Anne Brown and Todd Duncan in starring roles.

On October 19, *Othello,* presented by the Theater Guild, opens at the Shubert Theater with Paul Robeson in the title role. This production runs for 296 performances and sets a record for a Shakespearean drama on New York City's Broadway.

ASSO. On June 20, the National Congress of Racial Equality is organized.

CRIM. On May 25, white and black laborers fight over the promotion of 12 African American shipyard workers in Mobile, Alabama.

On June 16, a race riot in Beaumont, Texas, results in the death of two persons.

On June 20, 34 people (9 whites and 25 African Americans) are killed and more than 700 wounded in Detroit, Michigan, in one the country's bloodiest race riots. Of the 25 African Americans killed, 17 die at the hands of police. Six thousand federal soldiers come to Detroit to restore order. Before the riot, National Association for the Advancement of Colored People (NAACP) Executive Director Walter White warns Detroit city officials that because of competition for jobs, little affordable housing, and police brutality, an impending conflict based on social frustration is bound to occur. His appeals, however, are generally ignored as Communist-influenced rhetoric. African American leaders, radical unionists, and members of Jewish groups respond that the violence is provoked and sustained by "the KKK, the Christian Front, the Black Dragon Society, the National Workers League, the Knights of the White Camellia, the Southern Voters League, and similar organizations based on a policy of terror and white supremacy."

On August 1 and 2, a race riot explodes in Harlem, New York.

EDUC. W.E.B. Du Bois becomes the first African American admitted to the National Institute of Arts and Letters.

LAW. In December, William H. Hastie is awarded the National Association for the Advancement of Colored People (NAACP) Spingarn Medal for "his distinguished career as a jurist and as an uncompromising champion of equal justice."

MED. In December, the San Francisco *Sun-Reporter* is founded.

MILI. On January 5, William H. Hastie, civilian aid to Secretary of War Henry L. Stinson, resigns in protest over segregation and discrimination in the armed forces. Three years earlier, Hastie left his position as dean of Howard University's law school to assist the government in appealing for African American support for the war effort. Throughout his tenure, however, he experiences hostility and outright racist responses in and outside the government as he attempts to secure equal treatment for African American military personnel. Hastie publishes his reasons for resigning in the *Chicago Defender*.

OBIT. On January 5, scientist George Washington Carver dies in Tuskegee, Alabama, at the age of 78.

On December 15, musician and pianist Thomas W. "Fats" Waller dies at the age of 39 in Kansas City, Missouri.

POLI. On May 26, President Edwin Barclay of Liberia is the first African president to pay an official visit to a U.S. president at the White House.

SPOR. On March 13, Frank Dixon becomes the first African American miler in track by winning the Columbian Mile in New York City in the record time of 4 minutes, 9.6 seconds.

On July 10, Arthur Ashe, the first African American male to win the Wimbledon Tennis Championship, is born.

WAR. On June 2, the all-black Ninety-Ninth Pursuit Squadron flies its first combat mission and strafes enemy positions on the heavily fortified Italian island of Pantelleria.

On July 2, Lt. Buster Hall of Brazil, Indiana, becomes the first African American to shoot down a German fighter plane when his fighter group, the Ninety-Ninth Pursuit Squadron, escorts B-25 bombers over Sicily and is attacked by German Focke-Wulf 190 fighter planes.

On July 25, the USS *Leonard Roy Harmon* becomes the first U.S. warship named for an African American. It is launched at Quincy, Maine.

1944

ASSO. On April 24, the United Negro College Fund is incorporated.

EDUC. On September 18, 1,000 white students walk out of three schools in Gary, Indiana, to protest racial integration. Similar resistance by white students and their families occurs in Chicago and other northern and western urban centers.

EXPO. On January 28, Matthew Henson receives a joint medal from the U.S. Congress as codiscoverer of the North Pole.

LAW. On April 3, the U.S. Supreme Court in *Smith v. Allwright* declares that so-called white primaries that exclude African Americans are unconstitutional.

POLI. On August 1, Adam Clayton Powell Jr. is elected as the first African American congressmen from the eastern part of the country. He is elected for six consecutive terms as congressmen from Harlem, New York.

SCIE. In August, Charles Drew receives the National Association for the Advancement of Colored People (NAACP) Spingarn Medal for establishing a blood plasma bank at Presbyterian Hospital in New York City. The bank serves as a model for the banks operated by the America Red Cross.

1945

ARTS. In November, Paul Robeson is awarded the National Association for the Advancement of Colored People (NAACP) Spingarn Medal for his theatrical achievements and for his support of racial welfare.

Swing musician Nat King Cole becomes the first African American to have his own radio show, which runs for two years on NBC Radio. Later, he has his own network television program, *The Nat King Show*, also on NBC.

ASSO. From October 15 to 21, the fifth Pan-African Congress meets in Manchester, England. W.E.B. Du Bois is elected its president. Africans attending the conference feel that the world is changing and the time for anticolonial struggles should be at the forefront of the conference's discussions. Similarly, Du Bois considers the United States as a protector of the colonial system and opposes its political stance in the Cold War.

MED. On October 23, John H. Johnson publishes the first issue of *Ebony* magazine. The first issue sells 25,000 copies.

MILI. On June 30, Wesley A. Brown takes the oath of induction at the U.S. Naval Academy at Annapolis, Maryland. He is the sixth African American admitted to the Naval Academy. Three other African Americans were admitted during Reconstruction and two in the 1930s. All are forced out or resigned after racial hazing, excessive demerits, and racial violence.

On June 21, Col. B. O. Davis Jr. is named commander of Godman Field, Kentucky, and becomes the first African American to head an Army Air Force base in the United States.

OBIT. On April 12, President Franklin Delano Roosevelt dies in White Springs, Georgia, and Vice President Harry S. Truman assumes the office of president.

POLI. On April 25, the United Nations is founded at San Francisco, California. African American consultants, most notably W.E.B. Du Bois, Mary McLeod Bethune, Ralph J. Bunche, and Walter White, attend the opening session.

On November 3, Irving C. Mollison, a Chicago Republican, is sworn in as a U.S. customs judge in New York City.

SPOR. On October 23, Jackie Robinson signs with the Brooklyn Dodgers and is sent to their triple-A farm team, the Montreal Royals in the International League.

On March 29, National Basketball Association (NBA) New York Knicks guard Walt Frazier is born in Atlanta, Georgia. He leads his team to championships in 1970 and 1973 and is elected to the Basketball Hall of Fame in 1987.

WAR. On May 8, Nazi Germany surrenders to the Allied forces in Europe. This is known as Victory in Europe, or VE, Day.

On September 2, Japan surrenders to Allied forces in the Pacific. This is known as Victory over Japan Day, or VJ Day. This surrender signals the end of World War II. Official figures claim 1,154,720 African American soldiers are inducted

---

On returning to the United States after the fifth Pan-African Congress conference, W.E.B. Du Bois states: "We American Negroes should know ... until Africa is free, the descendants of Africa the world over cannot escape their chains ... the NAACP should therefore put in the forefront of its program the freedom of Africa in work and wage, education and health, and the complete abolition of the colonial system."

or drafted into the armed forces throughout the conflict in Europe, Africa, and Asia. Some 7,768 are commissioned as officers by August 31, 1945. Distinguished Unit Citations are awarded to the 969th Field Artillery Battalion, the 614th Tank Destroyer Battalion, and the 332nd Fighter Group.

At the height of the war, 3,902 African American women, of whom 115 are officers, enroll in the Women's Army Corps (WAC), and 68 officers enroll in the Navy auxiliary (WAVE). The highest-ranking black woman officers are Maj. Harriet M. West and Maj. Charity E. Adams.

1946

ARTS. Actor, singer, and dancer Gregory Oliver Hines is born in New York City on February 14.

CIVI. On June 3, the U.S. Supreme Court in *Irene Morgan v. Commonwealth of Virginia* bans segregation in interstate bus travel.

On December 5, President Harry S Truman creates the Committee on Civil Rights by Executive Order No. 9808. Two African Americans attorneys, Sadie M. Alexander and Channing H. Tobias, serve as members of the committee.

CRIM. On February 26, a race riot explodes in Columbia, Tennessee. Two people are killed and 10 wounded.

On August 10, a race riot tears through Athens, Alabama.

EDUC. On November 1, Dr. Charles S. Johnson becomes the first African American president of Fisk University.

LAW. In December, the National Association for the Advancement of Colored People (NAACP) awards the Spingarn Medal to the director of its Legal Defense and Educational Fund, Thurgood Marshall.

MILI. On March 13, Col. Benjamin O. Davis Jr. assumes command of Lockbourne Air Force Base in Ohio.

OBIT. On January 9, noted poet and writer Countee Cullen dies at the age of 42 in New York City.

On June 10, Jack Johnson, the first African American heavyweight champion, dies after an automobile accident near Raleigh, North Carolina.

On July 6, businessman, publisher, cosmetics manufacturer, and banker Anthony Overton dies in Chicago.

POLI. William H. Hastie is inaugurated on May 7 as the first African American governor of the U.S. Virgin Islands.

1947

ARTS. Helen L. Phillips becomes the first known African American singer to appear with the Metropolitan Opera chorus in what appears to be an accidental breaking of the color barrier. Apparently, the stage manager at the opera calls an agent seeking the agent's best soprano when several chorus members are missing. When Phillips arrives, the manager looks at her twice then tells her to hurry and go backstage. Jeff McMillan, an archivist at the Met, who says that there is no written policy barring African Americans from performing there, confirms her groundbreaking status. The first African American chorister to be granted a contract is Elinor Harper, who makes her debut at the opera in 1962. Helen Phillips is also the first African American soloist with Edwin Franko Goldman's band that plays in New York City's Central Park in the 1940s and 1950s. After World War II, Phillips makes more than 500 concert appearances for the U.S. State Department in Austria and West Germany then makes her Town Hall debut in 1953. As a graduate of Lincoln University in Jefferson City, Missouri, Phillips becomes a vocal coach before retirement.

CIVI. On January 3, the National Association for the Advancement of Colored People (NAACP) issues a state of the race report for the previous year, 1946. The report describes the first post–World War II year as one of the bleakest in NAACP history. The report describes the growing disillusionment among African Americans over the killing and lynching of blacks and the nonsensical "flamboyant promises about post war democracy and decency."

On April 9, the Congress of Racial Equality (CORE) and the Fellowship of Reconciliation, a group organized by Bayard Rustin, sends 16 black and white Freedom Riders through the South to test compliance with court decisions to prohibit segregation in interstate transportation. Outside of Chapel Hill, North Carolina, the group is assaulted and arrested. Rustin and three of his colleagues are sentenced to 30 days on a road gang, of which he serves 22 days.

On October 23, the NAACP takes the issue of American racism to the United Nations meeting at Lake Success, New York, by presenting a formal petition entitled "An Appeal to the World."

EDUC. On September 21, Archbishop Joseph E. Ritter states that he will excommunicate St. Louis Catholics who protest integration of Catholic parochial schools.

In October, Texas Southern University is established.

MED. On February 3, Percival Prattis, of *Our World in New York City* journal, becomes the first African American news correspondent admitted to the U.S. House and Senate press galleries in Washington, DC.

MILI. On March 15, John Lee becomes the first African American commissioned officer in the U.S. Navy.

SCIE. In October, the NAACP awards its Spingarn Medal to Dr. Percy Lavon Julian for his achievements as a scientist. Born in 1899, Dr. Julian becomes a foremost organic chemist and invents devices that either improve or save lives. His first invention is Aero-Foam, a substance that extinguishes oil and gas fires. In 1935, he produces a drug that alleviates pressure in the eyes and that prevents blindness in people with glaucoma. By producing synthetic progesterone and testosterone, he aids treatment of specific types of cancers. Julian's research with the soybean leads to the discovery of products that save lives in World War II and alleviate pain associated with arthritis. Dr. Julian has more than 138 chemical patents in his name.

SPOR. On April 10, Jackie Robinson joins the Brooklyn Dodgers baseball team to become the first modern African American to play in the major leagues (National League).

On July 6, Larry Doby becomes the second African American to play in major league baseball in modern times and the first to play in the American League.

Three additional African Americans join major league baseball teams: Dan Bankhead, a pitcher, joins the Brooklyn Dodgers; Willard Brown, an outfielder, joins the St. Louis Browns; and Henry Thompson, a third baseman, joins the St. Louis Browns.

1948

CIVI. On February 2, U.S. President Harry S Truman, in a special address to Congress, announces his intentions to adopt a civil rights program that includes a fair employment practices commission and strong antilynching and anti–poll tax measures.

On March 31, A. Philip Randolph tells the Senate Armed Services Committee that unless segregation and discrimination are banned in draft programs, he will urge African American youths to resist the military draft by using civil disobedience.

On May 3, the U.S. Supreme Court in *Shelley v. Kraemer* rules that federal and state courts cannot enforce restrictive covenants that bar persons from owning or occupying property because of their race.

On October 1, California's supreme court overturns a state statute that bans interracial marriages.

In October, the Spingarn Medal is awarded to attorney Channing H. Tobias for his "consistent role as defender of fundamental American liberties."

HHC. On February 12, 1st Lt. Nancy C. Leftenant becomes the first African American accepted to the Army Nursing Corps.

LAW. On January 12, the U.S. Supreme Court in *Sipuel v. Oklahoma State Board of Regents* declares that a state must allow blacks studying law to begin their studies at state institutions at the same time as other students. African American Ada Lois Sipuel is denied admission to the University of Oklahoma due to her race. The U.S. Supreme Court, however, concludes that to deny Sipuel entrance into the University of Oklahoma law school constitutes a breach of the Fourteenth Amendment's equal protection clause and that her admittance must occur simultaneously with other students.

MILI. On July 26, U.S. President Harry S. Truman issues Executive Order No. 9981, which directs equal treatment for everyone serving in the armed forces "without regard to race, color, religion, or national origin." After Truman signs the order, A. Philip Randolph and Grant Reynolds, who formed the League for Nonviolent Civil Disobedience against Military Segregation, disband the League and call off planned antimilitary marches and demonstrations in Chicago and New York.

OBIT. On May 22, noted writer and poet Claude McKay dies at the age of 58 in Chicago, Illinois.

POLI. From July 23 to 25, the Progressive Party in Philadelphia, Pennsylvania, nominates Henry Wallace for president. This new political party attracts some 150 African American delegates and alternates to its convention. Thirty-seven blacks run for state and local offices on the party ticket, and 10 blacks run for congress. The Progressive Party, however, attracts few black voters and force the Democratic Party to make serious gestures toward the African American community.

On September 18, Ralph Bunche is confirmed by the United Nations Security Council as acting UN mediator in Palestine. Three years earlier, Bunche was appointed as an advisor to the U.S. delegation at the San Francisco conference that drafted the United Nations charter. In 1949, he negotiates an armistice between Egypt and Israel. As a Harvard-educated student who received his doctorate in government and international relations, Ralph Bunche spent much of the 1930s studying the problems of African Americans. During World War II, he became a key expert on American policy pertaining to Africa and the Far East. The duplicity, or "two-ness" dilemma, that Du Bois often speaks of seems applicable to Bunche because of his work as a representative of

the U.S. government and yet one personally pledged to eliminate the scourge of foreign colonialism and U.S. racism.

1949

CIVI. In November, a chapter of the Congress of Racial Equality (CORE) in St. Louis, Missouri, presses its sit-in campaign to desegregate downtown business facilities.

CRIM. On August 28, white rioters prevent noted athlete, actor, and political activist Paul Robeson from singing at the Lakeland Picnic Grounds near Peekskill, Westchester County, New York. Many of his detractors are upset with Robeson's pro–Soviet Union views and statements that are interpreted as extremely anti-American. In response to his continued linking of the struggles against colonialism with the antiracist struggle in the United States, the U.S. State Department revokes his passport.

On September 4, rioters again prevent Paul Robeson from giving a concert in Peekskill, New York, and after the concert attack audience members.

LAW. On October 15, President Harry S. Truman appoints William H. Hastie as the first African American U.S. Circuit Court of Appeals judge.

MED. On October 3, WERD, the first African American–owned radio station, broadcasts in Atlanta, Georgia.

OBIT. On November 25, world-renowned dancer and entertainer, Bill "Bojangles" Robinson dies at age 71.

MILI. On June 3, Wesley A. Brown becomes the first African American to graduate as a

---

Of blacks in modern American, Ralphe Bunche writes: "Today, for all thinking people, the Negro is the shining symbol of the true significance of democracy. He has demonstrated what can be achieved with democratic liberties even when grudgingly and incompletely bestowed. But the most vital significance of the Negro … to American society … is the fact that democracy which is not extended to all of the nation's citizens is a democracy that is mortally wounded."

midshipman from the U.S. Naval Academy at Annapolis, Maryland. He retires 20 years later as a lieutenant commander in the navy's Civil Engineering Corps. Representative Adam Clayton Powell Jr. of Harlem, New York, sponsors him.

POLI. On January 18, U.S. Representative William L. Dawson is elected chairman of the House Expenditures Committee. He is the first African American to head a standing committee of Congress.

In November, the National Association for the Advancement of Colored People (NAACP) awards the Spingarn Medal to Ralph J. Bunche for his contributions to the (Gunnar) Myrdal study and his achievements as UN mediator of the Palestine conflict.

Swedish social scientist, Gunnar Myrdal led a research team of Americans, half of whom were African Americans in examining black life style in the United States. The resulting study, published in 1944 as, *An American Dilemma*, dramatically impacted how the public viewed institutionalized racism and the subsequent Civil Rights Movement.

SPOR. On March 1, Joe Louis retires as heavyweight boxing champion after holding the title for a record of 11 years and 8 months.

On June 22, Ezzard Charles defeats Jersey Joe Walcott for the world heavyweight boxing championship.

1950

ARTS. On April 16, Juanita Hall is the first African American to win a Tony Award for her portrayal of Bloody Mary in *South Pacific*.

CENS. The United States population is 150,697,361, of which 15,042,286 (10%) are African Americans.

CIVI. On June 9, the U.S. Supreme Court in three landmark cases overturns elements of segregation previously supported by the *Plessy v. Ferguson* (1896) doctrine of separate but equal racial practices in the United States. The court rules in favor of African American petitioners in *Sweatt v. Painter, McLaurin v. Okalahoma,* and *Henderson v. United States.*

LAW. In September, attorney Charles Hamilton Houston is posthumously awarded the National

Association for the Advancement of Colored People (NAACP) Spingarn Medal for his consistent and successful efforts in developing the NAACP legal campaigns for civil rights.

LIT. On May 1, writer and poet Gwendolyn Brooks is awarded the Pulitzer Prize in literature for her book of poetry *Annie Allen*. She is the first African American to be cited by the Pulitzer committee.

OBIT. On April 1, surgeon and developer of plasma and the blood bank concept, Dr. Charles Drew, dies in an automobile accident at the age of 45 near Burlington, North Carolina.

On April 3, historian, writer, publisher, and founder of the Association for the Study of Negro Life and History, Dr. Carter G. Woodson, dies in Washington, DC, at the age of 74.

On April 22, attorney, educator, and architect of the successful cases that lead to the *Brown v. Board of Education of Topeka, Kansas,* decision (1954), Charles Hamilton Houston, dies at the age of 54 in Washington, DC.

POLI. The U.S. government revokes Paul Robeson's passport. This stays in effect until the act is ruled unconstitutional by the U.S. Supreme Court in 1958.

On August 24, attorney Edith Sampson becomes the first African American representative, as an alternate delegate, for the United States to the United Nations.

On September 22, Ralph J. Bunche, director or the UN Trusteeship Division and former professor of political science at Howard University, is awarded the Nobel Peace Prize for his successful mediation of the conflict over Palestine. He is the first African American to receive a Nobel Prize.

SPOR. In an attempt to win back the heavyweight boxing championship on September 24, Joe Louis is defeated by Ezzard Charles.

Chuck Cooper becomes the first African American drafted by a National Basketball Association (NBA) team; the Boston Celtics. Later this year, Nat "Sweetwater" Clifton becomes the first African American to sign an NBA contract, with the New York Knicks. Earl Lloyd becomes the first African American to play in an NBA game, with the Washington Capitals.

WAR. On July 21, African American soldiers from the Twenty-Fourth Infantry Regiment recapture Yechon from North Korean soldiers after a 16-hour battle. This is the first U.S. military victory in the Korean War.

1951

CIVI. On June 23, the National Association for the Advancement of Colored People (NAACP) challenges the *Plessy v. Ferguson* (1896) doctrine that separate but equal facilities are beneficial to African American children on both the elementary and high school level. The judicial fight is argued before a three-judge federal court in both South Carolina and Kansas. The South Carolina court, despite a strong dissent from Judge Waites E. Waring, holds that segregation is not discrimination, whereas the Kansas Court decides that the separate facilities at issue are equal but that segregation has an adverse effect on black children.

On May 24, the Municipal Court of Appeals renders racial discrimination in Washington, DC, restaurants illegal.

CRIM. On December 25, Florida NAACP official Harry T. Moore is killed and his wife seriously injured by a bomb blast that wrecks their home in Florida.

EDUC. On July 14, the George Washington Carver National Monument is dedicated in Joplin, Missouri.

HHC. In December, noted nurse and health care administrator Mabel K. Staupers receives the NAACP's Spingarn Medal for leadership in the field of nursing.

HOUS. On February 16, the New York City Council passes a bill that prohibits racial discrimination in city-assisted housing developments.

On July 12, Governor Adlai Stevenson of Illinois calls out the National Guard to stop a mob of 3,500 rioting whites in Cicero, Illinois, who are trying to stop a black family from moving into their all-white neighborhood.

MED. On November 1, John H. Johnson founds *Jet* magazine.

MILI. On October 1, the last all-black military unit, the Twenty-Fourth Infantry Regiment, which received its colors from the U.S. Congress in 1866, is deactivated in Korea.

OBIT. On May 12, former congressman Oscar DePriest dies in Chicago, Illinois, at the age of 80.

WAR. On June 21, Brooklyn-born Pfc. William Thompson of the Twenty-Fourth Infantry Regiment is posthumously awarded the Medal of Honor for heroism in Korea. On August 6, 1950, at Masan, some 20 miles south of Yechon in South Korea, Thompson refused to join his company as it withdrew in the face of increasing and overwhelming enemy attacks from North Korean troops. Staying at his machine gun, he effectively provided covering fire until his unit had escaped. In the course of this action, he is mortally wounded. Thompson becomes the first GI to receive the Medal of Honor in Korea and the first African American to do so since the Spanish-American War. He is not officially recommended for this honor, however, until January 4, 1951, almost five months later because Lt. Col. Melvin Blair, Thompson's commander, refuses at first to submit a letter of recommendation.

1952

CIVI. In December, the National Association for the Advancement of Colored People (NAACP) awards its Spingarn Medal posthumously to the Florida state director of the NAACP, Harry T. Moore, for his civil rights leadership.

CRIM. This is the first year since the Colonial period that there is no reported lynching of an African American.

EDUC. On January 12, the University of Tennessee admits its first African American student.

LIT. Ralph Ellison wins the National Book Award for his novel *Invisible Man*. Though Ellison writs two other novels, *Shadow and Act* and *Going to the Territory*, it is *Invisible Man* that is his most powerful and lasting depiction of U.S. racism. When he was contemplating a career in music, a chance discussion with writer Richard Wright, author of *Native Son,* encourages him to concentrate on writing rather than music.

MILI. On February 12, the Medal of Honor is awarded posthumously to Sgt. Cornelius H. Charlton of the all-black U.S. Twenty-Fourth Infantry Regiment for heroism in Korea. Charlton was killed on June 2, 1951, after a series of firefights with the enemy, during which he led a platoon attack on a ridge held by Communist soldiers near Chipo-Ri, Korea. When his white commanding officer was seriously wounded, Charlton took command of his platoon and spearheaded three separate assaults up the steep ridge. He personally destroyed several enemy positions with grenades and rifle fire and, wounded in the chest by a grenade, waved away medics so he could single-handedly go after a group of Chinese on a far ridge. Holding his chest wound with one hand and an M-1 carbine with the other, he raced into the fire to be killed by an enemy grenade. Charlton was buried in a segregated cemetery in Beckley, West Virginia. The army claimed that it was an administrative oversight that he was buried in a segregated cemetery, and it did not offer to rebury him at Arlington National Cemetery with full military honors. When the military finally decides to rebury Sgt. Charlton at Arlington in 1989, the family states that this is simply a case of outright discrimination. John Shumate, a World War II navy veteran and commander of Beckley's all-white American Legion Post No. 32, proposes that Charlton be buried at the American Legion's cemetery. Sgt. Cornelius H. Charlton is reburied on March 10, 1989, at a ceremony attended by an assistant secretary of state, a local congressman, two army generals, and a full honor guard from Fort Knox, Kentucky. He is the only African American among the 251 other soldiers on top of the hill in the American Legion cemetery.

OBIT. On May 9, actor Canada Lee dies in New York City at the age of 45. Lee's role in *On Whitman Avenue* is memorable in that it addresses two of the most pressing social issues in the United States: the return of African American soldiers and their reintegration into northern cities.

On December 29, noted bandleader and music arranger Fletcher Henderson dies at the age of 55 in New York City.

1953

CIVI. In June, a bus boycott begins in Baton Rouge, Louisiana, that will affect a similar boycott two years later in Montgomery, Alabama.

HOUS. On August 4, African American families moving into the Trumball Park housing project in Chicago are resisted by white rioters. This conflict continues on and off for two to three years, forcing the Chicago Police Department to assign more than 1,000 policemen to the housing development to maintain order.

LAW. On June 8, the U.S. Supreme Court outlaws segregation in Washington, DC, restaurants.

LIT. James Baldwin's first novel and partially autobiographical account of his youth, *Go Tell It on the Mountain,* is published. His later essays, *Notes on a Native Son* (1955), *Nobody Knows My Name* (1961), *and The Fire Next Time* (1963), are highly influential in establishing the growing sense of racial exclusivity among African Americans. Baldwin, who does much of his writing in southern France and returns to the United States to lecture or teach, writes two highly controversial novels relating to the theme of homosexuality: *Giovanni's Room* (1956), about a white American expatriate who comes to terms with his homosexuality, and *Another Country,* which explores the homosexual relationships and tensions among New York City intellectuals. Though Baldwin's homosexuality becomes increasingly a topic of discussion along with his writing genius, these two novels evoke a negative reaction from many African American radicals, such as Eldridge Cleaver of the Black Panthers for Self Defense who argues that Baldwin's writings display an "agonizing, total hatred of blacks." In the next four years, James Baldwin writes three powerful novels that describe U.S. racism in its most virulent form: *Blues for Mister Charlie* (1964), *Going to Meet the Man* (1965), and *Tell Me How Long the Train's Been Gone* (1968).

POLI. On December 31, Hulan Jack is sworn in as Manhattan borough president. He is the first African American to hold a major elected position in a major U.S. city.

SPOR. On November 19, Roy Campanella, catcher for the Brooklyn Dodgers, is named the most valuable player of the National League for the second time.

WORK. In December, the National Association for the Advancement of Colored People (NAACP) awards its Spingarn Medal to Paul R. Williams for his achievements as an architect.

1954

ARTS. Tap dancer Gregory Hines makes his Broadway debut. He becomes largely associated with the rebirth of tap dance and as a dramatic actor in film and plays.

CIVI. On September 7 and 8, public schools in Washington, DC, and Baltimore, Maryland, are racially integrated.

LAW. On May 17, the U.S. Supreme Court overturns the *Plessy v. Ferguson* (1896) case that established the doctrine of separate but equal by deciding in *Brown v. Board of Education of Topeka, Kansas,* that segregation in public schools is unconstitutional. Chief Justice Earl B. Warren announces the decision. The lead attorney in the case is Thurgood Marshall.

MED. On January 29, Oprah Winfrey is born to an unmarried mother, Verita Lee, in Kosciusko, Mississippi. She is raised by her maternal grandmother, Hattie Mae, and father, Vernon Winfrey. They make sure that Oprah attends Tennessee State University, where she learns the skills that allow her to overcome racial obstacles. In 1984, she takes over an ailing television talk show in Chicago, *A.M. Chicago,* and within a month makes it a major competitor to Phil Donahue's program. Within three months, her on-air hours are expanded, and the show is renamed *The Oprah Winfrey Show.* Always wanting to be an actress, she lands the role of Sofia in *The Color Purple,* a film by Steven Spielberg adapted from Alice Walker's awarded-wining novel. Oprah is nominated for best supporting actress at the 1985 Academy Awards.

MEDI. On May 24, Dr. Peter Murray Marshall is installed as president of the New York County Medical Society and becomes the first African American to lead an American Medical Association unit.

In November, the National Association for the Advancement of Colored People (NAACP) awards its Spingarn Medal to Dr. Theodore K. Lawless for his research on skin-related diseases.

MILI. On October 27, Gen. Benjamin O. Davis becomes the first African American general in the U.S. Air Force.

On October 30, the U.S. Defense Department announces the elimination of all segregated regiments in the armed forces.

OBIT. On July 24, educator and civil rights leader Mary Church Terrell dies at the age of 90 in Annapolis, Maryland.

POLI. On August 19, Ralph Bunche becomes the first African American to be named undersecretary of the United Nations.

Charles Mahoney becomes the first African American delegate to serve on the United States delegation to the United Nations.

On November 2, Charles C. Diggs Jr. of Detroit, Michigan, becomes the state's first elected U.S. representative.

In *Brown v. Board of Education,* Thurgood Marshall argues that "it [Plessy] stands mirrored today as a legal aberration, the faulty conception of an era dominated by provincialism, by intense emotionalism in race relations .... and by the preaching of a doctrine of racial superiority that contradicted the basic concept upon which our society was founded. Twentieth century America, fighting racism at home and abroad, has rejected the race views of *Plessy v. Ferguson* because we have come to the realization that such views obviously tend to preserve not the strength but the weakness of our heritage."

RELI. Malcolm X becomes minister of the Nation of Islam's Temple Mosque No. 7 in Harlem.

WORK. On March 4, President Dwight D. Eisenhower appoints J. Ernest Wilkins assistant secretary of labor.

1955

ARTS. On January 7, opera singer Marian Anderson debuts at the Metropolitan Opera in New York City as Ulrica in Verdi's *Masked Ball.* She is the opera company's first African American singer.

Dorothy Dandridge is the first African American woman nominated for an Academy Award for best actress for her role in *Carmen Jones* and the first African American woman featured on the cover of *Life* magazine. Born in 1922, Dandridge started her career when she was six years old and sang with her sister, Vivian, in an act called the Wonder Kids. When the family moved to Los Angeles, a friend joined their singing group and called themselves the Dandridge Sisters. The group dissolved in 1941, but Dorothy was able to get a few bit parts in films. Her break came in 1953 when she costarred with Harry Belafonte in the *Bright Road,* and in 1954, she obtained the lead role in *Carmen Jones.* In 1957, she stars in the interracial drama *Island in the Sun,* and in 1959, she plays Bess in the musical *Porgy and Bess.* She makes 25 films in her career. As her career begins to decline, she reportedly turns to antidepressants and dies of an overdose in 1965

CIVI. On March 2, 15-year-old Claudette Colvin is arrested after refusing to give up her seat to a white man on a racially segregated bus in Montgomery, Alabama. An organization of African American woman, the Woman's Political Council (WPC), located at Alabama State University (ASU) and founded in 1946 by an ASU professor, Dr. Mary Francis Fair Burks, is ready to work with the National Association for the Advancement of Colored People (NAACP) to use this incident to force the local all-white Montgomery city commissioners and the segregated bus company to confront the U.S. Supreme Court's 1954 antisegregation decision. On May 24, the president of the WPC, Jo Ann Robinson, and other members of the organization send a letter of complaint regarding segregation and the continual incidents of racial bias on buses to the Montgomery city commissioners. The WPC circulates a notice for Montgomery blacks to hold a one-day boycott. They are surprised at the immediate response, the eagerness of the African American populace, and the success of the one-day boycott. Not receiving any satisfaction on these complaints from the city commissioners, however, the WPC approaches the local NAACP leader, E. D. Nixon, who, although agreeing with the intolerable racial situation, is reluctant to use the Claudette Colvin arrest as a test case because she is 15 years old, pregnant, and unmarried. Though the WPC is reluctant to go along with this assessment, it is only one of many differences they have with the more conservative civil rights organization. The WPC supports the idea that the African American population should attempt to obtain a franchise for a black-owned bus line, thereby forcing the city commissioners to decide between maintaining a segregated bus line on which blacks will not ride or having blacks successfully run a profitable bus franchise. The NAACP chooses not to support the idea of a black-owned franchise but instead argues that the goal should be for a racially integrated bus system.

On December 1, local seamstress and NAACP activist Rosa Parks is arrested after refusing to give up her seat to a white man on a racially segregated bus in Montgomery, Alabama. This incident provides an acceptable basis for the NAACP to support an aggressive political strategy to challenge racial segregation in busing and transportation in general.

On December 5, the 382-day Montgomery bus boycott begins after a mass meeting at Rev. Ralph Abernathy's church, the Holt Street Baptist Church. At this meeting, Rev. Martin Luther King Jr., a close friend of Rev. Abernathy, is elected president of the boycott organization, the Montgomery Improvement Association (MIA).

CRIM. Fourteen-year-old Emmett Till is kidnapped, tortured, and killed on August 28 in Money, Mississippi. The trail of Till's killers is facilitated by Till's uncle, Moses Wright, who identifies Till's kidnappers in a Mississippi courtroom in front of an all-white jury. The all-white jury acquits the two accused white males.

LAW. On May 31, in what is called Brown 2, the U.S. Supreme Court orders school integration to proceed in the face of a large number of states resisting implementation of the 1954 integration order in *Brown v. Board of Education.*

The Maryland supreme court in Baltimore bans segregation in public recreational facilities on November 7.

The Interstate Commerce Commission, which regulates interstate bus travel and waiting rooms, bans segregation on November 25.

MED. In December, Carl Murphy, publisher of the *Baltimore Afro-American,* receives the NAACP's Spingarn Medal for his contributions as a civil rights leader and for his role as a publisher of an influential newspaper.

OBIT. On March 12, innovative and influential jazz saxophonist Charlie "Bird" Parker dies in New York City at the age of 34.

On March 21, former NAACP Executive Director Walter White dies in New York City. Roy Wilkins replaces him as executive director.

On May 18, educator, civil rights leader, and founder of Bethune-Cookman College, Mary McLeod Bethune, dies in Daytona, Florida.

POLI. On July 9, E. Frederic Morrow is appointed an administrative aide to President Dwight Eisenhower and thereby becomes the fist African American to hold an executive position on the White House staff.

In December, Asa Philip Randolph and Willard S. Townsend are elected vice presidents of the AFL-CIO.

1956

ARTS. Singer, dancer, and actor Sammy Davis Jr. debuts on Broadway in the musical *Mr. Wonderful* and in the film *The Benny Goodman Story.*

CIVI. On May 30, civil rights advocates initiate a bus boycott in Tallahassee, Florida.

On September 12, African American students enter an elementary school under National Guard protection in Clay, Kentucky.

Inspired by the Montgomery bus boycott, massive numbers of African Americans defy the racial bus segregation laws of Birmingham, Alabama.

CRIM. In January, the two accused but acquitted killers of Emmett Till sell their confessions to *Look* magazine and gloat over their escape from justice.

On January 30, the home of the president of the Montgomery Improvement Association, the Reverend Dr. Martin Luther King Jr., is bombed.

Singer Nat King Cole is attacked onstage, on April 11, by white supremacists while performing at a theater in Birmingham, Alabama.

In Mansfield, Texas, white mobs prevent the enrollment of students on August 30 at Mansfield High School.

On September 2, the Tennessee National Guard is sent to Clinton, Tennessee, to disperse mobs demonstrating against school racial integration.

As a result of the victory by African Americans in their bus boycott in Montgomery, Alabama, the home of one of the leaders, Rev. F. L. Shuttlesworth, is destroyed by a bomb blast.

EDUC. On February 3, Autherine J. Lucy is admitted to the University of Alabama amid violent demonstrations and rioting. On February 7, she is suspended after a riot and expelled from the university on February 29.

On March 11 and 12, 100 southern U.S. senators and representatives sign a manifesto denouncing the U.S. Supreme Court decision on the integration of public schools.

On April 23, the U.S. Supreme Court refuses to review a lower court decision that prohibits segregation in interstate travel.

LAW. On June 5, a U.S. federal court rules that racial segregation on Montgomery, Alabama, buses violates the U.S. Constitution.

On November 13, the U.S. Supreme Court upholds a lower court decision that bans discrimination on city buses in Montgomery, Alabama. On December 20, federal injunctions prohibiting segregation on buses are served on city, state, and bus company officials. As a result, officials of the Montgomery Improvement Association (MIA) call off a year-long bus boycott, and buses are integrated on December 21.

On December 27, federal Judge Dozier Devane grants a temporary injunction against city officials in Tallahassee, Florida, who are attempting to block integration of the buses.

LIT. On September 19 and 20, African American writers attend the First International Conference of Black Writers and Artists at the Sorbonne in Paris, France.

OBIT. On November 5, noted jazz pianist Art Tatum dies in Los Angeles, California, at the age of 46.

SPOR. In December, baseball legend, hall of fame star, and the first African American to play major league baseball, Jack "Jackie" Roosevelt Robinson, receives the National Association for the Advancement of Colored People (NAACP) Spingarn Medal for his conduct on and off the playing field.

Althea Gibson becomes the first African American to win a major tennis title, the French Open.

1957

ARTS. Soprano Leontyne Price, the first African American opera singer to win international renown, makes her debut with the San Francisco Opera.

ASSO. In Chicago, lawyer W. Robert Ming is elected chairman of the American Veterans Committee on April 28. He is the first African American to lead a national veteran's organization.

On November 27, Dorothy Height is elected the president of the National Council of Negro Woman.

CIVI. On February 13 and 14, the Southern Christian Leadership Conference (SCLC) is formed in New Orleans, Louisiana, on the suggestion of social activists Bayard Rustin, Ella Baker, and liberal Jewish lawyer Stanley Levinson. Rev. Dr. Martin Luther King Jr. is elected president. The SCLC's mandate is to organize Christians and supportive liberal organizations into a progressive social-changing civil rights force.

On May 17, the largest civil rights demonstration ever held takes place in Washington, DC. It is the civil rights Prayer Pilgrimage and features gospel singer Mahalia Jackson.

In June, African Americans in Tuskegee, Alabama, boycott city stores in protest against a legislative act by the state of Alabama that places their homes outside the municipal limits of Tuskegee, thereby depriving them of the right to vote on city issues.

On September 4, Governor Orville Faubus of Arkansas orders 270 National Guard soldiers to stop any attempt to integrate Little Rock High School, thereby disregarding constitutional law and the 1954 U.S. Supreme court decision on desegregation in *Brown v. Board of Education*. When the federal court orders Faubus to remove the National Guard, he does so, leaving African American children exposed to the wrath of white anti-integration mobs. Defending the sovereignty of the federal court, President Dwight Eisenhower sends 1,100 paratroopers from the 101st Airborne to restore order, escort the black students into the school, and put the Arkansas National Guard under federal control. The troops remain in Little Rock for the entire academic year. Governor Faubus closes the other public schools as a show of defiance from 1958 to 1959. Eight of the nine African American students who attend Little Rock High School do so in the face of daily taunts, harassment, and curses both inside and outside the school. They eventually graduate from a desegregated Little Rock High School.

In December, Rev. Dr. Martin Luther King Jr. receives the National Association for the Advancement of Colored People (NAACP) Spingarn Medal for his leadership in the Montgomery bus boycott.

CRIM. On September 9, a new Nashville, Tennessee, school is destroyed by a bomb blast after its student body of 388 white students is integrated with one African American student.

LAW. On August 26, the U.S. Congress enacts the first major legislation against segregation since the end of Reconstruction in 1877 by approving the Civil Rights Act of 1957. The bill establishes a civil rights commission and a civil rights division of the Justice Department that is empowered to investigate civil rights infractions. Its enforcement powers are, however, limited.

An African American high school girl being educated via television during the period that the Little Rock, Arkansas schools were closed to avoid integration. Courtesy of Library of Congress.

City, Oklahoma, began a series of lunch counter sit-ins as a protest against segregated restaurants. The purpose of sit-in demonstrations is to make it difficult for segregated restaurants or businesses of any kind to function while demonstrators occupy the establishments. Though conceptualized as a form of peaceful protest, sit-in demonstrations quickly evolve into violent confrontations as violent prosegregationist mobs attempt to violently remove the demonstrators.

On October 25, baseball star Jackie Robinson, singer Harry Belafonte, and civil rights leader A. Philip Randolph lead 10,000 youths in a march for integrated schools in Washington, DC.

In October, Daisy Bates, the president of the Arkansas chapter of the NAACP, and nine of the students who integrated Little Rock, Arkansas's, Central High School are awarded the NAACP Spingarn Medal for their courage and leadership in the civil rights struggle.

CRIM. On September 20, a mentally disturbed woman stabs Rev. Dr. Martin Luther King Jr. in the chest while he is autographing a book in a Harlem department store.

EDUC. On May 27, African American Ernest Green is graduated from Little Rock, Arkansas's, Central High School with 600 white classmates.

LAW. On May 8, President Dwight Eisenhower orders the removal of federalized Arkansas National Guardsmen from Central High School in Little Rock, Arkansas.

MED. The Columbia Broadcasting System (CBS) airs reporter Mike Wallace's and Louis Lomax's five-part documentary *The Hate that Hate*

New York City becomes the first city to develop legislation against racial and religious discrimination in the housing market by adopting the Fair Housing Practice Law on December 5.

SPOR. On July 6, Althea Gibson is the first African American to win the women's single's tennis title at the Wilmington Championships in England.

Charles Sifford is the first African American to win a major professional golf tournament, the Long Beach Open.

1958

ARTS. Choreographer and dancer Alvin Ailey establishes in New York City the Alvin Ailey Dance Theater, which becomes world renowned.

CIVI. From May 12 to 13, civil rights leaders hold the Summit Meeting of National Negro Leaders to develop a campaign against discrimination. At the conference, President Dwight Eisenhower is severely criticized for a speech in which he asks civil rights leaders for patience in seeking full citizenship rights.

On August 19, members of the National Association for the Advancement of Colored People (NAACP) youth chapter in Oklahoma

Produced. This series gives Elijah Muhammad, the founder of the Nation of Islam, and its major minister, Malcolm X, national exposure.

OBIT. On April 10, noted musician and composer W. C. Handy dies in New York City at the age of 84.

POLI. On February 5, career diplomat Clifton R. Wharton Sr. is appointed minister to Romania. He is the first African American ambassador to head a U.S. embassy in Europe.

1959

ARTS. Singer Ray Charles has his first million-seller hit single, "What I'd Say."

Lorraine Hansberry's drama *A Raisin in the Sun* makes it debut on March 11 as the first Broadway play by an African American woman. It is also the first Broadway play in the modern era to have an African American director, Lloyd Richards.

In December, composer, pianist, and jazz pioneer Edward Kennedy "Duke" Ellington is awarded the National Association for the Advancement of Colored People (NAACP) Spingarn Medal for his contributions to the arts.

In December, Berry Gordy Jr. establishes Motown Records in Detroit, Michigan. Starting as a by-the-bootstraps business, Motown produces musical stars Diana Ross and Mary Wells.

CRIM. On April 27, an African American youth, Mack Charles Parker, is forcibly removed from jail by a mob of whites in Popularville, Mississippi, and lynched.

EDUC. In Prince Edward County, Virginia, the board of supervisors abandons its school system in an attempt to stop racial integration.

MILI. On May 22, Brig. Gen. Benjamin O. Davis Jr. is promoted to major general.

OBIT. On July 17, blues singer Billie Holiday dies at the age of 44 in New York City. She is best remembered for her rendition of a song that addresses the lynching of African Americans, "Strange Fruit."

1960

ARTS. Lorraine Hansberry's play *A Raisin in the Sun,* the first play by an African American woman to be produced on Broadway, becomes the first play by a black writer to win the New York Drama Critics' Circle Award.

ASSO. On August 1, Whitney Young Jr. is named the executive director of the National Urban League.

CENS. The United States population is 179,323,175, of which 18,871,831 (10.5%) are African Americans.

CIVI. On February 1, four freshman at North Carolina A&T College—Ezell Blair Jr., Joseph McNeil, Francis McCain, and David Richmond—stage a lunch-counter sit-in at a Woolworth's five-and-dime store in Greensboro, North Carolina. Though this is not the first sit-in demonstration in the South at segregated facilities, it triggers a series of similar actions mainly by college students throughout the South.

A sit-in in Chattanooga, Tennessee, on February 23 results in a race riot as mobs of whites attack African American demonstrators.

On February 25, students at Alabama State University stage a sit-in at the Montgomery state courthouse.

On March 15, two students from Atlanta University—Julian Bond and Lonnie King—develop a plan to deploy 200 students to 10 different eating establishments in Atlanta, Georgia. They target government-owned property and public places, including bus terminals and train stations and the state capital. At the federal building, Julian and his classmates are arrested after they attempt to eat in the municipal cafeteria. Hours later, they are released; however, the point of being arrested becomes a badge of honor for sit-in demonstrators as similar actions occur around the state. On September 27, Atlanta desegregates its municipal facilities.

On March 16, for the first time, lunch counters in a major southern city—San Antonio, Texas—are integrated after considerable pressure from local civil rights groups.

From April 15 to 17, delegates representing more than 50 colleges and 37 high schools meet at Shaw University in Raleigh, North Carolina, under the tutelage of Ella Baker, a Shaw alumna, to discuss and determine how the struggle against racism and segregation can be intensified. Baker addresses the students in a speech entitled "More than a Hamburger" in which she articulates a new set of goals and strategies for the civil rights campaigns. While maintaining a nonviolent approach to social change, Baker emphasizes the need for greater militancy beyond what many Southern Christian Leadership Conference (SCLC) leaders are willing to advocate for fear of upsetting sensitive racial relations. The name of the new organizations started by Baker is the Student Non-Violent Coordinating Committee (SNCC).

Rev. Martin Luther King Jr. is arrested on October 19 in Atlanta during a sit-in demonstration and is ordered by the court to serve four months in the Georgia state prison system due to a violated probated traffic sentence. King is released on October 26 from the Reidsville, Georgia, state prison after President John F. Kennedy expresses public concern for King's safety.

CRIM. One hundred fifty students are arrested in sit-in demonstrations in Nashville, Tennessee, after a bomb destroys the home of civil rights attorney Z. Alexander Looby. As a result, some 2,000 demonstrators march on city hall in protest.

On August 27, after 10 days of continual sit-in demonstrations in Jacksonville, Florida, a major race riot erupts in which 50 people are reported injured.

LIT. In December, noted author and poet laureate Langston Hughes receives the National Association for the Advancement of Colored People (NAACP) Spingarn Medal and is cited as "the poet laureate of the Negro race."

MED. On November 10, Andrew Hatcher is named associate press secretary to President John F. Kennedy.

OBIT. On November 28, the noted author of *Native Son,* Richard Wright, dies in Paris, France, at the age of 52. Wright's timeless novel examines the impact of racism on the human personality

and more significantly racism's influence on the collective conscious and unconscious mind of Americans.

RELI. On July 31, Elijah Muhammad, the leader of the Nation of Islam, calls for the creation of a black state within the United States.

1961

ARTS. On January 29, renowned opera singer Leontyne Price makes her debut at the Metropolitan Opera in New York City.

On September 28, *Purlie Victorious,* a play by noted actor Ossie Davis, opens on Broadway.

ASSO. On September 21, the Southern Regional Council (SRC) announces that the sit-in movement affected 20 states and more than 100 cities in southern and border states from February 1960 to September 1961. At least 70,000 blacks and whites are involved with and participate in the movement, an estimated 3,600 protestors are arrested, some 141 students are expelled from school, and 58 faculty members are fired by school authorities. The SRC concludes that one or more institutions or establishments in 108 southern cities and border states are desegregated as a result of the sit-in movement.

On September 22, the Interstate Commerce Commission (ICC) issues specific regulations that prohibited segregation on interstate buses and in terminal facilities.

CIVI. On May 4, 13 Freedom Riders organized by James Farmer's Congress of Racial Equality (CORE) begin a bus trip through the South that tests the Justice Departments willingness to protect the rights of African Americans to use bus terminal facilities on a nonsegregated basis. The first Freedom Riders run into trouble in Rock Hill, South Carolina, when John Lewis, one of the seven African American riders, attempts to use the white waiting room at the Greyhound terminal. He is brutally beaten by a white mob in full view and with no interference of the local police. The interracial Freedom Riders proceed southward through Alabama toward Mississippi. At Anniston, Alabama, however, the bus is firebombed, and the escaping passengers are beaten by waiting mobs of whites. With no police protection, CORE decides to abandon the rides; however, Student Non-Violent Coordinating Committee (SNCC) activists in Nashville, Tennessee, refuse to abandon the challenge, and on May 20, vow to continue the Freedom Rides to Montgomery, Alabama. With John Lewis remaining with the group, the buses arrive in Montgomery with 1,000 prosegregationist whites waiting with chains, ax handles, and knives. Lewis is knocked unconscious and others brutally beaten as the police watch. Even a presidential aide sent to observe the rides is injured. Attorney General Robert Kennedy sends 400 U.S. marshals to restore order. At this point, Rev. Martin Luther King Jr. and Rev. Ralph Abernathy join the conflict by holding a strategy meeting at Abernathy's church, at which 1,200 people attend. With the possibility of further massive violence in Montgomery, Alabama, Governor John Patterson orders the National Guard and state troopers to protect the protestors. When the Freedom Riders arrive in Jackson, Mississippi, they are arrested by waiting police and placed in Mississippi's notorious prison system.

On May 26, the Freedom Ride Coordinating Committee is established in Atlanta, Georgia.

On December 12, more than 700 demonstrators, including Rev. Martin Luther King Jr., are arrested in Albany, Georgia, after conducting five antisegregation marches to city hall. These arrests intensify the demonstrations.

In Baton Rouge, Louisiana, the police use leashed dogs and tear gas to stop mass demonstrations against segregation by 1,500 African Americans on December 15.

In December, renowned psychologist and educator Dr. Kenneth B. Clark receives the National Association for the Advancement of Colored People (NAACP) Spingarn Medal for pioneering studies that influenced the U.S. Supreme Court decision on school segregation.

EDUC. Two African American students, Charlayne Hunter and Hamilton Holmes, are prohibited from integrating the University of Georgia when their applications are suspended. A federal court orders the applications reinstated on January 11. Throughout this process, white

prosegregationist students and supporters riot. Classes resume on January 16.

On February 6, student members of SNCC in Rock Hill, South Carolina, refuse to pay fines after they are arrested for being sit-in demonstrators. This tactic, known as a "jail-in" or, more appropriately, "jail, no bail," is aimed at filling the jails with demonstrators, thereby financially forcing the county to feed and adjudicate protestors. For many southern states and counties, this tactic by the SNCC places a prohibitive financial burden on the state, thereby making segregation a burden.

LAW. On September 22, President John F. Kennedy names Thurgood Marshall to the U.S. Circuit Court of Appeals.

POLI. Congressman Adam Clayton Powell Jr. is elected chairman of the U.S. House Education and Labor Committee on January 3. Powell, whose father is minister of the Abyssinian Baptist Church in Harlem (of which Powell Jr. also serves as minister), received a master's degree in religious education from Columbia University in 1931. In 1937, he succeeded his father as minister of the Abyssinian Baptist Church and was elected to the New York city council in 1941 as the first African American council representative. In 1945, he was elected as a Democrat to the U.S. House of Representatives from the twenty-second congressional district, which includes Harlem, making him the first African American representative from New York. As one of only two black congressmen, Powell challenged the de facto segregation ban on African Americans using the Capitol's facilities, which were reserved only for members. He took visiting African American constituents to dine with him in the "whites only" House restaurant, actions that caused conflict between him and segregationists in his political party. In 1956, he supported Republican President Dwight Eisenhower for reelection, stating that the Democratic Party's civil right's platform was too weak. In 1958, he defeated efforts by New York Tammany Hall politicians to oust him from office. In 1960, Powell forced civil rights leader Bayard Rustin to resign from the Southern Christian Leadership Conference (SCLC) by threatening to discuss Rustin's morals charge in Congress. This year, Powell becomes the chairman of the powerful Education and Labor Committee. In this position, he presides over federal programs, minimum-wage increases, education and training for the deaf, vocational training, standards for wages and work hours, as well as aid to elementary and secondary education.

On February 11, Robert Weaver is sworn in as the government's director of the Housing and Home Finance Agency. This is the highest federal office held by an African American to this date.

On March 9, Clifton R. Wharton is sworn in as U.S. ambassador to Norway.

SPOR. Ernest Davis wins the Heisman Trophy for college football player of the year. He is the first African American to win the coveted award.

1962

CIVI. On August 1, Fannie Lou Hamer attempts to register to vote in Indianola, Mississippi. As a result, she is fired from her plantation job and she and her family are evicted from their land. Years later, when asked what provokes her to attempt to vote, she states that when Student Non-Violent Coordinating Committee (SNCC) workers came to her community to get African Americans to start a voting campaign, she is one of the first to volunteer. Fannie Lou Hamer becomes field secretary for the SNCC's Voter Education Project in Mississippi. On June 9, 1963, she and eight other women returning from a workshop in South Carolina are stopped and arrested by police in Winona, Mississippi. A black deputy sheriff following the orders of the white sheriff beats Hamer. She never fully recovers from her injuries.

On June 26, sit-in demonstrations and passive resistance begin in Cairo, Illinois, at segregated swimming pools, skating rinks, and other facilities for several months.

From July 10 to 21, more than 1,000 civil rights demonstrators in Albany, Georgia, are jailed after protesting at segregated businesses and public facilities. On the August 27 and 28, Martin Luther King Jr. and 75 other ministers and laymen, black and white, are arrested in Albany, Georgia, after a prayer demonstration against segregation.

CRIM. On September 9, two African American churches are burned to the ground near Sasser, Georgia. African American leaders ask President John F. Kennedy to halt the "Nazi-like reign of terror in southwest Georgia."

On September 11, two African American youths involved in a voter registration drive in Mississippi are wounded by a shotgun blast from the window of a home in Ruleville, Mississippi.

On September 17, four African American churches are burned to the ground in Dawson, Georgia. Three white males admit to torching the buildings. They are sentenced to seven years in prison.

EDUC. On January 16, a suit accusing the New York City Board of Education of using racial quotas to satisfy integration mandates is filed in the U.S. District Court on behalf of African American and Puerto Rican children.

On May 10, the *Southern School News* reports that 246,988 (7.6%) of the African American students in public schools in 17 southern and

---

Of the Student Non-Violent Coordinating Committee's (SNCC's) effect on her decision to attempt to register to vote, Fannie Lou Hamer states:

Nobody ever came out into the country and talked to real farmers and things because this is the next thing this country has done: it divided us into classes, and if you hadn't arrived at a certain level, you wasn't treated no better by blacks than you was by the whites. And it was these kids who broke a lot of that down. They treated us like we were special and we loved 'em…. We didn't feel uneasy about our language might not be right or something. We just felt we could talk to 'em.

border states and Washington, DC, attend integrated schools.

On May 28, a suit charging de facto racial segregation in Rochester, New York, public schools is filed by a chapter of the National Association for the Advancement of Colored People (NAACP) in New York.

On September 10, Supreme Court Justice Hugo Black vacates a lower court order and rules that the University of Mississippi must accept James H. Meredith's, an African American air force veteran, application to the university. When it becomes clear that the state of Mississippi will not respect the court-ordered integration or maintain law and order, President John F. Kennedy sends federal marshals to Mississippi and later federalizes the Mississippi National Guard. In the ensuing riots at the university, at least two people are killed and many injured.

On September 13, the governor of Mississippi, Ross R. Barnett, defies the federal court-ordered integration of the University of Mississippi and claims that he would rather go to jail than submit to such an order.

On September 20, Governor Ross Barnett personally denies James H. Meredith admission to the University of Mississippi. Four days later, on September 24, the U.S. Circuit Court of Appeals orders the Board of Higher Education of Mississippi to admit James Meredith to the university or be held in contempt. Governor Barnett again refuses to honor the federal court demand.

From September 28 to October 1, Governor Barnett is found guilty of civil contempt of the federal court order and must terminate his resistance or face arrest and a $10,000 fine for every day he is in contempt. Similarly, Mississippi Lt. Gov. Paul Johnson is also found guilty of civil contempt. On September 30, a large force of federal marshals escort Meredith into the University of Mississippi, and President Kennedy federalizes the Mississippi National Guard and white Mississippians are urged to obey the law and accept the decision of the federal court. A two-day riot ensues with gunfire and homemade bombs thrown at the marshals. Only with the arrival of 12,000 federal soldiers does the rioting stop. Paul Guihard, a European reporter, is killed in the rioting. In the midst of the armed resistance by white Mississippians is former U.S. Army Maj. Gen. Edwin A. Walker, who is arrested and charged with inciting insurrection and seditious conspiracy. Walker, who led federal troops during the Little Rock, Arkansas, integration crisis, calls for volunteers to oppose federal forces in Mississippi. Witnesses allege he leads students in charges against federal marshals during the campus riots. James Meredith registers at the University of Mississippi on October 1.

HOUS. Demonstrations against racial discrimination in housing for students attending the University of Chicago are staged from January 23 to February 5. The Congress of Racial Equality (CORE) charges the university with blatant racial bias and segregation in its off-campus student housing program.

On November 20, President John F. Kennedy issues an executive order

James Meredith walking to class accompanied by U.S. Marshals, October 1, 1962. Courtesy of Library of Congress.

barring racial discrimination in federally financed housing.

In November, economist and government official Robert C. Weaver receives the NAACP Spingarn Medal for his leadership in the movement for open housing.

MILI. On January 31, the U.S. Navy announces that Lt. Cdr. Samuel L. Gravely has assumed command of the destroyer escort USS *Falgout*. As such, he is the first African American to command a U.S. Navy warship.

RELI. On April 16, Archbishop Joseph Rumble excommunicates Louisiana segregationists for refusing to follow his order to desegregate all parochial schools under his jurisdiction.

SPOR. John "Buck" O'Neil becomes the first African American to coach a major league baseball team, the Chicago Cubs.

On February 22, Wilt Chamberlain sets a National Basketball Association (NBA) record of 34 successful free throws. On March 2, Chamberlain scores 100 points for the Philadelphia Warriors against the New York Knicks.

On July 3, Jackie Robinson, the first African American major league baseball player, is named to the Baseball Hall of Fame in Cooperstown, New York.

1963

CIVI. The Southern Christian Leadership Conference (SCLC) under the direction of Rev. Martin Luther King Jr. begins an antisegregation campaign in Birmingham, Alabama, on April 3. A series of demonstrations, some ending in police violence, continue into May and mark the centennial anniversary of the Emancipation Proclamation. Other civil rights organizations in Birmingham come into direct confrontation with Ku Klux Klan chapters, including the Alabama Christian Movement for Human Rights (ACMHR) led by Rev. Fred L. Shuttlesworth. The organizations code-name their antisegregation efforts Project C for Confrontation, and they address segregation at almost every single level of the city's social structure by utilizing both the adult and younger African American populace. Confronting the demonstrators is Public Safety Commissioner T. Eugene "Bull" Connor, who has a reputation for viciousness. Demonstrators utilize sit-in tactics and direct marches throughout the city, and some civil rights activists believe that Bull Connor will be goaded into using a level of violence against the demonstrators that will shock the nation and compel President John F. Kennedy to invoke federal mandates against recalcitrant segregationists in Alabama. On April 12, Good Friday, Rev. Martin Luther King Jr., Rev. Ralph Abernathy, and others are arrested and jailed. While in jail, King receives a series of letters from both Christian and Jewish religious leaders who complain that the tactics used in Birmingham are doing more harm than good for African Americans. In response, King writes a "Letter from Birmingham Jail" in which he derides those who ask the victims of persecution and racism to wait for a better day to protest.

At this stage of the struggle, Rev. James Bevel suggests that schoolchildren should be used to continue the demonstrations. Though many disagree, King and others prevail by arguing that the children must learn how to fight and struggle

---

In "Letter from Birmingham Jail," Martin Luther King Jr. writes:

I guess it is easy for those who have never felt the stinging darts of segregation to say, "wait…. Freedom is never voluntarily given by the oppressor; it must be demanded by the oppressed … nonviolent direct action seeks to create such a crisis and foster such a tension that a community which has constantly refused to negotiate is forced to confront the issue. It seeks so to dramatize the issue that it can no longer be ignored … any law that degrades human personality is unjust. All segregation statutes are unjust because segregation distorts the soul and damages the personality. It gives the segregator a false sense of superiority and the segregated a false sense of inferiority."

for their own freedom and future. On May 2 and 3, a children's crusade is launched in which thousands of African American youth, some as young as six years old, march in Birmingham and soon are confronted by police dogs, fire-fighters using high-powered hoses that rip the skin, police flaying with their nightsticks, and arrest. In the ensuing encounter, all of which is recorded by reporters and news media crews, the children fight back by hurling bottles and rocks. The intensity of the confrontation and brutality unleashed by Bull Connor concerns many white businessmen, who fear further escalation will radicalize the African American community into open, armed confrontation with whites, and they pressure city officials to find a way to the bargaining table.

On May 10, white businessmen agree to inte-grate downtown Birmingham, Alabama, and employ African Americans. The following night, Ku Klux Klan elements bomb the Gaston Hotel, the headquarters of the SCLC during the demon-strations, and dynamite the home of King's brother, Rev. A. D. King. In response, the black commu-nity burns cars and buildings and fires upon police. Only King's personal intervention stops the esca-lating violence. Though the SCLC does not gain everything it demands, Birmingham establishes a point of balance between the contending forces of segregation and desegregation.

On June 11, two African American students are escorted by federalized National Guard troops into the University of Alabama, despite the objections of Gov. George Wallace.

On August 27, the largest civil rights demonstration in history is held in Washington, DC. It is billed as the March on Washington, and an estimated 250,000 people attend, representing a variety of organizations and civil rights issues. At this march, Dr. King delivers his famous "I Have a Dream" speech in front of the Lincoln Memorial.

On October 22, 225,000 students boycott Chicago schools in a Freedom Day protest against de facto segregation.

In December, the National Association for the

Civil rights march on Washington, DC, 1963. A procession of African Americans carry signs for equal rights, inte-grated schools, decent housing, and an end to bias. Courtesy of Library of Congress.

Advancement of Colored People (NAACP) posthumously awards civil rights activist and president of the Jackson, Mississippi, chapter of the NAACP Medgar Wiley Evers the Spingarn Medal for his civil rights leadership.

CRIM. On April 23, William Lewis Moore is killed in Attalla, Alabama, during his one-man march against segregation.

On June 12, white segregationist Byron de la Beckwith murders Medgar Wiley Evers, age 37, the executive secretary of the NAACP chapter in Jackson, Mississippi. When Evers returns to his home at night, Beckwith, hiding in a bush 150 feet away, shoots Evers from behind in his driveway.

Four African American girls—Addie Mae Collins, Denise McNair, Carole Robertson, and Cynthia Wesley—are killed on September 15 when a bomb explodes inside the Sixteenth Street Baptist Church in Birmingham, Alabama.

On the same day as the bombing of the Sixteenth Street Baptist Church and the killing of the four girls, September 15, Virgin Lamar Ware is killed during a violent racist attack in Birmingham, Alabama.

After the assassination of John F. Kennedy on November 22, Malcolm X of the Nation of Islam characterizes the assassination as a "case of chickens coming home to roost," implying that it is an example of the kind of violence white Americans have traditionally used against African Americans. Malcolm X is eventually suspended from the Nation of Islam.

EDUC. On August 18, James Meredith becomes the first African American to graduate from the University of Mississippi.

OBIT. On August 27, scholar, protest leader, and a founding member of the NAACP, W.E.B. Du Bois dies in Accra, Ghana, at the age of 95.

POLI. On March 9, Carl T. Rowan is named ambassador to Finland.

SCIE. On March 30, U.S. Air Force Capt. Edward J. Dwight Jr. is selected for the fourth class of aerospace research pilots at Edwards Air Base and becomes the first African American astronaut candidate. He is dropped from the program in 1965.

SPOR. On July 22, Floyd Patterson loses his world heavyweight boxing championship to Sonny Liston.

WORK. On June 12 and 13, civil rights groups demonstrate at a Harlem, New York, site to protest discrimination in the building trades. Demonstrations continue throughout the summer and tie to issues relating to discrimination in housing, schools, and jobs.

1964

ARTS. On April 13, actor Sidney Poitier is awarded an Academy Award for best actor for his performance in *Lilies of the Field.*

ASSO. On June 28, Malcolm X founds the Organization of African American Unity (OAAU) in New York City.

BUSI. In December, the Independence Bank of Chicago is organized.

CIVI. In August, the Mississippi Democratic Freedom Party (MFDP) started by Fannie Lou Hamer organizes a caravan of cars to bring African American delegates from Mississippi to Atlantic City, New Jersey, to challenge the all-white Mississippi Democratic Party at the Democratic Party's national convention. The MFDP delegates are selected on August 6 under the leadership of Hamer and Victoria Gray, Annie Divine, and Aaron Henry at the MFDP's first state convention. Approximately 80,000 people put their names on the rolls. The 64 selected arrive in Atlantic City at the national convention to present their credentials. Many white liberals want to seat the MFDP delegates; however, President Lyndon Johnson, who is running for election, does not want to upset his southern white supporters, fearing that they will vote for Senator Barry Goldwater, his Republican opponent. In the midst of this confusion, Hamer is allowed to present the MFDP challenge to the Credentials Committee in a televised proceeding that reaches millions of viewers. She tells the committee and the nation how African Americans in many states across the country are prevented from voting through illegal tests, excessive taxation, and intimidation. Interestingly, her presentation further upset liberals, some of whom are black and fear a white backlash. Liberal white Senator Hubert Humphrey of Minnesota works out a compromise with the black MFDP challengers, agreeing that if loyalty is sworn by all delegates to the national party, two MFDP members will be given seats at this convention and the rest of the delegation can attend the convention as nonvoting guests. Most MFDP delegates, however, reject the token compromise. The duplicity of the Democratic Party causes many Student Non-Violent Coordinating Committee (SNCC) members to become more distrusting of liberal whites in the Democratic Party.

On December 10, the Noble Peace Prize is presented to Dr. Martin Luther King Jr. in Oslo, Norway. He is the third African American and the youngest person to receive the award.

In December, the executive secretary of the National Association for the Advancement of Colored People (NAACP), Roy Wilkins, receives the NAACP Spingarn Medal for "the advancement of the American people and the national purpose."

CRIM. From July 18 to 22, civil disobedience occurs in Harlem as well as in the Bedford Stuyvesant Section of Brooklyn, New York. Though heightening economic problems and a growing class of urban poor, known as the underclass, raise social tensions and conflicts with local police, an unwarranted shooting generally supplies the spark for explosive civil disobedience. In Harlem, the killing of a 15-year-old youth by an off-duty police officer quickly becomes a generalized rebellion against urban conditions. The use of Molotov cocktails (bottles filled with gasoline with a rag for a wick) symbolizes a new era of social conflict.

On July 25, a race riot explodes in Rochester, New York, and forces Gov. Nelson Rockefeller to mobilize the National Guard.

From August 2 to 30, race riots erupt in Jersey City, New Jersey; Paterson, New Jersey; Elizabeth, New Jersey; Philadelphia, Pennsylvania; and Dixmoor, a suburb of Chicago, Illinois.

On August 4, the bodies of three civil rights workers, 21-year-old African American James Chaney and two whites, 24-year old Michael Schwerner and 21-year-old Andrew Goodman, are found on a farm near Philadelphia, Mississippi. Missing since June 21, the three are apparently murdered on the night of their disappearance. Schwerner and Goodman are shot to death, but Chaney is beaten first with iron chains and then shot to death. The facts of their murders are not revealed until a $30,000 reward is posted and a Ku Klux Klan informer comes forward with the details. They are working with a civil rights project entitled Mississippi Freedom Summer that is mandated to register African American voters. During the summer, approximately 30 homes and 37 churches are bombed, 35 civil rights workers are shot at, 80 people are beaten, 6 are murdered, and 1,000 are arrested. In the face of this miniwar, SNCC activists begin to reject Rev. Martin Luther King's commitment to nonviolence amid growing racist attacks and suggest that armed defense is appropriate in specific circumstances.

One Harlem female resident describes her reaction to the civil disobedience:

I clean the white man's dirt all the time, I work for four families and some I don't care for, and some I like. And Saturday I worked for some I like. And when I get home and later when the trouble began, something happened to me. I went on the roof to see what was going on. I don't know what it was, but hearing the guns I felt like something was crawling on me, like the whole damn world was no good, and the little kids and the big ones and all of us was going to get killed because we don't know what to do. And I see the cops are white and I was crying. Dear God, I am crying! And I took this pop bottle and it was empty and I threw it down on the cops, and I was crying and laughing.

On August 26, major racial clashes occur in St. Augustine, Florida, as the civil rights campaign begins to confront segregation throughout Florida.

EDUC. Boycotts by schoolchildren around the country demonstrate their discomfort with racist educational policies. On February 3, New York City Public School officials report that 464,000 African American and Puerto Rican students boycott classes. On March 16, a second boycott results in 267,000 absentees from class. On February 25, 172,000 students boycott Chicago schools. On April 20, school officials in Cleveland, Ohio, report that 86 percent of the African American students participate in the one-day boycott against racist school policies such as a lack of cultural and political information relevant to the African American experience.

LAW. The Twenty-Fourth Amendment to the U.S. Constitution eliminates the poll tax requirement in federal elections. Historically, the poll tax is a criterion for voting; those who cannot afford the tax are automatically eliminated from the voting rolls. It is an effective device to eliminate the poorer, southern Africa American populous from voting.

On August 20, President Lyndon Johnson signs the Economic Opportunity Act.

POLI. On January 21, Carl T. Rowan is named director of the United States Information Agency.

On November 3, John Conyers Jr. is elected to the U.S. House of Representatives from Detroit, Michigan.

On December 3, J. Raymond Jones is elected leader of the New York Democratic organization known as Tammany Hall.

RELI. Minister Malcolm X resigns from the Nation of Islam on March 12. After months of debate regarding his role in the Nation of Islam and his comments referring to the assassination of President John F. Kennedy in November 1963 as a case of the "chickens coming home to roost," Elijah Muhammad, after suspending Malcolm X from the Nation, receives his resignation. Malcolm later claims that he left the religious organization after he obtained information about Elijah Muhammad's sexual indiscretions with his female secretary.

SPOR. On February 3, Cassius Clay defeats Sonny Liston for the heavyweight boxing championship. Clay becomes a member of the Nation of Islam and changes his name to Muhammad Ali.

1965

ARTS. In December, soprano singer Leontyne Price receives the National Association for the Advancement of Colored People (NAACP) Spingarn Medal for being "the outstanding soprano of our era."

BUSI. In December, African American–owned Seaway National Bank in Chicago is founded.

CIVI. On January 2, Rev. Martin Luther King Jr. starts a voter registration campaign in Selma, Alabama.

From March 7 to 25, some 600 civil rights marchers led by the

Martin Luther King and Malcolm X waiting for a press conference, 1964. Courtesy of Library of Congress.

Southern Christian Leadership Conference (SCLC) and Student Non-Violent Coordinating Committee (SNCC) propose a voter-rights march from Selma to the state capital of Alabama, Montgomery. As they approach the Edmund Pettish Bridge outside Selma, state troopers and county police, under the control of Sheriff James G. Clark, attack them. Many claim that Clark competes with Commissioner Bull Connor of Birmingham in racist brutality. Police on horses trample the civil rights marchers then teargas and beat them with clubs. Captured by television news crews and other media, the incident provides the marchers with national support, and leaders Rev. Martin Luther King Jr., Hosea Williams, and SNCC Chairman John Lewis reschedule another march for March 9. After the clash at the bridge, however, a federal judge issues a court injunction against the march to Selma. On the day of the march, nearly 1,500 protestors approach the bridge singing freedom songs. Reverend King and the leadership, with the exception of SNCC, find themselves in a dilemma. They want federal support, particularly from President Lyndon Johnson, for civil rights laws in support of voter registration drives throughout the South. To violate the court-ordered injunction will allow President Johnson to escape a responsibility to the civil rights movement; not to cross the bridge will jeopardize his credibility. Reverend King decides to cross the Pettus Bridge with other marchers; however, once across he stops, prays briefly, and turns around. The shock of not going farther infuriates groups such as the SNCC, who see King as betraying the cause. For the moment, the march is canceled. Later that evening, a white Unitarian minister from Boston, James Reeb, is clubbed to death by local whites. His murder and martyrdom cause a national outcry from liberal whites that forces President Johnson to act on behalf of the civil rights marchers. On March 15, President Johnson announces that he will submit voter-registration legislation to Congress. He also uses a rallying cry familiar to southern civil rights workers and first used by Reverend King in his 1963 March on Washington: "We shall overcome." On March 21, thousands of marchers and protestors led by Reverend King and protected by federalized Alabama National Guardsmen and U.S. Army soldiers begin the first leg of a march from Selma to Montgomery, Alabama. On March

25, the marchers enter the state capital of Montgomery, Alabama, and hold a rally attended by some 50,000 people.

On July 8, Roy Wilkins becomes the executive director of the NAACP.

On December 25, the national director of the Congress of Racial Equality (CORE), James Farmer, announces that he will resign from the position on March 1, 1966.

CRIM. On February 21, Muslim leader and civil and human rights activist El Hajj Malik El Shabazz, known as Malcolm X, is assassinated at the age of 39 at a meeting of his organization, the Organization of African American Unity (OAAU), at the Audubon Ballroom in New York City. Three blacks are later arrested, convicted of the crime, and sentenced to life imprisonment.

On February 26, civil rights activist Jimmie Lee Jackson dies at the age of 26 as the result of injuries suffered from being shot in the stomach by police officers in Marion, Alabama. Lee is involved in a civil rights night march well covered by the media when the marchers are attacked by police and state troopers. While attempting to shield his mother from a beating by a state trooper, Jackson is shot. The police also beat several reporters.

On March 25, civil rights worker and marcher from Selma to Montgomery, Alabama, Viola Liuzzo is shot to death by white terrorists on U.S. Highway 80 after the rally in the state capital. Three Klansmen are convicted of violating her civil rights and sentenced to 10 years in prison.

On June 2, African American Deputy Oneal Moore is killed by night riders in Varnado, Louisiana.

On July 18, African American Willie Wallace Brewster is killed by night riders in Anniston, Alabama.

From August 11 to 17, African American residents in the Watts section of Los Angeles, California, riot and destroy more than $35 million in property. Though the violence is provoked by a police stop of a driver suspected of drunk driving, deeper causes exist regarding the high level of unemployment, overcrowding in housing, poor health care facilities, inadequate public transportation, rising crime levels, and drug addiction. Residents' annoyance with police brutality provide the spark for what some call an urban rebellion or insurrection. In the midst of the disturbance, residents are heard to proclaim, "Burn baby burn" in reference to burning buildings and homes. This exclamation becomes a metaphor for urban disturbances across the country. Though Gov. Pat Brown calls out the National Guard to restore order, armed confrontations between the residents and the National Guard do not subside until, as one observer notes, Watts resembled "Germany at the end of World War II." Thirty-four people are killed, 900 injured, and more than 4,000 arrested.

On August 20, African American seminary student Jonathan Daniels is killed by a police deputy in Hayneville, Alabama.

CULT. In October, Maulena Karenga founds the United Slaves (US) organization in Los Angeles, California. A strong advocate of cultural nationalism, he founds the African American cultural festival of Kwanzaa, celebrated every year from December 26 to January 1. Each of the seven days represents a specific cultural, political, or economic value.

EDUC. Vivian Malone graduates from the University of Alabama on May 30. She is the first African American to do so.

LAW. On August 6, spurred by civil rights agitation and violence throughout the South, the U.S. Congress passes the Voters Rights Act of 1965. The act outlaws educational requirements for voting in states where half the voting-age population has been registered on November 1, 1964, or has voted in the 1964 election. It also empowers the attorney general to direct the Civil Rights Commission to assign federal registrars to enroll voters. Within months, some new 80,000 voters are registered. In Mississippi, voter registrants increase from 28,500 in 1964 to 251,00 in 1968.

On August 11, the U.S. Senate confirms Thurgood Marshall as the first African American U.S. solicitor general.

LIT. Alex Haley's *Autobiography of Malcolm X* becomes a major best seller.

MED. Bill Cosby is the first African American to star on a network television show, *I Spy.*

MILI. On April 16, U.S. Air Force Assistant Deputy Chief of Staff Gen. Benjamin O. Davis Jr. is promoted to lieutenant general, the highest rank attained to date by an African American in the armed forces.

OBIT. On January 12, noted playwright Lorraine Hansberry dies in New York City at the age of 34.

On February 15, singer and pianist Nat King Cole dies at the age of 45 in Santa Monica, California.

POLI. On May 19, Patricia R. Harris is named U.S. ambassador to Luxembourg. She is the first African American female ambassador.

1966

ASSO. On October 30, Huey Percy Newton and Bobby Seale found the Black Panther Party for Self Defense in Oakland, California. The organization's name is derived from an earlier Alabama civil rights organization, the Lowndes County Freedom Organization, and their political symbol, the black panther. Both Newton and Seale believe that self-defense is a prerequisite for survival within an aggressive society premised upon racism. In this regard, they develop a political program that fashions itself as a revolutionary vanguard.

CDIS. On July 5, the Oklahoma National Guard is mobilized for duty in Omaha, Oklahoma, after three nights of civil disobedience and rioting.

The Illinois National Guard is mobilized for duty in Chicago from July 12 to 15 after three days of civil disobedience and rioting.

On July 19, Ohio Gov. James A. Rhodes declares a state of emergency in Cleveland and mobilizes the National Guard to patrol the heavily African American Hough area of the city after growing violence between the police and residents.

On August 5, during a civil rights march, white residents in a Chicago, Illinois, suburb stone Rev. Martin Luther King Jr. The Southern Christian Leadership Conference (SCLC), under King's leadership, moves its campaign to a northern urban area due to the racial economic policies of many northern cities containing millions of African Americans and poor people. In Chicago, the movement discovers: (1) Racial discrimination is not only a southern problem but also exists in the North to a level that equals if not surpasses that of the South; (2) racial hatred and bias is directly involved with the economic structure of many northern cities. As a result of the Chicago experience, Reverend King begins to devise a program for a Poor People's Campaign that will transcend racial, class, and political backgrounds. He perceives a national program that will address the systematic and inextricable problems within the country's political and economic structures.

On August 7, a racial disturbance erupts in Lansing, Michigan.

On August 27, a racial disturbance erupts in Waukegan, Illinois.

The Ohio National Guard is mobilized to stop rioting in Dayton, Ohio, from September 1 to 2.

On September 6, racial rioting in Atlanta, Georgia, erupts.

The California National Guard is mobilized from September 27 to 29 to quell civil disturbances in San Francisco.

CIVI. On January 3, civil rights activist and North Carolina attorney Floyd B. McKissick is named the new national director for the Congress of Racial Equality (CORE).

Rev. Martin Luther King Jr. opens the northern campaign for civil rights in Chicago, Illinois, on January 7.

On January 18, Robert C. Weaver is sworn in as secretary of Housing and Urban Development, making him the first African American Cabinet member.

On March 9, Andrew F. Brimmer becomes the first African American governor of the Federal Reserve Board.

On May 16, Stokely Carmichael is named chairman of the Student Non-Violent Coordinating Committee (SNCC).

From June 7 to 26, some 30,000 civil rights protestors vow to continue James Meredith's march from Memphis to Jackson, Mississippi. Led by Rev. Martin Luther King Jr. of the SCLC, Floyd McKissick of CORE, Stokely Carmichael of the SNCC, and other civil rights leaders, the march of thousands reaches Jackson, Mississippi, on June 26. The SNCC, in an attempt to galvanize support from thousands of local blacks with whom they interact during the march, comes up with the slogan "Black Power." Later, Carmichael

recalls that he and his colleagues decide to change the emphasis of their march from a compliant desire for "Freedom Now" to an immediate demand for "Black Power." Self-power, Carmichael notes, seems the most natural desire for any group, in this case, Black Power. This new rallying cry immediately changes the emphasis for many civil rights activists from "Freedom Now," emphasized by SCLC, to the more militant. Many civil rights leaders and activists within the movement, such as Roy Wilkins, Bayard Rustin, and Rev. Martin Luther King Jr., view this new slogan as too militant, implying violence, and antiwhite. This development is viewed as the beginning of the Black Power movement.

CRIM. On January 3, an African American student activist, Samuel Younge Jr., is killed in a dispute over a whites-only restroom in Tuskegee, Alabama.

On January 10, Vernon Dahmer, an African American community leader, is killed in a Ku Klux Klan bombing in Hattiesburg, Mississippi.

On June 6, civil rights activist and the first African American student to integrate the University of Mississippi James Meredith attempts to underscore the importance of African American voter registration by walking 220 miles from Memphis, Tennessee, to Jackson, Mississippi. Near Hernando, Mississippi, on Highway 50, he is shot and wounded by a sniper.

On June 10, the Ku Klux Klan in Natchez, Mississippi, kills African American Ben Chester White.

On July 30, African American civil rights worker Wharlest Jackson is killed when police fire on civil rights protestors in Jackson, Mississippi.

CULT. Amiri Baraka founds the Spirit House Movers and Players in Newark, New Jersey, and pursues a cultural nationalist political orientation.

LAW. Constance Baker Motley is confirmed as the first African American woman U.S. district judge on the federal bench.

MED. In November, John H. Johnson, publisher of *Ebony* and *Jet* magazines, receives the National Association for the Advancement of Colored People (NAACP) Spingarn Medal for contributions to the enhancement of the Negro's self-image.

POLI. On January 10, SNCC Communications Director Julian Bond, who is elected to the Georgia state legislature, is denied his seat due to his opposition to the involvement of the United States in the Vietnam War.

On April 13, Rev. Martin Luther King Jr. denounces the role of the United States in the Vietnam War, which he states is "rapidly degenerating into a sordid military adventure." At this time, African American soldiers make up nearly 10 percent of the armed forces, but the number increases as the war progresses.

On November 8, Edward W. Brooke, a Republican from Massachusetts, is elected to the U.S. Senate and thereby becomes the first African American to do so since the Reconstruction era and the first ever elected by popular vote.

SPOR. On April 11, Emmett Ashford is the first African American major league baseball umpire.

On April 18, famed Boston Celtic basketball player Bill Russell is named head coach of the team. He becomes the first African American coach to manage a predominantly white team in professional athletics.

WAR. The Medal of Honor is awarded posthumously on April 21 to Pfc. Milton Lee Olive Jr. for bravery in Vietnam. On October 22, 1965, 18-year-old Olive is on a search-and-destroy patrol with the 173rd Airborne Brigade when he jumps on a live hand grenade thrown by the enemy. Absorbing the grenade's blast, he saves the lives of other solders around him. Olive is the first African American enlisted man to receive the Medal of Honor in Vietnam.

In 1966, the U.S. Department of Defense initiates a program, called Project 100,000, to recruit African American males into the military. The project enables recruiters to enlist African Americans who otherwise do not qualify for the military because of criminal records or lack of skills. The project is so successful that it supplies some 340,000 recruits for the Vietnam War, of which 136, 000 (40%) are African Americans, who make 10 percent of the country's population. Most of these African American recruits are assigned directly to combat units.

1967

ARTS. Pearl Bailey becomes a headline star in the Broadway production of *Hello Dolly!*, which runs for two years in New York and them tours nationally.

ASSO. On May 12, H. Rap Brown replaces Stokely Carmichael as chairman of the Student Non-Violent Coordinating Committee (SNCC).

CDIS. From June 2 to 5, interracial conflict erupts in the Roxbury section of Boston, Massachusetts.

From June 11 to 13, interracial conflict and rioting in Tampa, Florida, forces the governor to mobilize the National Guard.

Interracial conflict in Cleveland, Ohio, occurs from June 12 to 15. The National Guard is mobilized, and nearly 300 people are arrested.

On June 20, an interracial rebellion erupts in Buffalo, New York. Two hundred people are arrested.

Violent urban civil disobedience erupts in Newark, New Jersey, from July 12 to 17. Twenty-three persons are killed, 1,500 people are injured, and nearly 1,300 are arrested in a 23-square-mile destruction zone. More than 300 separate fires are reported as the rioting spreads to other cities such as New Brunswick, Englewood, Paterson, Elizabeth, Palmyra, Passaic, and Plainfield. When mobilized, the National Guard comes under intense rifle fire from residents.

From July 17 to 30, urban civil disobedience occurs throughout the United States. Although each disturbance increasingly takes the profile of a rebellion by the poor underclass of society, the level of violence waged against civil authorities becomes increasingly sophisticated. With disturbances in Cairo, Illinois, on July 17; Durham, North Carolina, on July 19; Memphis, Tennessee, on July 20; Cambridge, Maryland, on July 24; and Milwaukee, Wisconsin, on July 30, it is the Detroit, Michigan, disturbances that bring the political and social conflicts of the United States to a head. On July 23, with 43 people already dead, federal troops come into Detroit to confront an armed population that cite their own poverty and experience in fighting racism abroad, in the military, and at home in Detroit as cause for civil disobedience. In Detroit, the triggering event is the raiding by police of an after-hours drinking establishment in the black community where a party for two returning Vietnam veterans is in progress. Police efforts to close the club is enough to start a seven-day rebellion that uncovers a deep and troubling undercurrent of anger and frustration by Detroit's African American residents. Of the 59 uprisings, Detroit's is the deadliest. Not only is the National Guard unable to quell the disturbance, but neither can the combined efforts of 200 state police and 600 Detroit police bring order to the streets. A reluctant President Lyndon Johnson sends troops of the 101st Airborne, many of whom have just retuned from combat in Vietnam, and the elite 82nd Airborne, who arrive with armored cars and tanks. A total of 4,700 soldiers are needed to patrol and quell the urban rebellion in Detroit. An embarrassed Michigan Gov. George Romney sums it up from his perspective when he notes that part of the problem are President Johnson's pledge of a "Great Society" and his social welfare policies that raise expectations far beyond society's ability to fulfill them as it subsidizes social discontent through poverty programs.

On November 7, a report from the U.S. Senate Permanent Investigating Committee notes that there are 75 major riots in 1967, compared to 21 in 1966. The committee also reports that 83 persons are killed in the 1967 riots, compared to 11 in 1966 and 36 in 1965.

CULT. The beginning of the Black Arts Movement brings new forms of writing to the forefront that stress black beauty and pride and outstanding artists such as Sonia Sanchez, Nikki Giovanni, and Don Lee (Haki Madhubuti). Sanchez captures the violence and turbulence of the time in her work *We a BaddDDD People*. In 1968, Amiri Baraka and Larry Neal co-edit the anthology *Black Fire*, which reveals the extent to which black writers and thinkers have rejected the premises of integration in favor of a new black consciousness and nationalist political engagement.

LAW. On January 9, the first southern African American sheriff in the twentieth century, Lucius D. Anderson, is sworn in at Tuskegee, Macon County, Alabama.

On June 12, the U.S. Supreme Court adjudicates laws preventing interracial marriage in Virginia as illegal.

On June 13, President Lyndon Johnson names Solicitor General Thurgood Marshall to the U.S. Supreme Court.

On August 30, the U.S. Senate confirms Thurgood Marshall as the first African American associate justice of the U.S. Supreme Court.

OBIT. On July 17, noted innovator and famed jazz musician John "Train" Coltrane dies.

POLI. On January 9, Rep. Adam Clayton Powell Jr., the most prominent African American politician in the country, is ousted from his post as chairman of the House, Education and Welfare Committee on a charge that he misused congressional funds. Powell responds by charging specific members of congress with racism. Powell's political support is based on his longtime affiliation as pastor of the Abyssinian Baptist Church in Harlem, New York. Following in his father's footsteps as pastor of the church, Powell Jr. champions civil rights throughout the 1940s and becomes chairman of the Education and Labor Committee in 1961 and is instrumental in President Lyndon Johnson getting his antipoverty legislation through Congress. Complaints such as Powell's lavish lifestyle in the Caribbean, absenteeism from Congress, vacations at government expense, and charges of personal slander from one of his constituents,

At the forefront of the Black Arts Movement, Amiri Baraka declares: "The Black man must seek a Black politics, an ordering of the world that is beneficial to his culture, to his interiorization and judgment of the world. The Black Artist is desperately needed to change the images his people identify with, by asserting Black feeling, Black mind, Black judgement."

however, taint his political statue in an era when political stances and actions are equated with moral character. Congress censures Adam Clayton Powell Jr. on March 1, 1967, by a vote of 307 to 116. The Supreme Court overturns the censure, however, citing that Congress has no right to unseat a duly elected official.

On January 10, the Georgia state legislature reverses its earlier decision to bar Julian Bond from his duly elected legislative seat, and Bond continues to condemn the U.S. involvement in the Vietnam War.

Harlem voters ignore the U.S. congressional censure of Adam Clayton Powell Jr. and reelect him to Congress on April 11.

On November 7, Carl B. Stokes is elected mayor of Cleveland, Ohio, and Richard B. Hatcher is elected mayor of Gary, Indiana. Carl Stokes is sworn in on November 13 and becomes the first African American mayor of a major U.S. city.

On November 7, the National Association for the Advancement of Colored People (NAACP) awards its Spingarn Medal to Edward W. Brooke for his public service as the first African American senator since Reconstruction.

SCIE. On June 30, Maj. Robert H. Lawrence Jr. becomes the first African American astronaut. He is killed in a flight-training accident on December 8.

SPOR. On April 28, the World Boxing Association and the New York State Athletic Commission strip world heavyweight boxing champion Muhammad Ali of his title because he refuses to serve in the U.S. military.

On June 20, champion boxer Muhammad Ali is convicted in Houston, Texas, by a federal court for violating the Selective Service Act by refusing to be inducted into the U.S. armed forces.

Emlen Tunnell, defensive back for the New York Giants , is the first African American inducted into the Football Hall of Fame in Canton, Ohio.

1968

ARTS. Henry Lewis becomes the first African American to serve as musical director of a U.S. orchestra, the New Jersey Symphony.

James Earl Jones wins the Tony Award for his role in the Broadway dramatization of the life of boxer Jack Johnson, *The Great White Hope*.

On March 15, *Life* magazine names Jimi Hendrix "the most spectacular guitarist in the world."

On December 14, Sammy Davis Jr. receives the National Association for the Advancement of Colored People (NAACP) Spingarn Medal for his "superb and many faceted talent" and his contributions to the civil rights movement.

CIVI. On March 4, Rev. Martin Luther King Jr. announces plans to stage a massive Poor People's Campaign in Washington, DC. He states that he will lead a massive civil disobedience campaign in the nation's capital to emphasize the government's spending millions of dollars on the war in Vietnam when the money can be better utilized by providing jobs and better income for the country's poor. Reverend King holds a news conference and states that he will bring millions of poor African Americans, poor Hispanic Americans, and poor whites to Washington, DC, to develop a Poor People's Village on the Mall in front of the Lincoln Memorial. A major goal of this campaign is to get Congress to agree to a federally guaranteed income for the poor. Within these demands, Reverend King connects the Poor People's Campaign to the millions of dollars spent by the government "to slaughter, men, women, and children" while failing to protect African American civil rights in places like Albany, Georgia, and Birmingham and Selma, Alabama. He states that President Johnson is more concerned with winning the war in Vietnam than winning the war against poverty. This political position alienates Reverend King and many of the supporters for the Poor People's Campaign from President Johnson and more conservative African Americans who support both President Johnson and the war effort. This political and ideological division seemingly converts Reverend King into the major critic of the war effort and for some a political liability. Reverend King establishes April 20 as the date of the beginning of a Poor People's Campaign that continues until demands are met.

On April 9, Rev. Ralph Abernathy is elected to replace Reverend King as president of the Southern Christian Leadership Conference (SCLC).

On April 10, the U.S. Congress passes the Civil Rights Bill of 1968 that bans racial discrimination in the sale or rental of approximately 80 percent of the nation's housing. The bill also has a rider that placates the wishes of both civil rights advocates and southern white conservatives that makes it a crime to interfere with civil rights workers; however, it is also illegal to cross state lines to incite a riot or civil disturbance.

The Poor People's Campaign begins on April 29 and 30 with Rev. Ralph Abernathy of the SCLC leading a delegation representing poor whites, African Americans, indigenous groups, and Hispanic Americans to Capitol Hill for conferences with members of President Johnson's Cabinet and Congressional leaders.

On May 11, nine caravans of poor people arrive in Washington, DC, for the first phase of the Poor People's Campaign. Caravans arrive from different parts of the country and quickly set up a compound called Resurrection City on a 16-acre site in front of the Lincoln Memorial.

On June 24, Resurrection City is forced to close, and more than 100 demonstrators, including Rev. Ralph Abernathy, are arrested when they refuse to leave.

CRIM. On February 8, police officers shoot and kill three African American students from South Carolina State College at Orangeburg protesting the segregation policy of a local all-white bowling alley in Orangeburg. Tensions escalate when the students gather in front of the campus and taunt the police and some throw bottles, rocks, and lumber at the officers, hitting one in the face. Later that evening, without warning, nine highway patrolmen fire at the crowd of students on the grounds of the college. As a result, 3 students are shot dead and 27 others wounded. Most of those shot are hit in the back. The officers are acquitted of all charges, claiming that they were provoked and injured by rock-throwing students. One student, Cleveland Sellers of Student Non-Violent Coordinating Committee (SNCC), is convicted of rioting and serves nearly a year in prison. He is pardoned by Gov. James Hodges,

who apologizes to a group of survivors about their ordeal eight years later on the anniversary of the attack.

On February 29, the National Advisory Commission on Civil Disorders, also known as the Kerner Commission, issues a report that states that white racism is the fundamental cause of the riots and civil disturbances in U.S. cities. The commission poignantly states that the United States is "moving toward two societies, one black, one white—separate and unequal." Though this analysis is dramatic coming from a governmental commission, it is neither a surprise nor a revelation for many African Americans.

On March 28, a major racial disturbance erupts in Memphis, Tennessee, as Rev. Martin Luther King Jr. holds a march in conjunction with striking sanitation workers. The governor of Tennessee mobilizes the National Guard in response to the disturbance.

On April 4, Rev. Dr. Martin Luther King Jr. is assassinated in Memphis, Tennessee, while standing on the balcony of the Lorraine Motel. His assassination precipitates a national upheaval of angry citizens across race and class lines as civil disobedience and rioting occur in more than 100 cities. Some 20,000 federal troops and 24,000 National Guardsmen are mobilized to quell the disturbances. In Washington, DC, federal troops are forced to place machine guns and tanks near key governmental structures, including the Capitol. President Lyndon Johnson declares Sunday, April 6, a national day of mourning and orders all U.S. flags on government buildings and in all U.S. territories and possessions to fly at half-mast.

On the morning of June 5, Senator Robert F. Kennedy finishes his victory campaign speech in the California primary as he moves closer to becoming the Democratic Party's presidential candidate in November. While leaving the historic Ambassador Hotel in Los Angeles, he is shot and killed by Sirhan Sirhan. In the subsequent struggle, decathlon champion Rafer Johnson, former professional football star Rosie Grier, and others grab Sirhan, one holding his head, another with a finger in the trigger guard of Sirhan's pistol to prevent additional shots. Sirhan is eventually subdued and taken into police custody.

On June 8, James Earl Ray is captured in London, England, as the alleged assassin of Rev. Martin Luther King Jr.

From July 23 to 24, violent civil disobedience erupts in Cleveland, Ohio, after police allegedly ambush a group of African American radicals. Eleven people are killed, including three policemen.

EDUC. On March 19 and 20, Howard University students in Washington, DC, seize the administration building and demand that major reforms to the curriculum be put into place. A major concern for the students is a lack of Afrocentric educational courses in the university's curriculum.

On April 12, African American students occupy the administrative buildings at Boston University and demand that African American history courses be added to the curriculum and that the school be more aggressive in its recruitment of African American students.

On April 23, students of African heritage and radical whites seize five administrative buildings at Columbia University in New York City. They seek the end of the school's financial connection to prowar industries and government secret agencies.

OBIT. On April 9, Rev. Martin Luther King Jr. is buried after funeral services at Ebenezer Baptist Church and memorial services at Morehouse College in Atlanta. More than 300,000 people march behind his coffin, which is carried through the streets of Atlanta on a farm wagon drawn by two Georgia mules. Dignitaries from around the country and abroad attend the services.

POLI. On August 5, Senator Edward Brooke is named temporary chairman of the National Republican Convention in Miami, Florida. Three days later, civil disobedience erupts in Miami during the Republican National Convention. The Florida National Guard is mobilized to put down the disturbances.

In Chicago, Illinois, Rev. Channing E. Phillips, a Democrat from Washington, DC, is the first African American nominated by a major political party to be president of the United States. Phillips is nominated as the favorite son by the District of Columbia delegation and receives 67.5 votes.

On November 5, the largest number of African Americans—nine—is elected to the U.S. Congress. Among them is the first African American female representative to Congress, Shirley Chisholm from Bedford-Stuyvesant, Brooklyn, New York. Despite the controversy and congressional hearings on his political record, Adam Clayton Powell Jr. is reelected to Congress. The other representatives are William Dawson (Illinois), Charles Diggs (Michigan), Augustus Hawkins (California), Robert N. C. Nix (Pennsylvania), John Conyers (Michigan), Louis Stokes (Ohio), and William L. Clay (Missouri).

SPOR. Arthur Ashe becomes the first African America to win the U.S. Open Tennis Championship, defeating Tom Okker of The Netherlands at Forest Hills Stadium in New York on September 9.

John Carlos and Tommie Smith give a Black Power salute on the victory stand after winning the 200-meter event at the Olympics in Mexico City, Mexico, on October 16. They state that their salute is given as a protest against U.S. racism.

On October 15, Wyomia Tyus wins a gold medal in the 100 meters in two consecutive Olympiads.

On October 18, Bob Beamon sets a world record in the long jump at the Mexico City Olympic Games.

1969

ARTS. African American soprano, Jessye Norman makes her opera debut in Berlin, Germany in Wagner's *Tannhauser.*

ASSO. On March 27, the Black Academy of Arts and Letters is founded in Boston, Massachusetts. Dr. C. Eric Lincoln, professor of religion and sociology at Union Theological Seminary in New York, is elected president of the organization.

BUSI. In April, James Foreman of the Student Nonviolent Coordinating Committee (SNCC) leads a delegation of civil rights leaders to the National Black Economic Development Conference held in Detroit, Michigan. The delegates issue the "Black Manifesto" calling for "$500 million in reparations from white churches and Jewish synagogues." Articulated mainly by James Forman, they also want 60 percent of these institutions' assets surrendered to the conference to be used for the economic, social, and cultural rehabilitation of the black community. These figures are premised upon centuries of African slave labor in the United States under the aegis of Christian and other religious institutions. If anything, this manifesto confirms the Kerner Commission's 1968 report that the nation is indeed "two societies, one black, one white—separate and unequal."

CRIM. On March 10, James Earl Ray pleads guilty in a Memphis, Tennessee, court to charges naming him the assassin of Rev. Martin Luther King Jr. He is sentenced to 99 years in prison. The House Select Committee on Assassinations concludes that, although Ray fired the shot that killed Rev. Martin Luther King Jr., he is probably part of a much larger conspiracy.

On April 19, 100 African students carrying rifles and shotguns seize the Student Union at Cornell University in Ithaca, New York, to protest the university's racial policies pertaining to academic curriculum and student admission.

From May 21 to 23, local police and National Guardsmen fire on demonstrators at North Carolina A&T College. One student is killed and five policemen injured.

On August 30, the Florida National Guard is mobilized to quell racial disturbances in Fort Lauderdale.

From September 1 to 5, racial conflict erupts in Hartford, Connecticut. Five hundred people are arrested and scores injured.

On October 8, Chicago police and African American snipers exchange fire on Chicago's West Side. One black youth is killed and nine policemen wounded.

Two members of the Black Panther Party for Self Defense, Fred Hampton and Mark Clark, are killed in their beds during a police raid in Chicago on the night of December 4. Civil rights leaders are able to demonstrate that the two Black Panther Party members were set up by undercover Chicago police, drugged, and then murdered while they slept. Fred Hampton was considered by many radicals and civil rights activist to be an extremely effective leader and organizer.

EDUC. On October 17, Dr. Clifton R. Wharton Jr. is elected president of Michigan State University and becomes the first African American to head a predominately white university in the twentieth century.

The Ford Foundation gives $1 million to Morgan State University, Howard University, and Yale University to help prepare faculty members to teach courses in African American studies.

LAW. On June 16, the U.S. Supreme Court rules that the suspension of Adam Clayton Powell Jr. from the House of Representatives is unconstitutional.

On August 23, the U.S. Justice Department concludes that civil disobedience and rioting in the nation's urban centers in 1969 is down at least 50 percent from 1968. Officials express a belief that the period of large-scale racial rebellion is over.

The U.S. Supreme Court on October 29 states that school systems must end segregation "at once" and "operate now and hereafter only unitary schools." To emphasize the point, in the Mississippi case *Alexander v. Holmes,* the Court abandons the principle of "all deliberate speed" due to the "slowness" interpretation given it by segregationists.

LIT. Maya Angelou's memoir, *I Know Why the Caged Bird Sings,* is published.

MED. Gordon Parks, photographer and filmmaker, produces and directs *The Learning Tree,* the first film directed by an African American for a major film studio. He also makes the classic detective drama *Shaft* in 1971.

In December, photographer Moneta Sleet Jr. of *Ebony* magazine is awarded the Pulitzer Prize for his excellent work as a photographer. He is the first African American to be so honored.

POLI. On January 3, Rep. Adam Clayton Powell Jr. is seated in Congress.

On April 1, an alleged conspiracy by the Black Panther Party for Self Defense to bomb important city buildings in New York City results in the indictment and arrest of 21 Panthers.

In December, the director of the Washington bureau of the National Association for the Advancement of Colored People (NAACP), Clarence Mitchell Jr., receives the Spingarn Medal "for the pivotal role he played in enactment of civil rights legislation."

RELI. Thomas Kilgore Jr. becomes the first African American president of the National Council of Churches.

1970

ARTS. Playwright Charles Gordone receives the Pulitzer Prize for his play *No Place to Go*.

The Jackson Five singing and dance group have four consecutive number-one hits on the pop charts.

In November, painter Jacob Lawrence receives the National Association for the Advancement of Colored People (NAACP) Spingarn Medal.

BUSI. On February 13, Joseph L. Searles becomes the first African American member of the New York Stock Exchange.

CENS. The federal government reports that the United States population is 203,200,000, of which 22,600,000 (11.1%) are African Americans.

CIVI. From August 3 to 7, 2,000 delegates and observers attend the Congress of African Peoples Convention in Atlanta, Georgia.

CRIM. On May 12, the police kill six African Americans during a racial disturbance in Augusta, Georgia.

African American students demanding the termination of ROTC programs on the Ohio State University campus and the admission of additional African Americans students provoke the governor to mobilize the National Guard.

On August 7, four people are killed, including the presiding judge, in a courthouse shootout in San Rafael, Marin County, California. Among others killed is Jonathan Jackson, the brother of jailed Black Panther leader and writer George Jackson, whom authorities claim the attempted kidnapping of the judge aims to free. Political activist Angela Davis is charged with providing weapons for the attempted kidnapping and for the resulting killings in the courtroom. A national warrant for her arrest is issued.

On August 29, one policeman is killed and six wounded in an armed confrontation with members of the Black Panther Party in Philadelphia, Pennsylvania.

On August 31, Black Panther activist Lonnie McLucas is charged and convicted in New Haven, Connecticut, for the conspiracy to kill another Black Panther suspected of being an undercover police agent, Alex Rackley. Charges against other defendants in the case are dropped.

From September 14 to 15, one African American and two whites are injured in a shootout between political activists and police officers in a New Orleans, Louisiana, housing project.

On October 13, Angela Davis is arrested in New York City and charged with unlawful flight to avoid persecution for her alleged role in a California courtroom shootout that resulted in the death of four people, including the courtroom judge.

EDUC. On August 14, City University of New York (CUNY) initiates an open admissions policy designed to increase its number of poor and minority students.

LAW. On April 8, liberals and civil rights groups oppose U.S. Supreme Court nominee G. Harold Carswell, citing his racist views. The U.S. Senate subsequently rejects him.

U.S. President Richard M. Nixon signs a bill extending the Voting Rights Act of 1965 to 1975. This extension ensures that the government will evaluate those protective clauses in the 1965 Voting Rights Act that protect African Americans' ability to vote, particularly in southern states.

OBIT. The first African American U.S. Army general, Benjamin O. Davis Jr., dies in Chicago, Illinois, at the age of 93.

On July 30, author and news reporter Louis Lomax dies.

POLI. On June 16, Kenneth A. Gibson is elected mayor of Newark, New Jersey.

On June 23, Charles Rangel defeats Adam Clayton Powell Jr. in the Democratic primary in Harlem, New York.

NAACP Chairman Stephen Gill Spottswood tells the NAACP convention that the Nixon administration is "anti-Negro" and advocates "a calculated policy" inimical to "the needs and aspirations of the large" majority of citizens.

On November 3, 12 African Americans are elected to the 92nd Congress, including five new representatives: Ralph H. Metcalfe (Illinois), George Collins (Illinois), Charles Rangel (New York), Ronald Dellums (California), and Parren Mitchell (Maryland).

RELI. John M. Burgess is installed as the first African American bishop to head an Episcopal diocese in the United States, in Massachusetts.

SPOR. On February 16, boxer Joe Frazier knocks out Jimmy Ellis in the second round of the world heavyweight championship fight in New York City.

1971

ASSO. A civil rights organizer from the Southern Christian Leadership Conference (SCLC), Jesse Jackson, founds People United to Serve Humanity (PUSH) in Chicago, Illinois, on December 18.

BUSI. In December, the National Association for the Advancement of Colored People (NAACP) awards the Spingarn Medal to Rev. Leon H. Sullivan, founder of Opportunities Industrialization Centers of America (OIC) for his leadership.

CIVI. The U.S. Supreme Court rules unanimously that busing is constitutionally protected and an acceptable method for integrating public schools.

On June 14, the U.S. Justice Department files a suit against the St. Louis suburb of Black Jack, Missouri, charging the community with illegally using municipal procedures to block the construction of an integrated housing development.

On June 15, former United Negro College Fund Executive Director Vernon E. Jordan Jr. is appointed executive director of the National Urban League.

CRIM. On August 18, a white policeman is killed during a raid on the headquarters of the Republic of New Afrika (RNA) in Jackson, Mississippi. Ten members of the RNA, including its president, Dr. R. Obadele, are arrested.

On August 21, author, political activist, and member of the Black Panther Party George Jackson, one of three inmates know as the Soledad Brothers, is shot and killed in an alleged escape attempt at San Quentin Prison in California. Autopsy reports indicate that he is shot in the back.

On September 9, six Ku Klux Klansmen are arrested for the bombing of 10 schools in Pontiac, Michigan.

On September 9, inmates at Attica State Correctional Facility in New York revolt, take control of a major block of the institution, and hold several guards hostage. They issue a series of demands to the institution's administration, including better food, adjudication of their cases, elimination of prison guard's brutality, and a minimum wage for prison labor.

On September 13, 1,500 state police and correctional offices storm Attica State Correctional Facility. Thirty-two convicts are killed in the attack along with 10 guards held by the prisoners. Later evidence indicates that the guards die as a result of police gunfire.

On November 24, inmates at Rahway Prison in Rahway, New Jersey, rebel over prison conditions.

ENTE. On June 16, Tupac Amaru Shakur, internationally known rapper, film star, and celebrated spokesmen for rebellious inner city youth, is born to Afeni Shakur, a member of the Black Panther Party in New York City. Just months earlier, Afeni and other Panthers are acquitted of city and state criminal charges after a two-year trial. *Tupac Amara* are Inca words meaning "shining serpent" and *Shakur* is Arabic for "thankful to God."

LAW. On March 1, the U.S. Defense Department announces that a limited surveillance project has been initiated to gather civil-disturbance information for a collection plan aimed at civil rights groups.

On May 13, a jury finds all 21 members of the Black Panther Party arrested in New York City in 1969 for an alleged bombing plot not guilty. To date, this is one of longest criminal trials ever held in New York City.

On December 10, William H. Rehnquist is confirmed as an associate justice of the U.S. Supreme Court despite the opposition by civil rights organizations to his conservative judicial opinions.

MILI. On April 28, Samuel Lee Gravely Jr. becomes the first African American admiral in he U.S. Navy.

A U.S. Defense Department report states that African Americans constitute 11 percent of U.S. soldiers in Southeast Asia. The report also notes that 12.5 percent of all soldiers killed in Vietnam since 1961 are African Americans.

OBIT. Whitney Young Jr., the director of the National Urban League, dies while swimming off the coast of Nigeria. He is attending an international conference at the time.

Famed musician Louis "Satchmo" Armstrong dies in Corona, Queens, New York, at the age of 71.

On December 9, Ralph J. Bunche, Noble Peace Prize recipient and undersecretary of the United Nations from 1955 to his retirement in 1971, dies at the age of 67 in New York City.

POLI. On January 4, the Congressional Black Caucus is formed with 17 members.

On January 21, 12 African American congressmen boycott President Richard Nixon's State of the Union Address because of Nixon's refusal to respond to petitions of grievances by African Americans.

On February 25, President Nixon meets with members of the Congressional Black Caucus and then appoints a panel to study a list of grievances and recommendations made by the group of congressmen.

On March 23, Rev. Walter Fauntroy, a former aide to Martin Luther King Jr., becomes the first nonvoting congressional delegate from the District of Columbia since Reconstruction.

On May 18, President Nixon rejects 60 of the demands made by the Congressional Black Caucus.

SPOR. On June 28, the U.S. Supreme Court unanimously overturns the selective service evasion conviction of boxer Muhammad Ali.

On August 9, Leroy "Satchel" Paige is the first player from the Negro Leagues to be elected to the National Baseball Hall of Fame in Cooperstown, New York. When accepting the award, Paige states, "There are many Satchels and many Joshes," referring to Josh Gibson, a noted Negro League catcher. In 1948, Paige joined the Cleveland Indians. With Paige on the mound, Cleveland won the World Series. In 1952, he was selected as a pitcher to the American League All-Star Team. According to a noted baseball historian, Satchel Paige is the greatest pitcher of all time. Based on his estimates, Satchel Paige threw 55 no-hitters and won more than 2,000 of 2,500 games he pitched.

1972

ARTS. In December, the National Association for the Advancement of Colored People (NAACP) awards the Spingarn Medal to photographer, writer, filmmaker, and composer Gordon B. Parks.

Rhythm and blues singer and musical innovator Stevie Wonder releases his hit album *Talking Book*.

ASSO. On June 22, the National Black MBA Association is incorporated with more than 2,000 minority members.

BUSI. On June 29, the annual report of the NAACP notes that there are more unemployed blacks in urban areas than at any time since the 1930s. The report also claims that school desegregation is increasing throughout the nation.

On July 13, the Bureau of the Census reports that African American unemployment averages 9.9 percent in 1971, compared with 5.4 percent for whites. The report also notes that 31.8 percent of all African American families are headed by women, an increase from 28 percent in 1970.

CIVI. On July 4, the NACCP adopts an emergency resolution charging President Richard Nixon with "leading the mob in its assault upon the Fourteenth Amendment's Equal Protection clause."

CRIM. From January 10 to 12, racial conflict in Baton Rouge, Louisiana, results in the deaths of two African American youths and two deputy sheriffs.

On June 17, Frank Wills, a Washington, DC, security guard, discovers a break-in attempt at the headquarters of the Democratic National Committee at the Watergate Hotel. Known as the Watergate conspiracy, it opens the door for further examinations of President Nixon's administration.

On October 11, prisoners in a Washington, DC, jail revolt against living conditions.

On November 6, two members of the Symbionese Liberation Army, a West Coast self-proclaimed anti–U.S. government group, ambushes and kills Marcus A. Foster, superintendent of schools in Oakland, California. Two members of the group are later convicted of the killing, but the conviction of one attacker is overturned on a legal technicality.

EDUC. On April 19, a National Education Association study reveals that African Americans have lost 30,000 teaching jobs since 1954 in 17 southern and border states because of desegregation and discrimination. For many African Americans, racial integration proves to be costly when African American–owned institutions, born in the midst of racial segregation, begin to loose economic support as white-owned institutions allegedly become more amenable to blacks. This is apparent in the educational institutions of the South and raises a serious challenge to African American funding groups such as the Negro College Fund to save the historically black colleges and universities.

HHC. On July 25, the public learns of a medical study that used African American males as so-called guinea pigs in a 40-year syphilis experiment. Beginning in 1932, the U.S. Public Health Service (USPHS) initiated a major study of syphilis, a sexually transmitted disease that can cause paraly-

sis, insanity, and heart failure. The study is officially called the Tuskegee Study of Untreated Syphilis in the Male Negro. The USPHS recruited 622 African American men, all of whom were poor sharecroppers and the majority of them illiterate. Of this number of subjects, 431 had advanced cases of syphilis, the rest were free of the disease and served as controls. The program was called a treatment program but was in fact an experiment designed to chart the progression and development of the disease. To gain the confidence of the men, the USPHS hired an African American nurse, Eunice Rivers, and utilized Tuskegee Institute as the center of operations for the experiment. Although penicillin, which could in most cases cure the disease, was available by the early 1940s, the sharecroppers never received it but were instead given ineffective placebos to convince them they were receiving a cure. Though the study (experiment) was to last six months, it was continually extended. The survivors and descendants of those who participated in the study sue the U.S. government and settle for $9 million.

LAW. On June 4, Angela Davis is acquitted by a white jury in San Jose, California, of charges associated with the 1970 shootout in San Rafael County, California.

On June 29, the U.S. Supreme Court rules 5–4 that the death penalty is cruel and unusual punishment that violates the Eight Amendment to the Constitution. Six hundred persons await execution, of which 483 are African Americans or members of other minority groups.

MED. On April 11, a Memphis, Tennessee, lawyer and minister, Benjamin L. Hooks, becomes the first African American selected to the Federal Communications Commission.

MILI. Maj. Gen. Frederic E. Davidson becomes the first African American to assume command of a U.S. Army Division, the Eighth Infantry Division.

On September 28, the secretary of the army clears the military records of 167 soldiers dishonorably discharged in 1906 because they refused to identify alleged participants in the so-called Brownsville Raid.

On October 12 and 13, 46 African American and white sailors are injured in a race riot on the aircraft carrier USS *Kitty Hawk* off the coast of Vietnam.

OBIT. On January 27, gospel singer Mahalia Jackson dies in Evergreen, Illinois, at the age of 60.

Civil rights activist and U.S. Rep. Adam Clayton Powell Jr. dies at the age of 63 in Miami, Florida.

On December 8, Rep. George Collins dies at the age of 47 in an airplane crash near Midway Airport in Chicago, Illinois.

POLI. On January 25, the first African American congresswoman, Shirley Chisholm, begins her presidential campaign.

On March 10, 3,000 African American delegates and 5,000 observers attend the three-day African American Political Convention in Gary, Indiana, the first of its kind in the twentieth century. The three cochairs of the convention, Charles Diggs, Amiri Baraka, and Ronald Walters, reflect a wide range of political perspectives at the conference. The African Nationalist perspective, represented by Amiri Baraka and Maulana Karenga, interprets "Black Power" to mean that African Americans should control their own communications and create separate cultural institutions distinct from the white United States. This viewpoint, however, clashes that of African American political officials represented by Mayor Carl Stokes of Cleveland, Ohio, and Mayor Richard Hatcher of Gary, Indiana. According to Ronald Walters, it is this body of people who are contending for the national leadership of the black community in the early seventies, and this new group of black elected officials joins the civil rights leaders and becomes a new leadership class, but a conflict in outlook exists between them and the more indigenous, social, grassroots-oriented nationalist movement. The NAACP and a few other civil rights organizations withdraw from the convention after a resolution critical of busing and the state of Israel are adopted.

On March 27, an all-white jury acquits the two surviving Soledad Brothers, Fleeta Dumgo and John Cluchette, of charges that they killed a white guard at Soledad Prison in 1970. The third Soledad Brother, George Jackson, was killed in an alleged escape attempt in August 1971.

On July 10, Shirley Chisholm, in her bid for the Democratic Party presidential nomination at its Miami Beach convention, receives 151.95 votes out of a possible 2,000 on the first ballot.

On November 17, Barbara Jordan of Texas and Yvonne Brathwaite Burke of California are elected to the U.S. Congress. Republican Senator Edward W. Brooke of Massachusetts is overwhelmingly reelected for a second term.

RELI. On December 7, African American W. Sterling Cary is elected president of the National Council of Churches.

SPOR. On October 24, baseball great and the first African American to play in the modern major leagues Jack Roosevelt "Jackie" Robinson dies in Stamford, Connecticut, at the age of 53.

Baseball great Roberto Clemente, who played for the Pittsburgh Pirates, dies in a plane crash.

1973

EDUC. The National Association for the Advancement of Colored People (NAACP) awards the Spingarn Medal to California Superintendent of Public Instruction Wilson C. Riles.

OBIT. On June 4, writer and educator Arna Bontemps dies at the age of 72 in Nashville, Tennessee.

POLI. On April 16, Leila Smith is the first African American woman to be elected mayor of a U.S. city, Taft, Oklahoma. She holds this position for 13 years.

On May 29, Thomas Bradley is elected the first African American mayor of Los Angeles.

On June 5, Cardiss R. Collins, wife of deceased Chicago Rep. George Collins, is elected to succeed her husband.

On October 16, Maynard Jackson is elected mayor of Atlanta, Georgia.

On November 6, Coleman Young is elected mayor of Detroit, Michigan.

1974

CIVI. On October 15, the Massachusetts National Guard is mobilized to restore order in the wake of court-ordered busing of children.

U.S. District Court Judge W. Arthur Garrity rules in favor of a group of African American parents that files a class-action suit against the Boston School Committee. The ruling finds the school committee guilty of violating the equal protection clause of the Fourteenth Amendment. To achieve racial balance in the Boston schools, the judge orders the busing of several thousand students between mostly white south Boston, Hyde Park, and Dorchester and mostly black Roxbury. The crisis is intensified by the fact that educational segregation patterns are reflected in housing segregation patterns. Consequently, poorer neighborhoods reflect poorly maintained and supplied educational facilities. Although many schools receive higher-valued teachers due to the political and economic strength and influence of the local community, the reverse tends to be the case in poorer neighborhoods. Schools in higher-income and white communities reflect the higher socioeconomic status of whites in the Boston area, whereas the poorer schools are derelict, overcrowded, and deficient in school supplies, even desks, books, and chalk for blackboards. This relationship not only reflects economic or class factors but also more visible, racial characteristics. Whites mostly oppose busing and organize demonstrations and resistance boycotts to prevent their children from being bused into black communities and black children from being bused into white communities. Violence continues for about two years despite the arrest of dozens of people and the closing of bars.

CRIM. On June 30, an African American shoots and kills Mrs. Martin Luther King Sr. and Deacon Edward Boykin during church services at Ebenezer Baptist Church in Atlanta, Georgia. The assailant, Marcus Chennault of Dayton, Ohio, is convicted and sentenced to death.

On August 15, Joanne Little is acquitted of murder in the August 24, 1974, killing of a white jailer who tried to sexually molest her. In court, her defense attorney states that she stabbed the jailer with an ice pick only after he made sexual advances.

LAW. In November, the National Association for the Advancement of Colored People (NAACP)

awards the Spingarn Medal to United States District Court Judge Damon J. Keith.

OBIT. On May 24, world-renowned musician, composer, and bandleader Edward Kennedy "Duke" Ellington dies in New York City at the age of 75.

POLI. On April 22, the Joint Center for Political Studies reports that 2,991 African Americans hold elective office in 45 states and the District of Columbia, compared to 2,621 in April 1973 and 1,185 in 1969. Michigan has the largest number, at 194 elected officials, followed by Mississippi's 191.

From May 19 to 27, approximately 500 delegates and observers, half of whom are African Americans, attend the sixth Pan-African Congress in Dar es Salaam, Tanzania.

On November 5, Walter E. Washington becomes the first African American elected mayor of Washington, DC, in the twentieth century.

SPOR. On October 3, Frank Robinson is named manager of the Cleveland Indians baseball team and becomes the first African American manager in the major leagues.

1975

LAW. On September 2, Joseph W. Hatcher of Tallahassee, Florida, becomes the state's first African American supreme court justice since Reconstruction.

MILI. On September 1, Gen. Daniel "Chappie" James Jr. is promoted to the rank of four-star general and named the commander in chief of the North American Air Defense Command.

OBIT. On April 18, the holder of more than 138 chemical patents and a pioneer and synthesizer of cortisone drugs, Dr. Percy Lavon Julian, dies at the age of 76.

On February 25, leader of the Nation of Islam, Elijah Muhammad, dies in Chicago, Illinois, at the age of 77. His son, Wallace D. Muhammad, succeeds him.

On April 10, singer, entertainer, and operative for the French underground during World War II

Josephine Baker dies at the age of 68 in Paris, France.

On May 27, former heavyweight boxing champion Ezzard Charles dies in at the age of 53 in Chicago, Illinois.

On August 9, saxophonist and bandleader Julian "Cannonball" Adderly dies in Gary, Indiana, at the age of 46.

On December 17, a jazz pioneer Nobel Sissle dies at the age of 86. Sissle, a bandleader and decorated veteran of the 369th Regiment in World War I, returned to the United States and teamed with Eubie Blake to write a number of songs for Broadway shows. Some of the more popular include "I'm Just Wild about Harry," "Love Will Find a Way," and "Shuffle Along."

POLI. On January 14, President Gerald Ford names William T. Coleman secretary of transportation. He is the second African American to hold a Cabinet position.

RELI. On July 1, Nation of Islam (NOI) leader Wallace D. Muhammad, son of NOI founder Elijah Muhammad, announces a change in the religious order's racial construct by allowing members of all races to join.

SPOR. On April 8, Henry "Hank" Aaron of the Atlanta Braves brakes Babe Ruth's major league baseball record when he hits his 715th home run in Atlanta, Georgia.

Lee Elders becomes the first African American to compete in the Masters Golf Tournament, but fails to qualify for the final two rounds on April 11.

On July 5, renowned tennis champion Arthur Ashe wins the men's single's title at the Wimbledon Championships in England.

In December, Henry "Hank" Aaron receives the National Association for the Advancement of Colored People (NAACP) Spingarn Medal for his home-run record and his sportsmanship.

1976

ARTS. In December, Alvin Ailey receives the National Association for the Advancement of Colored People (NAACP) Spingarn Medal "in recognition of his international pre-eminence in the field of dance."

ASSO. On November 6, Benjamin Hooks is named to succeed Roy Wilkins as executive director of the NAACP.

EDUC. On January 7, Dr. Mary Frances Berry becomes the chancellor of the University of Colorado.

LAW. On October 25, Clarence "Willie" Norris is granted a full pardon by Gov. George Wallace. Norris is the last surviving member of the nine African American defendants who in 1931 were arrested and charged with raping two white female hoboes on a freight train traveling through Alabama.

LIT. Alex Haley publishes the Pulitzer Prize-winning novel *Roots*.

MILI. On August 18, Vice Adm. Samuel L. Gravely Jr. becomes commander of the U.S. Third Fleet and the first African American to hold that military position.

OBIT. On January 23, singer, actor, and political activist Paul Robeson dies at the age of 77 in Philadelphia, Pennsylvania.

POLI. A Freedom of Information suit is filed on April 5 against the federal government to force the release of federal Bureau of Investigation (FBI) documents that indicate that the government was spying on U.S. citizens involved in the civil rights movement during the 1960s. In a letter dated April 25, 1967, the governments states that its program, named the Counter Intelligence Program (COINTELPRO), is designed "to expose, disrupt, misdirect, discredit or otherwise neutralize the activities of black nationalist, hate-type groups, their leadership, spokesmen, membership and supporters, and to counter their propensity for violence and civil disorders." Another letter specifically names the Student Nonviolent Coordinating Committee and the Southern Christian Leadership Conference (SCLC) as organizations that have "radical and violence prone leaders, members and followers."

On July 5, the mayor of Newark, New Jersey, Kenneth Gibson, becomes the first African American president of the U.S. Conference of Mayors.

On July 12, Barbara Jordan of Texas is the keynote speaker at the Democratic National Convention.

On December 16, Andrew Young Jr., a civil rights activist, member of the SCLC, and Georgia congressmen, is appointed U.S. ambassador and chief delegate to the United Nations.

On December 21, President Jimmy Carter names Patricia R. Harris secretary of the Department of Housing and Urban Development.

RELI. Dr. Joseph H. Evans is elected the first African American president of the predominantly white American Church of Christ.

1977

CULT. From January 15 to February 12, the second World Festival of Black and African Art (FESTAC) opens in Lagos, Nigeria. The largest delegation outside of Nigeria is from the United States.

From January 23 to 30, an estimated 130 million viewers watch an eight-part television production of Alex Haley's novel *Roots*.

EDUC. On October 26, Dr. Clifford R. Wharton Jr. is named chancellor of the state of New York.

LIT. Author Toni Morrison publishes her novel *Song of Solomon*. In 1987, her novel *Beloved* establishes her as a major literary talent (see 1993).

In November, the National Association for the Advancement of Colored People (NAACP) awards the Spingarn Medal to Alexander P. Haley "for his unsurpassed effectiveness in portraying the legendary story of an American of African descent."

MILI. On February 11, Clifford Alexander Jr. is confirmed as the first African American secretary of the army.

OBIT. On January 2, noted jazz pianist Erroll Garner dies in Los Angeles, California, at the age of 53.

Civil rights activist, founder of the Mississippi Freedom Democratic Party (MFDP), and speaker who delineated the differences between civil and human rights activism Fannie Lou Hamer dies at the age of 59 on March 14.

Noted writer, civil rights activist, and literary voice for the civil rights movement James Baldwin dies in New York City at the age of 63.

In February, comic actor Eddie "Rochester" Anderson dies at the age of 71. Anderson is often criticized for his racially stereotyped performances of an African American chauffer or butler in the 1930s and 1940s Charlie Chan detective movies and with white comedian Jack Benny.

On March 27, Shirley Graham Du Bois, author and widow of W.E.B. Du Bois, dies at the age of 69 in Beijing, China.

On September 1, singer and actress Ethel Waters dies at the age of 80 in Chatsworth, California.

POLI. President Jimmy Carter names Eleanor Holmes Norton director of the Equal Employment Opportunity Commission (EEOC). From 1977 to 1982, Norton is largely responsible for enforcement of Title VII of the Civil Rights Act of 1972 and the Equal Employment Act of 1972. She is given credit for cutting in half the backlog of cases and increasing the productivity of EEOC area offices by 65 percent. Before coming to work for the government, she is an assistant legal director of the American Civil Liberties Union and gives legal advice to the Mississippi Freedom Democratic Party under the leadership of Fannie Lou Hamer when it challenges the all-white Mississippi Democratic delegation at the Democratic National Convention of 1964 (see 1990.)

On March 8, Henry L. Marsh III is elected mayor of Richmond, Virginia.

1978

CIVI. On June 28, the U.S. Supreme Court orders the University of California Medical School at Davis to admit Allan P. Bakke as a student. Bakke, a white, charges reverse discrimination due to the school's attempt to integrate its medical school by establishing a quota that reserves 16 of the 100 seats for nonwhite students. Central to Allan Bakke's argument is that by using race—black or white—as a criterion, he is denied a seat.

CRIM. On November 18, Rev. Jim Jones from California leads more than 900 people, most of whom are African Americans, in a mass suicide and murder pact at the Peoples Temple in Jonestown, Guyana.

POLI. In November, the National Association for the Advancement of Colored People (NAACP) awards the Spingarn Medal to Ambassador Andrew J. Young.

SCIE. On January 16, three African Americans are named to the NASA space program as astronauts: Maj. Frederick D. Gregory, Maj. Guion S. Bluford, and Dr. Ronald E. McNair.

SPOR. On February 15, Leon Spinks defeats Muhammad Ali for the heavyweight boxing championship of the world. Ali regains the title on September 15 and becomes the first fighter to win the title three times.

1979

BUSI. On January 30, Franklin A. Thomas is named the first African American president of the Ford Foundation.

In November, an African American is awarded a Nobel Prize in an area other than peace for the first time. Professor Arthur Lewis receives the award in the area of economics.

CIVI. On June 27, the U.S. Supreme Court rules in *Weber v. Kaiser Aluminum and Chemical Corporation* that employers and unions can establish voluntary programs, including the use of quotas, to facilitate so-called minority employment. This problematic decision, however, does not address the level or quality of employment, thereby allowing companies the loophole of satisfying the court decision but not necessarily providing quality jobs for so-called minorities.

In November, the National Association for the Advancement of Colored People (NAACP) awards Rosa L. Parks the Spingarn Medal for her role as the catalyst in the Montgomery bus boycott of 1955 and 1956.

CRIM. In Greensboro, North Carolina, Ku Klux Klansmen fire on a crowd of antislave demonstrators, killing five people on November 3.

On November 15, the Anti-Defamation League of B'nai B'rith releases a study that indicates a rise in Ku Klux Klan membership in 22 states. The study notes that although a rise in membership is around 2,000 during in a 20-month period ending in November 1979, the rise in Klan sympathizers during this same period jumps from 30,000 to 100,000.

MILI. On February 23, Frank P. Peterson is named the first African American general in the U.S. Marine Corps.

Hazel Johnson is promoted to brigadier general in the U.S. Army, thereby making her the first African American woman general officer in the U.S. military.

OBIT. Civil rights leader and founder of the Brotherhood of Sleeping Car Porters and Maids Asa Philip Randolph dies at the age of 90 in New York City.

POLI. On July 19, Secretary of Housing and Urban Development Patricia R. Harris is named secretary of the Department of Health, Education, and Welfare in President Jimmy Carter's administration.

On August 15, UN Ambassador Andrew Young is pressured to resign after having an unauthorized meeting with representatives of the Palestine Liberation Organization. His resignation causes controversy between the African American and Jewish American communities.

On August 22, 200 African American leaders meeting in New York City express support for Andrew Young and demand that African Americans be given a voice in shaping future U.S. foreign policy.

On August 31, Donald McHenry is selected to replace Andrew Young as U.S. ambassador to the United Nations.

SPOR. On September 23, Lou Brock steals his 935th base in the major leagues, thereby becoming the all-time leader in stolen bases.

1980

ARTS. On October 8, Jamaican reggae singer and composer Robert "Bob" Nester Marley collapses onstage during a concert in Pittsburgh, Pennsylvania. This is his last performance.

CENS. The population of the United States is 226,500,000, of which 26,500,000 (11.7%) are African Americans.

CRIM. On April 8, Georgia state troopers mobilize to stop a racial disturbance in Wrightsville's. Similar racial incidents occur throughout the year in Chattanooga, Tennessee; Oceanside, California; Kokomo, Indiana; Wichita, Kansas; and Johnston County, North Carolina. Much of this activity is associated with renewed efforts of the Ku Klux Klan to influence a growing conservative movement in government.

From May 17 to 19, a major racial disturbance occurs in Miami, Florida, where 16 people are killed and more than 300 injured. Racial violence again explodes on July 5 and continues until July 17. Nearly 40 people are injured.

On May 29, Vernon Jordan, president of the National Urban League, is critically wounded in an attempted assassination in Fort Wayne, Indiana.

The unprovoked murder of six African Americans in Buffalo, New York, pressures the authorities on October 13 to establish a national investigation to determine the cause.

EDUC. In October, the National Association for the Advancement of Colored People (NAACP) awards the Spingarn Medal to historian and author Rayford W. Logan.

On September 29, the Schomburg Center for Research on Black Culture opens a new $53.8 million building next to its original structure. The Schomburg Center contains the largest collection of historical data on African Americans.

MED. On November 17, WHMM-TV becomes the first African American public broadcasting television station.

OBIT. The winner of four gold medals in track and field at the 1936 Berlin Olympic Games, Jesse Owens, dies in Tucson, Arizona, at the age of 66.

1981

ASSO. On September 9, Vernon E. Jordan resigns as president of the National Urban League and joins a Washington, DC, law firm. He is succeeded by John E. Jacob, the National Urban League's vice president.

BUSI. On August 10, Jesse Jackson's civil rights organization, PUSH, receives an offer from the Coca-Cola Bottling Company to invest $34 million in African American businesses, thereby ending a national boycott by PUSH of the company's soft-drink products.

CRIM. On March 5, the U.S. government grants the Atlanta, Georgia, city government $1 million to finance mental health and social programs in the wake of a mysterious series of abductions and killings of at least 22 African American youths.

On April 29, a Buffalo, New York, grand jury indicts Joseph G. Christopher, a white U.S. Army soldier, on murder charges stemming from the racially motivated slaying of three African Americans in September 1980.

On July 17, Wayne B. Williams, a 23-year-old photographer, is indicted by an Atlanta, Georgia, grand jury for murdering 2 African American youths among the 28 killed in a series of murders and disappearances in Atlanta. Williams, who denies the charges, is convicted on February 27, 1982. After he is sentenced to two life terms, Williams appeals the conviction, but it is upheld on December 5, 1983.

On September 28, Joseph Paul Franklin, an avowed racist, is sentenced to life imprisonment for the murder of two African American joggers in Salt Lake City, Utah.

EDUC. On March 6, former dean of arts and sciences at Tufts University, Dr. Bernard Harleston, is appointed president of the City College of the City University of New York.

OBIT. On April 12, former heavyweight boxing champion Joe Louis dies at the age of 66 in Las Vegas, Nevada. He won the title in 1937 and held it until his retirement in 1949, the longest reign of any heavyweight champion.

On September 8, former National Association for the Advancement of Colored People (NAACP) Executive Director Roy Wilkins dies in New York City at the age of 80.

POLI. On September 19, more than 300,000 demonstrators from a variety of labor and civil rights organizations converge on Washington, DC, on what is billed as a Day of Solidarity to express their disagreement with President Ronald Reagan's administration and overall social policies.

On October 27, former UN Ambassador Andrew Young is elected mayor of Atlanta, Georgia.

Four African Americans are elected mayors of urban centers: on October 28, Edward M. McIntyre is elected the first African American mayor of Augusta, Georgia; on November 3, Coleman Young is reelected mayor of Detroit, Michigan; Thurman L. Milner is elected mayor of Hartford, Connecticut; and James Chase is elected mayor of Spokane, Washington.

On November 30, four African American newcomers are elected to Congress: Mervyn Dymally of California, Augustus Savage of Illinois, Harold Washington of Illinois, and George W. Crockett Jr. of Michigan.

SPOR. On January 14, the president of Lincoln University in Missouri, James Frank, is installed as the first African American president of the National Collegiate Athletic Association (NCAA).

WORK. On January 9, the U.S. Labor Department announces that African American unemployment in December 1980 is 14 percent.

1982

ARTS. Singer, dancer, and actor Michael Jackson wins eight Grammy Awards for his album *Thriller*.

CRIM. From December 28 to 31, a race riot rages in Miami, Florida, triggered by the shooting of an African American by Miami police.

LIT. Alice Walker's novel *The Color Purple* is published, bringing the author critical acclaim.

MILI. On August 11, U.S. Army Lt. Gen. Roscoe Robinson Jr. is promoted to four-star general and becomes the second African American in the U.S. military to hold that rank.

OBIT. On June 8, baseball great Leroy "Satchel" Paige dies at the age of 75 in Kansas City, Missouri.

On October 4, Heman Marion Sweatt dies in Atlanta, Georgia, at the age of 69. Sweatt became known as a result of the 1950 U.S. Supreme Court case *Sweatt v. Painter* in which the Court ruled that the University of Texas could not build or maintain a separate law school for one student due to his racial background, thereby supposedly addressing the issue of equal education. The court ruled that this was simply the "separate but equal" concept of *Plessy v. Ferguson* that was overturned in *Brown v. Board of Education*. The Supreme Court further explained that what makes a good educational institution is the student's ability to interact with a strong faculty, experienced administrators, influential alumni, tradition, and prestige.

Noted modern jazz pianist and composer Thelonious Monk dies. Monk is an innovator of the 1940s jazz evolution.

POLI. On June 29, President Ronald Reagan signs a bill that extends for 25 years specific provisions of the Voting Rights Act of 1965.

WORK. On February 5, the U.S. Labor Department reports the African American unemployment rate drops from 17.3 percent to 16.8 percent, yet it is twice the unemployment rate of white Americans.

1983

CIVI. On November 2, President Ronald Reagan signs into law a bill that designates the third Monday in January as a federal holiday in commemoration of Rev. Dr. Martin Luther King Jr.'s birthday on January 15.

CULT. On September 17, Vanessa Williams, a 20-year-old student from Syracuse University, becomes the first African American to win the Miss America title. On July 23, 1984, nude photos of Vanessa Williams are published in a national magazine. Williams resigns her title, which is then given to the first runner-up, Suzette Charles, who is also African American.

Jesse Jackson, 1983. Courtesy of Library of Congress.

LAW. On April 11, Charles Thomas becomes the first African American on the Virginia Supreme Court.

In *Memphis Fighters v. Stotts,* the U.S. Supreme Court rejects a judicial order to retain less-senior African American employees during layoffs.

OBIT. Noted pianist and composer Eubie Blake dies in New York City on February 12 at the age of 100.

On May 15, renowned photographer of Harlem, New York, James Van Der Zee dies at the age of 96 in Washington, DC.

POLI. On April 29, Harold Washington is sworn in as the first African American mayor of Chicago, Illinois.

Jesse Jackson, the director of PUSH, declares his candidacy for the presidency of the United States on November 2. His candidacy generates a high level of support in Midwestern states, surprising some pundits. He wins several states, including South Carolina and Louisiana.

On November 8, W. Wilson Goode becomes the mayor of Philadelphia, Pennsylvania.

SCIE. On August 30, Colonel Guion S. Bluford, Jr. becomes the first African American astronaut to travel into space when he participates as a mission specialist on the *Challenger.*

1984

CRIM. On November 11, African Americans, some of whom are celebrities, launch a series of protests against apartheid (legalized racial separation) in South Africa and the Reagan administration's supportive political policy toward South Africa. By December, nearly 40 people have been arrested for picketing the South African embassy in Washington, DC, and its other offices throughout the nation.

MED. *The Cosby Show*, a television program depicting the family life of a middle-class African American family, debuts on NBC. The program receives an Emmy Award in 1986.

OBIT. On March 28, minister, educator, and civil rights leader Dr. Benjamin E. Mays, who served as president of Morehouse College for 27 years, dies in Atlanta, Georgia, at the age of 89.

On April 1, popular singer Marvin Gay is shot and killed at the age of 44 by his father, Marvin Gay Sr., in Los Angeles, California. The shooting is judged to be accidental.

On April 26, noted jazz pianist and bandleader William "Count" Basie dies in Hollywood, Florida, at the age of 77.

On November 11, Rev. Martin Luther King Sr., longtime civil rights activist and father of Rev. Dr. Martin Luther King Jr., dies in Atlanta, Georgia, at the age of 84.

POLI. On March 13, African American Republican James L. Usry becomes mayor of Atlantic City, New Jersey.

Jesse Jackson terminates his bid for Democratic Party nominee for president of the United States in a speech as the Democratic National Convention in San Francisco on July 17.

SCIE. On August 30, Lt. Col. Guion S. Bluford Jr., one of the crew members on the space shuttle

Challenger, becomes the first African American to fly into outer space.

SPOR. On April 3, John Thompson becomes the first African American coach to win a Division 1 NCAA national basketball title.

From August 4 to 11, Carl Lewis becomes the first athlete since Jesse Owens's triumph at the 1936 Berlin Olympic Games to win four gold medals in track and field at the Olympics. Lewis's victories occur in the 100 and 200 meters, long jump, and 4 × 100-meter relay.

On October 7, Walter Payton of the Chicago Bears football team surpasses Jim Brown's (of the Cleveland Browns) career rushing record of 12,312 yards.

WAR. On October 25, U.S. Marines, Army Rangers, and a number of special forces units invade the country of Grenada in the Caribbean and depose the political leadership. The invasion is sparked by a series of international incidents, including the deaths of U.S. military personnel in the Middle East and a concern that Grenada might become a military threat to the United States due to its political relationship with the Communist government in Cuba.

WORK. On February 4, the Department of Labor reports that the unemployment rate among African Americans has remained at a record high 20.8 percent.

1985

ARTS. On January 4, opera star Leontyne Price makes her farewell performance at New York's Metropolitan Opera House. She plays the lead role in *Aida.*

CRIM. On January 25, Bernhard H. Goetz, a white male, shoots and wounds four African American youths, one critically, whom he alleges are about to rob him in a crowed New York City subway car. He is charged with the minor offense of illegal possession of a firearm. The shooting evokes a heated national and racially explosive debate on the right of the public to use extreme force.

Philadelphia Mayor W. Wilson Goode apologizes to the city for the armed attack by Philadelphia police and firefighters involved in the helicopter bombing of the home and headquarters of the militant group MOVE on May 13. The resulting fire kills 11 African Americans, including five children, and destroys 61 nearby homes.

EDUC. On July 31, Dr. Laval S. Wilson is named the first African American school superintendent in Boston, Massachusetts.

OBIT. On January 13, educator and former ambassador to Sweden Jerome Holland dies in New York City at the age of 69. He was also the first African American on the New York Stock Exchange board of directors.

On March 23, the first female African American ambassador and a presidential Cabinet member, Patricia Roberts Harris, dies at the age of 60 in Washington, DC.

On July 1, author, lawyer, and first African American woman Episcopal priest in the United States Pauli Murray dies at the age of 74 in Pittsburgh, Pennsylvania.

POLI. On January 4, Rep. William H. Gray is elected chairman of the House Budget Committee, the highest congressional post held by an African American.

On January 24, Tom Bradley, four-term mayor of Los Angeles, receives the National Association for the Advancement of Colored People (NAACP) Spingarn Medal for public service.

On November 5, state Senator L. Douglas Wilder is elected lieutenant governor of Virginia and becomes the first African American to hold this office in a southern state since Reconstruction.

SCIE. On April 29, Colonel Frederick D. Gregory becomes the first African American astronaut to pilot a space shuttle (the *Challenger*). This mission transports a space lab.

SPOR. On July 13, Arthur Ashe, the first African American male to win the Wimbledon Tennis Championships is inducted into the International Tennis Hall of Fame.

1986

BUSI. Oprah Winfrey forms her own production company, Harpo Productions. In 1989, she becomes the first African American woman to own a television and production studio company, making her one of the wealthiest women in the world.

CRIM. On December 20, a mob of white youths chase and kill Michael Griffith in the Howard Beach neighborhood of Queens, New York.

HHC. On October 23, the Centers for Disease Control and Prevention in Atlanta, Georgia, reports that African Americans account for 25 percent of U.S. victims of acquired immunodeficiency syndrome (Aids).

LAW. On July 2, the U.S. Supreme Court in *Wygant v. Jackson Board of Education* rejects a school board's plan for laying off white teachers while retaining less-senior black teachers, but it also rejects the Reagan administration's position that affirmative action should be limited to actual victims of discrimination, thus broadly upholding affirmative action.

The U.S. Supreme Court in *Local 93 of International Association of Fire Fighters v. City of Cleveland* upholds the promotion of minorities ahead of white applicants with higher test scores and greater seniority. This decision is an attempt to view affirmative action as a means to remedy past discrimination.

LIT. Playwright August Wilson receives the Pulitzer Prize for his play *Fences*. He receives another Pulitzer Prize in 1990 for *The Piano Lesson*.

OBIT. On May 11, Frederick Douglas "Fritz" Pollard, football player and coach and the first African American named to an All American football team (playing for Brown University) dies in Silver Spring, Maryland, at the age of 92 (see 2005).

POLI. On January 16, the bust of Martin Luther King Jr. is unveiled in the Great Rotunda of the U.S. Capitol.

On January 20, millions of African Americans and supporters celebrate the first Martin Luther King Jr. federal holiday.

On March 6, a commission selected by Mayor W. Wilson Goode of Philadelphia, Pennsylvania,

concludes that the mayor and other public officials are grossly negligent during the May 1985 bombing of the headquarters of the MOVE organization.

Edward Perkins becomes the first African American ambassador to South Africa on October 15.

On November 5, Gov. Evan Mecham of Arizona provokes a national furor when he decides to begin a process to rescind Martin Luther King Jr.'s. birthday as a state holiday.

SCIE. Ronald E. McNair, PhD, is mission specialist for the *Challenger* space craft. He is a physicist with a bachelor's degree in science from North Carolina A&M University and doctorate from Massachusetts Institute of Technology. Earlier in his career, as a member of the *Challenger* 41-B crew in 1984, he was the second African American astronaut to fly in space. This was his second mission.

On January 28, McNair is killed with six other astronauts when the shuttle *Challenger* explodes after liftoff.

On October 29, the National Academy of Sciences reports that approximately 25,000 Americans thus far have died from acquired immunodeficiency syndrome (AIDS).

SPOR. On February 7, during her freshman year at Stanford University, Debi Thomas becomes the first African American to win the senior women's U.S. Figure Skating Championship and World Figure Skating Championship. She is also named *Wide World of Sports* Athlete of the Year. Two years later she adds a second national title with a bronze medal in the Olympics.

1987

ASSO. On January 14, the National Urban League's report *State of Black America* presents strong criticism of President Ronald Reagan. The report states, "Black Americans enter 1987 besieged by the resurgence of raw racism, persistent economic depression and the continued erosion of past gains."

BUSI. Businessman Reginald Lewis buys Beatrice Foods, an international packaged-goods company, for $2.5 billion. This is the largest leveraged buy-out in U.S. history, and Lewis becomes the wealthiest African American. A graduate of Harvard Law School, Lewis starts his economic ascendancy by first purchasing the McCall Pattern Company. Before his death, Reginald Lewis donates millions of dollars to Howard University and the National Association for the Advancement of Colored People (NAACP).

CRIM. On January 17, white racists attack African Americans celebrating the birthday of Martin Luther King Jr. in Forsyth County, Georgia. On January 24, an interracial group of demonstrators marches in Forsyth County, Georgia, protesting racist attacks and an apparent complicity on the part of local police officials in Forsyth County.

On June 16, Bernhard H. Goetz is found innocent of the attempted murder of four African American youths he shot on a New York City subway.

LAW. On May 6, Thurgood Marshall, the first African American associate justice of the Supreme Court, criticizes plans for a national bicentennial celebration of the U.S. Constitution. He reminds Americans that the original document is anything but a perfect one and, in doing so, alludes to its gender bias and racist constructs.

LIT. On April 16, African American playwright August Wilson receives the Pulitzer Prize for his play *Fences*.

MILI. On November 5, Lt. Gen. Colin L. Powell becomes the national security advisor to President Ronald Reagan.

OBIT. The former NAACP president in Montgomery, Alabama, labor leader, and an important figure in the initial development of the Montgomery bus boycott, E. D. Nixon dies in Montgomery, Alabama, on February 25 at the age of 87.

On August 24, civil rights activist and major planner of the March on Washington and the Freedom Rides Bayard Rustin dies at the age of 75 in New York City.

Noted writer John O. Killens dies in Brooklyn, New York, on October 27 at the age of 71.

On November 25, Chicago Mayor Harold Washington dies in Chicago, Illinois. African American Alderman Eugene Sawyer succeeds him.

On December 1, novelist and civil rights activist James Baldwin dies at the age of 63 in St. Paul de Vence, France.

On December 15, civil rights leader Septima Poinsette Clark, who played a role in establishing the Southern Christian Leadership Conference and the Student Non-Violent Coordinating Committee, dies on St. John Island, South Carolina, at the age of 89.

POLI. On April 7, Chicago Mayor Harold Washington is reelected by an overwhelming margin.

Jesse Jackson announces that he will, for the second time, attempt to gain the Democratic Party nomination for the U.S. presidency.

Carrie Saxon Perry is elected mayor of Hartford, Connecticut, on November 3 and in doing so becomes the first African American woman mayor of a major city in the northeastern United States.

SCIE. On June 5, a Los Angeles physician, Dr. Mae C. Jemison, is named the first African American astronaut.

SPOR. On April 8, Al Campanis, a Los Angeles Dodgers baseball executive, is fired for slurring African Americans on television when he questions the managerial potential of black baseball players. Campanis makes his comments on a television program honoring the accomplishments of legendary baseball player Jackie Robinson, the first African American to play major league baseball.

1988

BUSI. On June 29, Berry Gordy's Motown Record Company is sold to an MCA/Boston Ventures partnership for $61 million.

CENS. On August 31, the U.S. Census Bureau reports that the median income for African American families in 1987 is about $18,098, compared to the $32,274 median income for white Americans. The Census Bureau also reports that the poverty level in 1987 among white Americans is 10.5 percent, but among African Americans it is, 33.1 percent. The Census Bureau notes the poverty rate for all children is 10.5 percent, compared to the 45.8 percent found among African American children.

CIVI. On August 27, 60,000 people march in Washington, DC, to commemorate the 25th anniversary of the 1963 March on Washington.

On September 13, President Ronald Reagan signs the bipartisan Fair Housing Bill that expands protection against housing discrimination.

CRIM. On February 12, approximately 200 students from the University of Massachusetts occupy the African American Studies building to protest the brutal beating of two African American students by six white men.

On August 4, a major fire destroys the first African American Phi Beta fraternity house at the University of Mississippi. Investigators suspect that arson is the cause of the fire.

CULT. On December 21, Rev. Jesse Jackson and a group of African American leaders call for the abandonment of the term *black* to describe African Americans. The argument is that the term *African American* defines a geographical, cultural, and political origin for African descendants.

EDUC. On July 14, the National Association for the Advancement of Colored People (NAACP) presents its 73rd Spingarn Medal posthumously to Dr. Frederick D. Patterson, founder of the United Negro College Fund.

On November 4, television star Bill Cosby and his wife, Camille, donate $20 million to Spelman College in Atlanta, Georgia. This is the largest single monetary gift given by an African American to an African American college.

HHC. On December 22, Morehouse Medical School President Louis W. Sullivan is named U.S. secretary of the Department of Health and Human Services.

LAW. On March 3, Juanita Kidd Stout is sworn in as justice of the Pennsylvania Supreme Court and becomes the first African American woman to sit on a state supreme court.

On May 3, Mayor W. Wilson Goode and his top aides are cleared of criminal responsibility in the 1985 bombing attack on MOVE headquarters in Philadelphia, Pennsylvania. In this attack, 11 people are killed and 60 homes destroyed. Though cleared of criminal charges after the two-year investigation, the jury criticizes the mayor and this aides for their gross incompetence in handling the militant group.

LIT. On March 31, famed novelist Toni Morrison wins the Pulitzer Prize for her novel *Beloved.*

OBIT. Noted blues singer Memphis Slim dies at the age of 72 in Paris, France, on February 24.

On March 12, African American painter Romare Bearden dies in New York City at the age of 75.

On October 7, dancer and entertainer Billy Daniels dies in Los Angeles, California, at the age of 73. He is noted for the song "That Old Black Magic."

On October 24, S. B. Fuller, an African American businessman and founder and president of Chicago's Fuller Products Company, dies in the Chicago, Illinois, suburb of Blue Island at the age of 83.

On December 15, attorney Wiley A. Branton, who represented the African American students in the Little Rock integration crisis and who served as dean of the Howard University Law School, dies at the age of 65 in Washington, DC.

On December 20, Max Robinson dies in Washington, DC, at the age of 49. He is the first African American anchor of a major news network, ABC.

POLI. On March 8, Jesse Jackson wins five states in the presidential primaries on Super Tuesday.

On August 2, the Congressional Black Caucus sends a letter to Japanese Premier Noboru Takeshita protesting Japan's anti–African American remarks and ongoing anti-African practices.

On October 23, Jesse Jackson criticizes Vice President George Bush and the Republican Party for using photographs of convict Willie Horton to spread racial fear and raise concerns about African American crime during the presidential campaign.

On December 5, Rep. William H. Gray, Democrat from Pennsylvania, wins a three-way race for chairman of the House Democratic Caucus and becomes the first African American admitted to the highest ranks of congressional leadership.

RELI. On March 15, Washington, DC, Auxiliary Bishop Eugene Antonio Marino is named both the first African American archbishop of Atlanta and the first African American Roman Catholic archbishop in the United States.

On September 24, the Episcopal Church elects the Most Reverend Barbara C. Harris of Massachusetts as its first African American woman bishop.

SPOR. On January 16, the CBS sports commentator Jimmy "The Greek" Snyder comments during a Washington, DC, television program that if any more African Americans take coaching positions, there will not be any left for whites. Snyder's remarks provoke viewer complaints about their racist implications. He is quickly fired by CBS.

On January 31, Doug Williams, the first African American to quarterback a Super Bowl team, passes for a record of 340 yards and ties a record with four touchdown passes in leading the Washington Redskins to a 42–10 victory over the Denver Broncos. Williams is also named the most valuable player of Super Bowl XXII, played in San Diego, California.

On April 12, Frank Robinson, who was fired from his job as the first African American manager of a major league baseball team by the San Francisco Giants, is hired by the Baltimore Orioles.

In September, African American athletes at the Seoul, Korea, Olympic Games brake a number of records. Jackie Joyner-Kersee brakes her own world record in winning the heptathlon. She also wins a gold medal in the long jump. Carl Lewis wins the long jump and the men's 100 meters. Florence Griffith Joyner establishes records in the 200 meters and wins gold medals in the 100 meters and 4 × 100-meter relay. Her three gold medals and one silver medal represent the second best effort for a woman in Olympic history. Kenny Monday wins the 163-pound wrestling

event and becomes the first African American to win a gold medal in wrestling.

On December 3, Barry Sanders of Oklahoma State University wins the Heisman Trophy.

WORK. On February 5, the U.S. Labor Department announces that the African American unemployment is 12.2 percent, Hispanic unemployment is 7.2 percent, but the national average is 5.7 percent.

1989

ARTS. On June 4, singer Ruth Brown wins a Tony Award for her role in the Broadway play *Black and Blue*. For the same play, Henry LeTang, Frankie Manning, and Fayard Nichols share a Tony Award for choreography.

BUSI. On October 21, African American businessmen Peter Bynoe and Bertram Lee of the National Basketball Association (NBA) Denver Nuggets become the first African Americans to hold a substantial minority ownership interest of a major league sports franchise.

CENS. The U.S. Census Bureau states that the poverty rate for African Americans in 1988 is 31.6 percent, compared to 10.1 percent for white Americans and 26.8 percent for Hispanic Americans.

CRIM. An African American motorcyclist is shot and killed by Miami, Florida, police after a long chase. The killing is a catalyst for three days of violent disturbances between January 16 and 18.

On August 29, Yusuf K. Hawkins, a 16-year-old African American youth, is murdered in the Bensonhurst section of Brooklyn, New York, by a gang of white youths. Hawkins's death inflames racial passions and tensions throughout the city. Six white youths are arrested for the murder.

On September 2, clashes between African American students and police in Virginia Beach, Virginia, lead to the injury of 43 people and 260 arrests. The clash occurs during an annual student retreat in the popular resort town.

CULT. On September 16, Debbye Turner of Missouri is crowned Miss America. She is the third African American woman to wear the crown.

EDUC. On January 11, critics of the National Collegiate Athletic Association deride the association's decision to approve a new rule, Proposition 42, that eliminates athletic scholarships for freshmen who do not meet minimum academic standards. Consequently, all students on athletic scholarships must maintain at least a C average. Critics charge racial bias, however, and manipulation of academic standards.

HHC. On April 13, the Centers for Disease Control and Prevention state that 27 percent of all reported cases of acquired immunodeficiency syndrome (AIDS) occur among African Americans, although African Americans make up only 12 percent of the total population.

LAW. The U.S. Supreme Court rules in *Richmond v. J. Croson and Co.* that the Fourteenth Amendment prohibits set-asides for minority contractors, thus going against spirit of *Weber v. Kaiser Aluminum and Chemical Corporation* and against the letter of *Fullilove v. Klutznich* and implying that all such plans face strict scrutiny.

MED. On September 20, Euzhan Palcy becomes the first African American woman to direct a full-length feature film for a major U.S. studio when her film, *A Dry White Season,* premiers.

On September 19, Gordon Parks's *Learning Tree* becomes one of the first films registered by the National Film Registry of the U.S. Library of Congress.

MEDI. On March 1, former Morehouse Medical School President Dr. Louis W. Sullivan is confirmed as secretary of the Department of Health and Human Services by a vote of 98–1. The negative vote comes from southern conservative Senator Jesse Helms.

MILI. On February 2, African American Lt. Cdr. Evelyn Fields is named the first woman to command a U.S. Navy ship.

On September 21, Gen. Colin Powell becomes the first African American to serve as the chairman of the U.S. Joint Chiefs of Staff.

OBIT. Noted African American poet Sterling A. Brown dies in Tacoma Park, Maryland, on January 13 at the age of 87.

Noted nurse and health care specialist Mabel K. Straupers dies at the age of 99 in Washington, DC.

On February 26, trumpet player Roy Eldridge dies in Valley Spring, New York, at the age of 78.

On May 10, the first African chancellor of the New York City Public Schools, Richard R. Green, dies after a severe asthma attack.

On August 7, outspoken African American chairman of the House Select Committee on Hunger Mickey Leland dies in an airplane crash in western Ethiopia near the Sudan border. Although investigators rule this an unfortunate accident, controversy surrounds the circumstances of Leland's death.

Huey P. Newton, cofounder of the Black Panther Party for Self Defense, is shot to death in an Oakland, California, neighborhood on August 22. Circumstances surrounding his murder suggest some level of drug involvement.

On December 1, dancer, choreographer, and director Alvin Ailey dies in New York City at the age of 58. Alvin Ailey's American Dance Theater is world renowned for its excellence.

On December 24, the first African American mayor of New Orleans, Ernest Nathan "Dutch" Morial, dies at the age of 60 in New Orleans, Louisiana.

POLI. On January 3, Rep. John Conyers, Democrat from Michigan, is elected chairman of the U.S. Government Operation Committee of the House of Representatives.

On February 10, Rep. Ronald H. "Ron" Brown is elected chairman of the Democratic Party and becomes the first African American to head a major national political party.

On March 7, Republican National Committee Chairman Lee Atwater resigns his trusteeship position at Howard University after students demonstrate against his decisions and positions on civil rights, which they define as his racist strategy during Republican George Bush's 1988 presidential campaign.

On June 14, Democrat William Gray is elected majority whip of the House of Representatives. He is the first African American to hold this position.

Gwendolyn S. King becomes the first African American commissioner of the Social Security Administration on August 1.

On August 6, National Urban League President John E. Jacob announces at the organization's annual conference that recent Supreme Court decisions are a direct threat to the interest of African Americans.

Maynard Jackson, the first African American mayor of Atlanta, Georgia, is reelected to office on October 3. He previously served as mayor from 1974 to 1982 and was replaced by Andrew Young, who also was mayor for two terms.

On November 7, L. Douglass Wilder is elected governor of Virginia and becomes the first African American governor of a U.S. state. Other election victories include David Dinkins as the first African American mayor of New York City.

SCIE. On November 22, U.S. Air Force Col. Frederick D. Gregory commands the space shuttle *Discovery* as the first African American to lead a space mission.

SPOR. On January 22, San Francisco 49ers tight end Jerry Rice receives the Most Valuable Player Award during the team's victory against the Cincinnati Bengals in Super Bowl XXIII.

Bill White, a former New York Yankee baseball star and radio announcer, is named president of the National League. He assumes the position on April 1.

Former football offensive end Art Shell of the Oakland Raiders is named head coach of the Los Angeles Raiders and becomes the first African American head coach since 1925.

On November 1, Frank Robinson is named the American League's baseball manager of the year.

WORK. On January 23, the U.S. Supreme Court bans a Richmond, Virginia, program that sets aside 30 percent of the city's public works funds for minority-owned construction companies in *Richmond v. J. Croson and Co.* The court states that the Fourteenth Amendment prohibits set-asides for minority contractors. The 6–3 ruling, written by Associate Justice Sandra Day O'Connor, says that the program constitutes reverse discrimination. In dissent, Associate Justice Thurgood Marshall argues that it constituted "a full scale retreat from the court's long-standing solicitude to race-conscious remedial efforts directed toward deliverance of the century-old promise of equality of opportunity." This decision dramatically goes against the *United Steelworkers v. Weber* (1979) and *Fullilove v. Klutznick* (1980) decisions that support minority preferential hiring and training in the workplace as well as government programs that reserve places for minorities.

On March 10, the U.S. Labor Department reports that African American unemployment is 11.9 percent in February, compared to white unemployment of 4.3 percent.

On June 12, the U.S. Supreme Court in *Martin v. Wilks* rules that employees may challenge affirmative-action plans after they have gone into effect. Though Congress in the 1991 Civil Rights Act overrules this decision, it reflects the tenor of the times for white workers who sense that a level of racial privilege enjoyed in the past has waned. In a separate ruling the same day, the Court rules against a belated challenge to a discriminatory seniority system.

1990

ARTS. Stage and screen actor Denzel Washington wins an Academy Award for best supporting actor for his role in *Glory*, the epic Civil War drama of the black Fifty-Fourth Massachusetts Volunteer Infantry that fought gallantly at Fort Wagner, South Carolina, in July 1863.

On August 14, popular singer and composer Curtis Mayfield is paralyzed in an accident at an outdoor concert in Brooklyn, New York.

BUSI. On November 9, Freedom National Bank in Harlem, New York, one of the country's largest African American commercial institutions, is declared insolvent by federal regulators. Founded in 1965, the bank has 22,000 depositors and $91 million in deposits. Most of its depositors are protected by the Federal Deposit Insurance Corporation (FDIC) and are issued refunds to accounts less than $100,000.

CENS. The federal government reports that the population of the United States is 248,709,878, of which 29,987,060 (12.1%) are African Americans.

CRIM. On January 18, Washington, DC, Mayor Marion S. Barry Jr. is arrested by local police and

Federal Bureau of Investigation agents who videotape him smoking crack cocaine in a sting operation. He is later convicted and sentenced to a federal prison.

CULT. On March 3, Carole Gist becomes the first African American to win the Miss USA title.

On September 8, Illinois African American law student Marjorie Judith Vincent is crowned Miss America at the annual pageant.

EDUC. On February 23, Bishop College in Dallas, Texas, is sold at a bankruptcy auction to businessman Comer J. Cottrell, who says he will try to keep it open as a predominately African American institution.

On March 29, the U.S. Department of Education announces that enrollment of African American students at private colleges and universities rose by 7.1 percent between 1986 and 1988. During the same period, African American enrollment in public institutions of higher learning rose by only 0.2 percent.

On April 23, Derrick A. Bell Jr., the first African American law professor at Harvard University, takes a sabbatical to protest the university's inability to hire an African American female to its tenured faculty.

Eleanor Holmes Norton serves as professor of law at the Georgetown University Law Center in Washington, DC. She is also elected as a nonvoting representative to Congress from the District of Columbia.

ENTE. On January 3, Tupac Shakur (as a roadie, dancer, and rapper with his firsts major group, Digital Underground), records "This Is an E.P. Release." Over the next six years, his quick rise to fame and recognition is fueled by artistic skills in films such as *Juice* (1992), *Poetic Justice* (1993), *Above the Rim* (1994), and *Gang Related* (1996) and more significantly as a rapper and producer of, *2Pacalypse Now* (1991), *Strictly 4 My N.I.G.G.A.Z.* (1993), *Me Against the World* (1995), *All Eyes on Me* (1996), and his controversial *"Hit 'Em Up"* (1996). Though these albums sell in the millions, singles such as "Dear Mama" go platinum in seven months.

HHC. On March 22, the U.S. Department of Health and Human Services issues a report that indicates the health gap between African Americans and white Americans is widening, with the life expectancy of Africans Americans being 69.4 years, compared to whites' 75.6 years. The infant mortality rate is even more staggering at 17.9 per 1,000 for African Americans, compared to 8.6 per 1,000 for white Americans.

INVE. On April 8, two noted African American scientists are admitted to the National Inventors Hall of Fame: Percy Julian, who created drugs that combated glaucoma and devised methods to mass-produce cortisone, and famed agriculturalist, chemist, and educator George Washington Carver.

LAW. The U.S. Supreme Court in *Metro Broadcasting v. FCC* upholds an affirmative-action plan to increase minority broadcasting owners, returning to *Fullilove v. Klutznich.*

OBIT. On January 1, African American fashion designer Patrick Kelly dies at the age of 40 in Paris, France.

Longtime civil right activist, aide to Rev. Martin Luther King Jr. during the Montgomery bus boycott and the Southern Christian Leadership Conference (SCLC) civil rights campaigns throughout the 1950s and 1960s Rev. Ralph Abernathy dies in Atlanta, Georgia, at the age of 64.

On April 23, Clifton R. Wharton, the first African American U.S. State Department career officer to reach the ranks of minister and ambassador, dies at the age of 90 in Phoenix, Arizona. He joined the U.S. Foreign Service in 1924 and was appointed ambassador to Sweden in 1961.

On April 25, master musician and tenor saxophone great Dexter Gordon dies at the age of 67 in Philadelphia, Pennsylvania. Gordon received an Academy Award nomination for his role in the jazz film *'Round Midnight.*

On May 16, entertainer, singer, and dancer Sammy Davis Jr. dies at the age of 64 in Beverly Hills, California.

Actor and director Raymond St. Jacques Jr. dies in Los Angeles, California, at the age of 60.

POLI. In November, Arizona voters defeat two propositions that would have established Rev. Martin Luther King Jr.'s birthday as a paid holiday for state workers. As a result of this decision, numerous associations who would have held their national conventions in Arizona withdraw until Arizona establishes King's birthday as a state holiday. This has an immediate financial impact on Phoenix, the state capital.

State Rep. Daniel T. Blue, a North Carolina Democratic, is elected on December 7 as the first African American speaker of a southern legislature body since Reconstruction.

RELI. On May 13, George Stallings is ordained the first bishop of the African American Catholic Church. Stallings renounced the Roman Catholic Church in 1989, citing its failure to meet the needs of African American Catholics. The new church also has a more Afrocentric liturgy.

SPOR. On January 8, the National Collegiate Athletic Association (NCAA) modifies its 1989 Proposition 42 and permits first-year student-athletes to receive financial aid based upon need. They retain, however, a provision that bars participation in sports by first-year students failing to meet minimum educational requirements.

On November 15, the U.S. Golf Association, following a decision by the Professional Golfers Association (PGA), announces that it will require clubs hosting golf tournaments to ban discrimination against minorities and women.

WORK. The U.S. Labor Department releases comparative unemployment figures for African Americans, which is 11.3 percent, and for white Americans, which is 4.6 percent.

1991

ARTS. On March 25, actress Whoopi Goldberg receives an Academy Award for best supporting actress in her role in *Ghost*. She is the second African American woman to be so honored.

BUSI. From April 17 to 19, African American leaders meet in Abidjan, Ivory Coast, for the first Summit Meeting of Africans and African Americans. Organized by Rev. Leon H. Sullivan,

who calls for closer economic and social ties between Africans and African Americans, also urges European powers to cancel African countries' foreign debt, citing the enormous profits European colonialism enjoyed in the past. At the summit, Sullivan in his keynote speech tells Africans, "Hold on, Africa, we are coming! Home of our heritage, land of our past, we can help. We have 2 million college graduates in America. We earn $200 billion a year. Three centuries ago they took us away in a boat, but today we have come back in an airplane."

On July 10, U.S. President George Bush lifts U.S. trade and investments sanctions against the racist, apartheid government of South Africa. The sanctions originally placed on South Africa, due to its racist governing policies, are lifted because of an improvement in their policies. Top Democratic Party and African American leaders and lobbyists cite, instead, the growing number of prisoners and the denial of the vote to the majority African population as reasons to counter, argue against, and demonstrate against President Bush's political policies and administrative philosophy.

On October 21, the Federal Reserve Board reports that African Americans are twice as likely to be turned down for a mortgage than white Americans in the same income group.

CDIS. On August 19, a Hasidic Jewish driver strikes and kills a seven-year-old African American youth. The incident explodes into further violence as Jewish and largely African Caribbean residents face off and fight each other and the police for four days in the Crown Heights section of Brooklyn, New York.

CENS. On March 8, the U.S. Census Bureau reports in 1990 a 13.2 percent increase in the number of African Americans in the country, placing their population at 30 million. The bureau also indicates that 77 percent of white American children and 37 percent of African American children live in two-parent households. These results are immediately challenged, however, by African American and other minority groups around the country, claiming that their population numbers are purposely undercounted for political representation purposes.

On April 18, the U.S. Census Bureau reports that four to six million people have been overlooked and that African Americans are undercounted by 6 percent compared to non–African Americans.

CRIM. On March 3, Los Angeles police beat motorist Rodney G. King after he is stopped for an alleged speeding violation. Much of King's beating is videotaped and distributed to major media outlets on March 4 and 5. Writer and columnist Earl Ofari Hutchinson suggests, "Black professionals or business owners tell harrowing tales of being spread-eagle over the hoods of their expensive BMW's or Porsches while the police ran makes on them and tore their cars apart searching for drugs. In polls taken after the Rodney King beating, blacks were virtually unanimous in saying that they believed any black person could have been on the ground that night being pulverized by the police. These were eternal reminders to the "new" black bourgeoisie that they could escape the hood, but many Americans still considered them hoods." Despite the graphic videotape evidence, the officers involved are acquitted of using excessive force.

On June 28, Miami police shoot an African American suspect and trigger widespread civil disturbance throughout the black communities.

EDUC. On October 4, the world's largest public circulating library is dedicated to the memory of the former Chicago mayor as the Harold Washington Library Center.

LAW. On June 27, citing "advancing age and medical condition," U.S. Supreme Court Associate Justice Thurgood Marshall announces his retirement from the bench at the age of 82. In his final dissent (in the case of *Payne v. Tennessee*), Marshall notes that the Court's conservative majority is recklessly overturning decisions protecting the rights of African Americans and minorities. It becomes apparent to Justice Marshall and his law clerks that Chief Justice Rehnquist's court is going to use the *Payne* case to trample on the principle of stare decisis, that is, the principle that once the Court has decided an issue, that decision becomes the law that

Americans can count on. Rehnquist announces, in the June 27 decision, that the Court is declaring victim-impact statements constitutional, a position with which Marshall strongly disagreed.

On July 1, President George Bush nominates Judge Clarence Thomas, a conservative African American from the U.S. District of Columbia Court of Appeals, to fill the vacancy left by retiring Justice Thurgood Marshall.

On November 21, President Bush reverses himself and signs the compromise Civil Rights Act of 1991, making it easier for workers to sue in job discrimination cases. This also makes it easier for so-called reverse-discrimination suits to be adjudicated.

OBIT. On February 25, Adrienne Mitchell is the first African American woman to die in combat. She is killed in her military barracks in Saudi Arabia during the Persian Gulf War.

On April 28, civil rights leader, speaker, founder of the community Soul City, and former director of the Congress of Racial Equality Floyd B. McKissick dies in Soul City, North Carolina, at the age of 69.

On July 17, Roman Catholic Bishop Harold R. Perry, the first African American Roman Catholic bishop in the twentieth century and the first African American minister to deliver the opening prayer in the U.S. Congress, dies at the age of 74 in New Orleans, Louisiana.

On October 11, comedian Redd Foxx, who created the role of Fred Sanford in the TV hit *Sanford and Son,* dies at the age of 68 on the set of another TV series, *The Royal Family,* in Los Angeles, California.

POLI. On June 3, the U.S. Supreme Court extends its ban on race-based juror exclusion in its ruling in *Edmonson v. Leesville Concrete Co.,* stating potential jurors in a civil case cannot be peremptorily challenged on the basis of race alone.

On June 20, Rep. William H. Gray, the third-ranking Democrat in the U.S. House of Representatives and the highest-ranking African American in Congress, resigns his position and becomes the new president of the United Negro College Fund. He succeeds Christopher Edley.

On August 2, civil rights leader John Lewis, former chairman of Student Non-Violent Coordinating Committee (SNCC) and a supporter of Rev. Martin Luther King Jr. is named Democratic deputy whip of the U.S. House of Representatives.

WAR. On January 16, the Persian Gulf War begins with a U.S. military attack on Iraq. A disproportionate number of African American soldiers are involved in the military campaign. Some critics of the war claim that because of the realities of the all-volunteer army, many African Americans and the poor join the military as a way to survive economically, thereby placing themselves in a vulnerable position in a needless war.

On March 21. the U.S. Department of Defense reports that African Americans make up 24.5 percent of the combat force in Operation Desert Storm and are 15 percent of the fatalities.

On April 15, Cpl. Freddie Stowers is posthumously presented the nation's highest military award, the Medal of Honor, for heroism in World War I. The citation reads:

> Stowers unit the 371st Infantry Regiment was poised to attack a German position, when a German NCO came forward to indicate his fellow comrades were willing to surrender. Germans started climbing out of their trenches with their arms up in surrender. The 371st advanced without firing, when a whistle was blown and the Germans jumped back into their trenches and started firing on the 371st killing those African American soldiers in the forward squads. In the midst of the ensuing battle, Corporal Stowers led his squad in a relentless firing on the Germans, destroying a machine gun position that had previously inflicted 40 percent of his company's casualties. Stowers was eventually seriously wounded while moving to destroy another German machine gun position. Due to his heroism, German units were pushed out of the area allowing the final phase of the attack to continue on.

It takes 73 years for his actions to be recognized. The other reality is that from the Spanish-American War onward, African American military personnel are excluded from receiving the nation's highest military award due to institutional racism. When announcing this award, the U.S. Army refuses to recognize past racism when they claim Cpl. Freddie Stowers did not receive the award when alive due to bureaucratic oversight.

1992

ARTS. Noted filmmaker Spike Lee releases his epic movie *Malcolm X* to generally favorable critical acclaim. Known for his provocative and bold films that expose the inner motivations and dynamics of African American life and racial presumptions in U.S. society, Lee's films are often on the cutting edge of controversy: *Jungle Fever* addresses social issues connected with interracial love; an African American woman's sexuality in *She's Gotta Have It;* race and class issues in *Do the Right Thing* (see 2001).

Dancer, actor, and singer Gregory Hines receives a Tony Award for the musical *Jelly's Last Jam.* He also receives Tony Award nominations for his performances in *Eubie, Comin' Uptown,* and *Sophisticated Ladies.* Starring in 25 films either as a dancer or in a dramatic role, his performances capture the attention of both audiences and film critics. His notable cinematic performances are in *The Cotton Club, White Nights, Running Scared,* and *Tap.* He hosts his own show, *The Gregory Hines Show,* in 1997 and plays in a recurring role in *Will & Grace* as Ben Doucette. Hines's idol is Sammy Davis Jr., whose dancing style he tried to emulate as a child.

On March 18, singer Donna Summers receives a star on Hollywood's Walk of Fame.

ASSO. On February 15, National Association for the Advancement of Colored People (NAACP) Director Benjamin L. Hooks announces that he will retire in 1993. Hooks has headed the association since 1977.

CDIS. On April 29, a superior court in Simi Valley, a suburb of Los Angeles, California, acquits the four white police officers involved in the videotaped beating of motorist Rodney King. Within a few hours, the largest urban disturbance since the New York City Conscription Riot of 1863 erupts throughout Los Angeles and smaller surrounding municipalities. Federalized National Guard units and U.S. Army troops struggle to contain the pent-up anger and frustration vented upon the city. Similar upheavals occur in other major urban centers.

CENS. The U.S. Census Bureau announces that the gap between the median incomes of white households and African American households narrowed slightly in the 1980s. The median income for African Americans in 1989 is $19,758, or 63 percent of the $31,435 median income for white Americans. The report also indicates a measurable gain in high school graduates among African Americans. In college degrees, the number increases from 8.4 percent in 1980 to 11 percent in 1990.

CRIM. On February 10, former heavyweight boxing champion Mike Tyson is convicted of raping an 18-year-old Miss America contestant in Indianapolis, Indiana. He appeals the case on grounds that the jury did not represent the racial composition of the county. He is sentenced to six years in prison.

On April 16, former Philadelphia Police Chief Willie L. Williams is named chief of the Los Angeles Police Department.

On April 23, former Washington, DC, Mayor Marion S. Barry Jr. is released from Loretto Prison in Pennsylvania after serving six months for cocaine possession.

On August 5, the U.S. Attorney's office announces that a federal grand jury has indicted the four white police officers acquitted in the beating of Rodney King. Their indictment cites the violation of Rodney King's civil rights.

EDUC. Dr. Derrick A. Bell Jr. is fired by Harvard University when he refuses to return to the school because of its inability to hire an African American female law professor as tenured faculty.

LAW. On February 1, U.S. Immigration and Naturalization Service (INS) officials forcibly repatriate Haitian refugees picked up at sea while fleeing their homeland. The U.S. government's rationale for rejecting Haitians is that U.S. law only provides for exile if a person or group is fleeing from political oppression,

whereas Haitians are fleeing for economic reasons. African American leaders, along with high-ranking white Democrats, say the policy is racist and that the distinctions between political and economic oppression are not exclusive of each other.

On June 18, the U.S. Supreme Court rules in *Georgia v. McCollum* that defendants in a criminal case cannot bar potential jurors solely on the basis of race.

On June 22, the U.S. Supreme Court rules 5–4 that a St. Paul, Minnesota, law making it a crime to engage in inflammatory racist or sexist speech is unconstitutional.

On June 26, a direct threat to the existence of traditional or historical African American colleges and universities is posed when the U.S. Supreme Court rules 8–1 that so-called race-neutral policies do not relieve the state of Mississippi from its obligation to eliminate segregation in the public university system.

LIT. On July 6, author Terry McMillan publishes her novel *Waiting to Exhale,* which is acclaimed for its portrayal of an older woman who finds herself in love of a younger man. The film version is also a major success. The works of two other African American woman novelists, Toni Morrison and Alice Walker, create a further sensation by moving onto the *New York Times* bestseller list, and the three jointly hold sway for three weeks.

On October 8, the Nobel Prize for Literature is awarded to West Indian poet and playwright Derek Walcott, who makes his home in the United States.

MED. On April 30, the last episode of *The Cosby Show* is aired. It is one of the most popular family-oriented TV programs in the history of the industry; however, the show is also controversial because of the upper-middle-class status of the Huxtable family and Bill Cosby's role as a doctor and Phylicia Rashad's role as an attorney. Some critics argue that it is not a real portrayal of a middle-class African American family, whereas others say there should no stereotype for what is a middle-class family and that the Huxtables simply present one version.

OBIT. Blues singer Willie Dixon dies in Burbank, California, on January 29 at the age of 76. He is best known for his songs "Hoochie Koochie Man" and "My Babe."

On February 10, Author of the Pulitzer Prize-winning *Roots* and the award-winning *The Autobiography of Malcolm X* Alexander Haley dies in Seattle, Washington, at the age of 70.

On February 26, the first African American woman to head a large white educational institution, the University of Houston in Texas, Marguerite R. Barnett, dies at the age of 49 in Wailuku, Hawaii.

On May 13, Mary Wells, who became well known as a singer on the Motown label, dies in Los Angeles, California, at the age of 49.

On August 25, actor Frederick O'Neal dies at the age of 86 in New York City. He was the first African American president of the Actor's Equity Association.

On October 5, Eddie Kendricks, tenor singer with the popular vocal group the Temptations, dies in Birmingham, Alabama, at the age of 52.

Movie, theater, and television actor Cleavon Little dies at the age of 53 in Sherman Oaks, California. Little is best known for his performance in the movie *Blazing Saddles* and received a Tony Award for the title role in the musical *Purlie*. He was also celebrated as one of the early actors in the long running hit television program *Saturday Night Live!*

POLI. On January 27, the U.S. Supreme Court limits the scope of the Voting Rights Act of 1965.

Tom Bradley announces that he will not seek a sixth term as mayor of Los Angeles, California.

On November 4, Carol Moseley Braun of Illinois defeats a white male opponent and becomes the first African American female and Democrat in the U.S. Senate.

Sixteen new House members—11 men and 5 women—bring the total number of African Americans in Congress to a historic high of 40. Among the new House members are the first post-Reconstruction representatives from Alabama (Earl Hilliard), Florida (Corrine Brown, Alcee Hastings, and Carrie Meek), North Carolina (Eva Clayton and Melvin Watt), South Carolina (Jim Clyburn), and Virginia (Bobby Scott).

On November 6, President Bill Clinton names attorney and former National Urban League Director Vernon E. Jordan Jr. chairman of his transition team, making him the first African American to head a transition team of a U.S. president. Jordan's deputy director is an African American woman, Alexis Herman.

On December 12, President-elect Clinton names Democratic National Chairman Ronald H. Brown to be the U.S. secretary of commerce in the new administration.

On December 12, President-elect Clinton names Jesse Brown, a Vietnam War veteran and the director of Veterans of America, to be secretary of veterans affairs.

On December 21, President-elect Clinton names Hazel R. O'Leary, a Minnesota Power Company executive, as secretary of energy. She is the first African American and woman to hold that office.

On December 22, President-elect Clinton names educator and businessman Clifton R. Wharton Jr. as undersecretary of state, the highest position held by an African American in the State Department.

On December 24, President-elect Clinton names Rep. Mike Espy, an African American Democrat from Mississippi, as secretary of agriculture.

SCIE. On September 12, astronaut Mae Jemison becomes the first African American woman to go into space on the space shuttle *Endeavor*. Jemison joined the National Aeronautics and Space Administration (NASA) in 1987 and served as a mission specialist on the space shuttle *Discovery* in 1991.

SPOR. On January 10, former Stanford University football coach Dennis Green is named head coach of the Minnesota Vikings. He is the second African American coach in the National Football League in the modern era.

WORK. On February 7, the U.S. Department of Labor announces that the unemployment rate for African Americans has increased to 13.7 percent from 12.7 percent.

1993

EDUC. On September 1, Condoleezza Rice is named provost of Stanford University, the youngest person and first African American to hold this position.

LIT. On October 7, writer Toni Morrison is awarded the Nobel Prize in Literature. She is the first African American writer to be so honored.

OBIT. On February 6, champion tennis player, humanitarian, and political activist Arthur Ashe dies.

On June 26, legendary Brooklyn Dodgers catcher Roy Campanella dies in Los Angeles.

POLI. On January 21, Rep. Mike Espy of Mississippi is confirmed as the first African American secretary of the Department of Agriculture.

RELI. Pope John Paul II apologies for the Roman Catholic Church's role in support of slavery from the fifteenth to the nineteenth century.

SPOR. On August 17, African American athlete Jackie Joyner-Kersee wins her 17th consecutive heptathlon, edging out Germany's Sabrine Braun in the World Track and Field Championships in Stuttgart, Germany.

1994

BUSI. There are 75 African American publishing companies in the United States.

CRIM. On February 5, white supremacist Bryon de la Beckwith is convicted of the murder of Medgar Evers more than 30 years after Evers is ambushed and shot in the back in Jackson, Mississippi.

1995

CIVI. On October 16, the Nation of Islam under the leadership of Minister Louis Farrakhan helps sponsor and promote a gathering of largely African American males in Washington, DC,

known as the Million Man March. An estimated 300,00 marchers participate.

LAW. The U.S. Supreme Court in *Adarand Constructors v. Pena* strikes down a statute requiring 10 percent of federal highway funds to go to minority contractors but, instead, broadly asserts that any such programs using racial classifications are constitutional.

POLI. On March 16, after 130 years, the state of Mississippi becomes the last state to ratify the Thirteenth Amendment to the U.S. Constitution, which abolished slavery in the United States in 1865.

On May 6, Ron Kirk becomes the first African American mayor of Dallas, Texas, by winning 62 percent of the vote.

On December 12, Willie Brown defeats incumbent Mayor Frank Jordan to become the first African American mayor of San Francisco.

1996

BUSI. *Publishers Weekly* reports that the number of bookstores specializing in African American books has increased from a dozen a few years earlier to more than 200 nationwide.

CIVI. Nearly 1,000 civil rights activists protest the small number of African American and Latin American law clerks hired by U.S. Supreme Court justices.

OBIT. Tupac Shakur dies on September 13 after being shot four times in the chest by an assailant in a passing vehicle. His mother, Afeni Shakur establishes a record label, Amaru Records, in his memory one year later.

MILI. On October 1, Lt. Gen. Joe Ballard becomes the first African American to head the U.S. Army Corps of Engineers.

At the Million Man March, Louis Farrakhan reminds the marchers that this is a "Holy Day of Atonement and Reconciliation," to "reconcile our spiritual inner beings and to redirect our focus to developing our communities, strengthening our families, working to uphold and protect our civil and human right, and empowering ourselves through the Spirit of God, more effective use of our dollars, and through the power of the vote."

SPOR. On September 6, baseball player Eddie Murray joins Hank Aaron and Willie Mays as the only baseball players to make at least 500 home runs and 3,000 hits.

1997

CIVI. On October 27, an estimated 500,000 woman of African heritage converge on Washington, DC, to hold a Million Woman March that is in many ways similar to the Million Man March two years earlier. Two Philadelphia women—Phil Chionesu, a small-business owner, and Asia Coney, a public housing organizer—organize this gathering to protest and speak out against domestic violence, inadequate access to quality health care, educational opportunities, responsible governmental efforts against the proliferation of illegal drugs, and violence within local communities. Rep. Maxine Waters, rapper Sister Souljah, and South African activist Winnie Mandela are among the speakers who address the marchers.

MEDI. On November 19, African Americans Dr. Paula Mahone and Dr. Karen Drake lead a team of 40 specialists in the first successful delivery of septuplets in Carlisle, Indiana.

POLI. On December 6, Lee Brown defeats Rob Mosbacher to become Houston, Texas's, first African American mayor.

SPOR. On April 13, Eldrick "Tiger" Woods wins the 61st Masters Tournament in Augusta, Georgia, at the age of 21, the youngest person and the first African American to win the tournament.

On July 7, former heavyweight boxing champion Mike Tyson is dropped from the rankings by the World Boxing Association (WBA) for biting Evander Holyfield's ear in their championship bout.

On November 9, the National Basketball Association (NBA) hires its first two women to officiate games, Dee Katner and Violet Palmer.

1998

CRIM. On December 2, former Secretary of Agriculture Mike Espy is acquitted of all 30 charges of corruption levied against him by independent counsel Donald Smaltz. Espy was the first African American to hold this position.

LIT. The National Literary Hall of Fame for Writers of African Descent opens at Chicago State University in Illinois.

MILI. On July 18, the African American Civil War Memorial is dedicated in Washington, DC.

OBIT. On July 16, Dr. John Henrik Clarke, noted historian, scholar, professor, and advisor to leaders such as El Hajj Malik el Shabazz (Malcolm X) dies at the age of 83 at St. Luke's Hospital in New York City.

On September 21, Florence "Flo-Jo" Griffith Joyner, Olympic gold medalist in track, dies in Mission Viejo, California, at the age of 39.

On November 15, Kwame Toure (Stokely Carmichael) dies at the age of 57 in Ghana, West Africa. Toure played a major role in the development of the Student Non-Violent Coordinating Committee (SNCC) into a militant civil rights organization and was often critical of Rev. Dr. Martin Luther King Jr. as being too moderate. In the early 1960s, Toure was effective in developing Alabama's Lowndes County Freedom Organization (LCFO), which challenged the all-white Democratic Party of Alabama for state political power. From this struggle emerged the symbol of the black panther for the LCFO as opposed to the white rooster that was the symbol of the Democratic Party in Alabama. In the 1965 Selma to Montgomery, Alabama, march, Toure and another key SNCC activist, Willie Ricks, developed the term *Black Power* as a demand for the marchers. The demand for Black Power was immediately interpreted by many as a call for a more militant approach to civil rights than the Southern Christian Leadership Conference's (SCLC's) and the National Association for the Advancement of Colored People's (NAACP's) call for "Freedom Now!" Toure was also instrumental in the development of the Black Panther Party for Self Defense.

SPOR. Basketball star Michael Jordan wins his sixth NBA championship with the Chicago Bulls.

On June 29, head coach Lenny Wilkens of the Atlanta Hawks becomes only the second person to be elected to the NBA Hall of Fame twice: once as a player, then a coach.

1999

CRIM. On September 9, a Texas jury imposes the death sentence upon Lawrence Russell Brewer, the second white supremacist convicted in the murder of James Byrd Jr. Byrd was brutally killed when he was tied up and dragged behind a pickup truck.

OBIT. On November 1, Chicago Bears Hall of Fame running back Walter Payton dies at the age of 45.

SPOR. On June 16, African American track star, Maurice Greene breaks the world track and field record in the 100 meters in Athens, Greece. His time is 9.79 seconds.

On September 11, 17-year-old African American tennis player Serena Williams defeats Martina Hingis to win her first major tennis championship, the U.S. Open.

On November 7, Eldrick "Tiger" Woods is the first golfer to win four consecutive tournaments since Ben Hogan in 1953.

TWENTY-FIRST CENTURY

2000

BUSI. On June 22, the Nashville, Tennessee, based American General Life and Accident insurance company agrees to pay $206 million to primarily poor African American customers to settle allegations the company overcharged their clients for burial insurance.

CENS. The U.S. Census Bureau reports that women own 38 percent of African American–owned businesses. This represents a larger percentage than in the nation's business community as a whole, of which women own only 26 percent. The census also indicates that so-called minority firms, however, account for only 15 percent of all businesses in the nation.

The U.S. Census Bureau reports that it changed its classification of racial categories. Whereas in earlier years the two dominant categories were two—black and white—it has expanded the categories to six. For the first time in U.S. history, African Americans are no longer the largest so-called minority group. According to the Census Bureau, 35.3 million Hispanic Americans, 34.7 African Americans, and 1.8 million Americans who considered themselves as a mixture of African, American Indian, Asian, Pacific Islander, or European white live in the United States.

The U.S. Census Bureau notes that in 1960, only 37.7 percent of African Americans between the ages of 25 and 29 had completed high school; however, by 2000, 86.8 percent have completed high school. Similarly, African American college and university enrollment was 136,000 in 1960 but rose to 1,548,000 in 2000.

LIT. In January, Randal Robinson, a graduate of Virginia Union University and Harvard Law School as well as the founder and president of TransAfrica, a lobbying group that was extremely successful in putting U.S. political pressure on the Apartheid government of South Africa and securing the release of political prisoner Nelson Mandela, publishes the controversial book *The Debt: What America Owes to Blacks*. Robinson argues that just as the Japanese Americans were compensated for the horrors they suffered during World War II in American so-called relocation camps, African Americans are also due financial indemnification for slavery and "246 years of an enterprise murderous both of a people and their culture."

MED. Oprah Winfrey launches her highly successful magazine, *O*, and her influential Oprah's Book Club. Oprah Winfrey is reputed to be one of the wealthiest women in the world and one of the few African Americans on the *Forbes* 1998 list of the top 40 entertainers in the U.S. entertainment industry.

OBIT. On June 9, renowned African American artist Jacob Lawrence dies at age 82.

POLI. After the 2000 elections, George W. Bush nominates Colin L. Powell as the first African American secretary of state. The son of Jamaican immigrants, Powell served as the chairman of the Department of Defense's Joint Chiefs of Staff from 1989 to 1993. During his term as chairman, he oversaw U.S. military operations in Operation Desert Storm during the Persian Gulf War of 1991.

Presidential candidate Al Gore asks African American Donna Brazile to manage his presidential campaign. Born in 1960 in Louisiana, Brazile was graduated from Louisiana State University and worked on the presidential campaigns of Jesse Jackson, Michael Dukakis, and Bill Clinton. In her published recollections *(Cooking with Grease: Stirring the Pots in America)* of working in the Jackson presidential campaign, Brazile notes that "Reverend Jackson was at the time the best at mobilization and politics, and he understood the marriage between electoral politics and grassroots progressive movements. He created a coalition of conscience, bringing together white women, Hispanics, environmentalist, peace activist, gays, lesbians and organized labor."

Every year since 1993, when John Conyers was elected as a Democratic congressman from Detroit, he has introduced a bill in Congress, titled HR 40, that asks Congress to establish a federal commission to investigate slavery and the legacy of racial discrimination. To date, the bill has never reached the floor of the House of Representatives.

RELI. In July, after 214 years in existence, the African Methodist Episcopal (AME) Church names Vashti Murphy McKenzie as the first African American woman bishop. She is named the bishop of the 18th Episcopal District in Southeast Africa, which comprises approximately 200 churches and 10,000 members in Lesotho, Botswana, Swaziland, and Mozambique. Earlier, she was pastor for 10 years of Baltimore, Maryland's, Payne Memorial Church, in which she increased the membership from 300 to 1,700. Assuming her new post, she declares that her tasks are to concentrate on programs for grassroots economic development, construction of schools, and expanded health care delivery.

SPOR. On June 18, professional golfer Eldrick "Tiger" Woods wins the 100th U.S. Open, breaking several United States Golf Association records in the process.

On July 8, professional African American tennis player Venus Williams defeats Lindsay Davenport 6–3, 7–6 to win her first Wimbledon Championship.

2001

ARTS. Director Spike Lee releases his controversial film *Bamboozled,* a powerful satire about the minstrel components of modern African American television shows.

Denzel Washington and Halle Berry receive Academy Awards for best actor and best actress for their respective roles in the films *Training Day* and *Monster's Ball.*

CRIM. On September 11, several hundred African Americans are among the almost 3,000 who die as the result of terrorists attack on the World Trade Center in New York City and the Pentagon. Scores more die in the rescue attempts by the police and fire departments.

President George W. Bush names former Sanford University provost and expert on Russian politics Condoleezza Rice as national security advisor.

SPOR. Tiger Woods becomes the first professional golfer of any race to hold all four major golf championships at the same time: the Masters, PGA, U.S. Open, and the British Open.

2002

ARTS. On April 12, the *Voice of America* radio magazine honors African American artists with a number of awards. Special recognition is given to the National Association of Black Owned Broadcasters (NABOB), who represents the interest of African American owners of radio and television stations in the United States. The award ceremony recognizes a number of African American artist, such as the rhythm and blues group the Isley Brothers, popular singer Janet Jackson, and radio station owner Cathy Hughes. NABOB also presents blues musician Bo Diddley with the Pioneer in Entertainment Award. Opera singer Leotyne Price is honored with the Lifetime Achievement Award, and popular singer Patti LaBelle sings some of her greatest hits including "Marmalade."

BUSI. The U.S. Census Bureau reports that estimated revenues for African American businesses this year are $92.7 billion. This represents an increase of 30 percent from 1997 and an increase over the national growth by 22 percent.

Thirty-eight percent of African American businesses are in the area of health care and other service industries and health care and retail trade. The census bureau observes that African American business owners are more likely to hold graduate degrees when they start or acquire ownership in their businesses—about 25 percent—than the national average of 19 percent.

OBIT. On August 9, famed African American dancer, actor, and singer Gregory Hines dies at age 57 in Los Angeles, California.

2003

BUSI. *Black Enterprise Magazine's* annual ranking of the largest African American–owned industrial and service firms, auto dealerships, advertising agencies, banks, insurance companies, asset managers, and private equity firms reports that for 2002 the revenues for the top 100 African American–owned companies in the area of auto dealerships and industrial and service businesses alone are $20.9 billion, an increase of $600 million over 2001.

LAW. The U.S. Supreme Court in *Grutter v. Bollinger* upholds by a decision of five to four the University affirmative action policy in the use of racial preferences in the admission of students to the University of Michigan Law School. The Court notes that race can be one of many factors considered by colleges when selecting their students because it furthers "a compelling interest in obtaining the educational benefits that flow from a diverse student body."

POLI. In a speech before the United Nations Security Council, U.S. Secretary of State Colin Powell argues, based on what eventually turns out to be faulty or at best misleading intelligence reports, that Saddam Hussein, president of Iraq, not only has weapons of mass destruction but possibly the ability to use them in an attack on neighboring countries. The evidence attempts to directly associate Saddam with terrorist networks affiliated with Al Qaeda. The Security Council is not convinced by Powell's argument and votes against any military action against Iraq. The United States, with the support of Great Britain, invades Iraq on March 19.

2004

CENS. The U.S. Census Bureau reports that as of July 1, the estimated African American population, including those of more than one race, is 39.2 million (13.4%) of the entire population. This represents an increase of 500,000 from the previous year.

POLI. At the 2004 Presidential Democratic Convention in Boston, Massachusetts, Barack Obama, a little known 42-year-old state senator from Illinois who is running for the U.S. Senate, electrifies the convention by giving a keynote address that proclaims only good and efficient government can improve the life chances for all Americans. African American columnist Clarence Page notes that Obama's speech and his entire persona made him the "quintessential crossover candidate, a Colin Powell for the party of the Revs. Jesse Jackson and Al Sharpton." In November, Obama Barack is elected to the U.S. Senate from Illinois.

In November, President George W. Bush nominates Condoleezza Rice as the first African American woman secretary of state. Rice was born on November 14, 1954, in Birmingham, Alabama. She earned her PhD from the Graduate School of International Studies at the University of Denver, became a professor of political science at Stanford

---

At the 2004 Presidential Democratic Convention, Barack Obama receives a standing ovation when he proclaims, "Yet even as we speak, there are those who are preparing to divide us, the spin masters and negative ad peddlers who embrace the politics of anything goes. Well, I say to them tonight, there's not a liberal America and a conservative America; there's the United States of America. There's not a black America and white America and Latino America and Asian America; there's the United States of America."

University, and served as that university's provost for six years. She acted as George W. Bush's national security advisor during his first term.

WORK. The U.S. Census Bureau reports that 27 percent of the African American population 16 years of age or older works in management, professional, and related occupations, with some 50,600 as physicians and surgeons, 69,400 as postsecondary teachers, 44,800 as lawyers, and 53,800 as chief executives. When these figures are compared to the entire African American population, however, the median income is $30,134, compared to $34,241 for Hispanics and $46,697 for whites (non-Hispanics). The poverty rate for African Americans, 24.7 percent, has not changed in the last two years, yet 48 percent of African American are homeowners.

2005

CULT. On January 13, Maurice Barboza, founder of the Black Revolutionary War Patriots Foundation, unveils a model of a black Revolutionary War soldier that will be part of a planned memorial for the Mall in Washington, DC. Designed by engineer and sculptor Ed Dwight, the bronze memorial will stretch 90 feet as it charts the history of black soldiers in the American Revolution. Barboza commented that Ed Dwight, who won the competition to design the memorial in 1990, was continually harassed because "*they* wanted it to be abstract" and that "in this city, our nation's capital, there was issue with putting black faces on the National Mall."

OBIT. On August 10, famed photographer George H. Scurlock dies at age 85 in Washington, DC. George Scurlock and his brother Robert, who died in 1994, learned their trade from their father, Addison Scurlock, the founder of the family business in 1911. Inheriting their father's desire for perfection when capturing images of not only the famous but also the common folk, the family documented an array of African American lifestyles throughout most of the twentieth century. Included in their collection are photos of Paul Lawrence Dunbar, Countee Cullen, Dr. Charles Drew, Booker T. Washington, W.E.B. Du Bois, Marion Anderson, Billie Holiday, Lena Horne, and many others. A collection

of more than 50,000 images from the Scurlock family archives are housed in the Smithsonian Institution's National Museum of American History.

On July 27, opera singer Helen L. Phillips, who broke the so-called color barrier at the Metropolitan Opera House, dies at age 85 in the Washington Heights neighborhood of Manhattan (see 1947).

On August 11, Theodore Roosevelt Radcliffe dies at age 103 in Chicago, Illinois. Known for his prowess on the pitcher's mound and behind the plate, he was nicknamed Double Duty by baseball enthusiast and philanthropist Damon Runyon. Born in Mobile, Alabama, on July 7, 1902, Ted moved to Chicago after World War I, played semiprofessional baseball, and then played with more than a dozen Negro League teams. He managed the Memphis Red Sox and Chicago American Giants. His biggest thrill was hitting a home run in the West's 7–4 victory in the 1944 All-Star Game, after which he recalled, "My mama met me at home plate."

Radcliffe also had unpleasant memories, particularly of their traveling team driving through the Deep South, where racism was solid and dangerous. Ted Radcliffe was an all-star pitcher and catcher and a manager during a career in the Negro Leagues that spanned more than two decades. He was 44 years old when Jackie Robinson came into the major leagues with the Brooklyn Dodgers in 1947. in the 1960s, he was a scout for the Cleveland Indians.

SCIE. In October, Captain Merry L. David becomes the first and only African American woman to fly in the United States Air Force's elite spying unit of U-2 planes. Her solo flights exceed 70,000 feet and last 9 hours.

SPOR. On August 7, Frederick (Fritz) Douglass Pollard is inducted posthumously into the Pro Football Hall of Fame in Canton, Ohio. Named after the famous African American abolitionist, Pollard, who died in 1986 at age 92, first gained renown as a two-time all-American running back at Brown University, where in 1916 he was the first African American athlete to play in the Rose Bowl. He joined the Akron Pros of the American Professional Football Association

(APFA) in 1919. Two years later, he played and coached the Akron team, and in 1922 the APFA was renamed the National Football League (NFL). Pollard, who stood five feet, nine inches and weighed 165 pounds, played and occasionally coached for four NFL teams and after 1926 helped organize and coach a number of all-black teams that barnstormed the country in an era when many NFL teams refused to sign black players. Fritz Pollard played high school football in Chicago against George Halas, who later became a Hall of Fame coach and owner of the Chicago Bears. Halas never allowed Pollard to try out for the Bears, however, and even refused to schedule games for Pollard's all-African American teams.

OBIT. Rosa Parks, known as the Mother of the Civil Rights Movement, dies on October 25, in Detroit, Michigan.

GLOSSARY

American Colonization Society (ACS). Founded in 1816, its initial members were prominent slave-holders such as Bushrod Washington, a nephew of George Washington and Henry Clay. Their expressed purpose was to export emancipated or manumitted Africans out of the United States, preferably to Liberia, West Africa, or a Caribbean country.

Angolans. Indigenous population from the southwestern coastal area of West Africa.

Asiento. In Castilian Spanish, it means to "take a seat" as when men conducting business who sit down to discuss and sign a contract. The Asiento was in fact a subcontract, first given by the Catholic Church in the sixteenth century (1518) to the Dutch to purchase and bring Africans as enslaved laborers to Spanish colonies in the New World. In 1713 England obtained the Asiento and contractually transported enslaved Africans to her colonies. By the time of the American Revolution, England was transporting approximately fifty thousand enslaved Africans per annum to her colonies.

Bamboozle. To be tricked, deceived or led astray. Malcolm X revived this term as a contemporary social commentary on the social and political status of African American leadership. He argued that they were "bamboozled" into thinking racism could be legislated out of society.

BPP. The Black Panther Party (BPP) was first conceived of in rural black belt Lowndes County, Alabama (situated between Selma and the state capital of Montgomery) in 1964. Members of the Student Non-Violent Coordinating Committee (SNCC) started working with poor, landless, vote-less and economically dependent African Americans whose livelihood depended upon a small elite class of white plantation owners. Political activists such as Stokely Carmichael and other members of SNCC organized residents into a political party that they called the Black Panther Party. This organization became a part of the Lowndes County Freedom Organization (LCFO), whose political symbol was the Black Panther. When asked why they chose the black panther as a political symbol, LCFO Chairman, John Hulett stated that, "The black panther is an animal that when it is pressured it moves back until it is cornered ... then it comes out fighting for life or death. We felt we had been pushed back long enough and that it was time for Negroes to come out and take over." Two years later, in October 1966, the Black Panther Party for Self Defense was founded in Oakland, California by Huey P. Newton and Robert (Bobby) Seales. While the former BPP was rurally based and focused on issues such as voting rights, terrorist night rides perpetrated by the Klan , and institutionalized racial segregation, the California-based BPP was largely located in urban inner city areas and focused on police brutality, urban education and housing, the Vietnam War, self defense, and rising incarceration levels of African American youth.

CORE. An acronym for the Congress of Racial Equality. The expressed purpose of this organization, started in 1942, was to find an interracial methodology, primarily pacifist, nonviolent way to address institutionalized racism. Finding political solace in the teachings and practices of Indian leader Mohandas Gandhi, founding leaders of CORE such as James Farmer and Bayard Rustin before and after World War II developed strategies of nonviolent protest, such as sit-in's, that were later utilized throughout the 1950s and 1960s Civil Rights era.

Cotton Gin. A mechanical device that separated cotton from is plant stem. Traveling through the southern states, Eli Whitney noticed that trusted slaves had developed a device that quickly separated cotton from its stem, thereby providing more cotton to be bailed while protecting the hands of slaves from the plants sharp thorns. Whitney improvised on what he saw and patented it in 1793 as the cotton gin.

Dred Scott. In 1857, the U.S. Supreme Court, in *Dred Scott v. Sanford,* decided that petitioner Dred Scott was not a free man although he lived in places were slavery was illegal. The Court also concluded that the U.S. Congress could not support the Missouri Compromise (1821) or the Kansas-Nebraska Act, which would prevent slave owners from bringing their property into new U.S. territory. The Court (Chief Justice Roger B. Taney) claimed that the 5th Amendment protected slave owners from the loss of their slaves. Consequently, wherever Dred Scott lived, his status as human property was considered permanent by law.

Durante Vita. Spanish term meaning, "throughout their life." Implying that an enslaved person was so enslaved for life.

Emancipation Proclamation. The preliminary Emancipation Proclamation, as issued by president Abraham Lincoln on September 22, 1862, asserted that if the southern states continued their armed struggle against the Union, he would evoke a full Emancipation Proclamation for any enslaved Africans under Union control on January 1, 1863. The southern Confederacy refused to negotiate for a truce, and consequently a full proclamation was issued on January 1, 1863, thereby converting the war from one aimed at keeping the Union together to a war against slavery.

Head Right System. A tenure system that encouraged English colonist to establish new settlements by providing them with land and indentured servants or slaves to work the land.

Indentured Servant. During British rule in North America, this term underscored a contract labor system that allowed Europeans to sign a work-agreement for a period of five, seven, or twelve years. This was helpful in forcing a large segment of Great Britain's population out of faltering urban centers and jails. This labor system allowed the colonial government as well as private contractors to pay the steerage cost for Europeans emigrants to travel to the colonies under a contractual agreement that ensured a certain amount of profits from their forced labor would be returned to the contractors, private or governmental. Unlike the enslaved colonial population, indentured servants could make appeals to colonial officials about mistreatment. Often, white indentured servants would simply break their contract by escaping to another colony. Once this occurred, they simply took on another identity, worked as freemen to obtain finance to hold the papers on newly purchased slaves or imported indentured servants, thereby quickly raising their social and economic status to property owners.

Indigenous People. A people whose origins are associated with the earliest knowledge of that specific land or territory.

Minutemen. Local farmers who sided with the "Sons of Liberty," an anti-British, pro-independence political movement in the British North American colonies. As an irregular military force, they fought against the British forces at Lexington and Concord, Massachusetts on April 19, 1775. The Minuteman eventually became the nucleus for the American Revolutionary Army.

Montgomery Improvement Association. Organized by a number of civil rights activist from various associations such as the NAACP, Women's Political Council (WPC), and local churches. Their associations voted to have Rev. Dr. Martin Luther King Jr. act as their spokesmen and president in 1955 as they organized the Montgomery Bus Boycott in Alabama.

National Association for the Advancement of Colored People. Known as the NAACP, this civil rights association was formed in 1909 with the expressed mandate to fight institutionalized American racism from a judicial perspective. Though a multiracial organization, it increasingly became identified as an African American organization.

Osawatomie. The name of a major battle that occurred on August 30, 1856 in the Kansas territory, near the town of Osawatomie. Five antislavery activists under the command of John Brown were killed, including one of his sons, Frederick. In response, Brown's followers burned the town of Osawatomie, earning him the nickname "Osawatomie Brown."

Pottawatomie. In response to an attack by proslavers on the town of Lawrence, Kansas Territory, May 21 and May 22, 1856, John Brown and his raiders attacked proslavers two days later on the Pottawatomie settlement, killing five.

Privateer. A privately owned commercial ship that operated with a government license, though it was not a government-owned vessel. During war, these vessels supplemented government-owned warships.

PUSH. An acronym for People United to Serve Humanity. Founded by Rev. Jesse Jackson in 1971, its purpose is to provide a social activist structure for campaigns such as voting rights issues and the inducement of large major corporations to address issues such as jobs and education within poor African American communities.

SCLC. The Southern Christian Leadership Conference began to take shape in Atlanta, Georgia on January 10 and 11, 1957 after a meeting called the "Southern Negro Leaders Conference on Transportation and Integration" occurred and highlighted the on-going need for African Americans to organize around fundamental grievances within and outside their communities. After the first meeting, the following was agreed upon as a mandate for the SCLC: (1) the church had functioned effectively as the institutional base of protest movements; (2) aggressive nonviolent action by African Americans was necessary if the system of segregation was to be overthrown; (3) an organized mass force was needed to supplement the activities of the NAACP, which was under fierce attack throughout the South; and (4) movements could be generated, coordinated, and sustained by activist clergy and organized African American masses working in concert.

Settlers. Individuals or groups of colonists who migrate and establish homesteads on land populated by an indigenous people. Settlers are often referred to as pioneers, and their migration usually resulted in hostile interaction between them and the indigenous populace.

Spingarn Medal. An annual medal awarded by the National Association for the Advancement of Colored People (NAACP) to African Americans who have made a significant achievement in their profession, from science to sports, from politics to art. The prestigious award is in the form of a gold medal that is valued at one hundred dollars. The award is named after literary scholar Joel Elias Spingarn, who was also chairman of the NAACP board of directors in 1914. The board's stated purpose was to ensure that Americans knew of the achievements of African Americans and that the award serve "as a reward for such achievement and a stimulus in the ambition of colored youth." The first award was presented to biologist, Ernest E. Just in 1915.

SNCC. The Student Non-Violent Coordinating Committee was founded on April 16–18, 1960 in Raleigh, North Carolina. Ella Baker, a long-time civil rights activist and executive member of SCLC, called for the formation of SNCC as a means to develop and achieve among students "a more unified sense of direction for *training and action in Nonviolent Resistance*." She wanted to assure students that, although "Adult Freedom Fighters" would be present "for counsel and guidance," the conference would be "youth centered."

Virginia House of Burgess. Legislative body of the Virginian Colony under British rule.

BIBLIOGRAPHY

BOOKS

Adero, Malaika. *Up South: Stories, Studies and Letters of this Century's African American Migrations.* New York: The New Press, 1993.

Anderson, Osborne P. *A Voice from Harper's Ferry: A Black Revolutionary Who Was There.* 1861. Reprint New York: World View Publishers, 1974.

Andrews, William L., ed. *Three African-American Novels.* New York: New American Library, 1990.

Aptheker, Herbert. *American Negro Slave Revolts.* New York: International Publishers, 1993.

Astor, Gerald. *The Right to Fight: A History of Africans in the Military.* New York. Da Capo Press, 2001.

Bank, William M. *Black Intellectuals: Race and Responsibility in American Life.* New York: W. W. Norton, 1998.

Bearden, Romare, and Harry Henderson. *A History of African-American Artists: From 1792 to the Present.* New York: Pantheon Books, 1993.

Bennett, Lerone, Jr. *Before the Mayflower: A History of Black America.* New York: The Penguin Group, 1988.

Berry, Faith. *Langston Hughes: Before and Beyond Harlem.* Westport, CT: Lawrence Hill and Company, 1983.

Buckley, Gail. *American Patriots: The Story of Blacks in the Military from the Revolution to Desert Storm.* New York: Random House, 2001.

Carson, Clayborne. *In Struggle: SNCC and the Black Awakening of the 1960's.* Cambridge, Massachusetts: Harvard University Press, 1981.

Cliff, Michelle. *Free Enterprise.* New York: Plume/Penguin Book, 1993.

Cohen, Stan. *John Brown: The Thundering Voice of Jehovah.* Missoula, MT: Pictorial Histories Publishing, 1999.

Davis, Burke. *Black Heroes of the American Revolution.* San Diego, CA: Harcourt Brace, 1976.

Deagan, Kathleen, and Darice MacMahan. *Fort Mose: Colonial America's Black Fortress of Freedom.* Gainesville: University Press of Florida, 1995.

Douglass, Frederick. *My Bondage and My Freedom.* Chicago: Ebony Classics, Johnson Publishing Company, 1970.

Du Bois, W.E.B. *Black Reconstruction in America, 1861–1880.* New York: Atheneum, 1983.

Durham, Philip, and Everett L. Jones. *The Adventures of the Negro Cowboys.* New York: Dodd Mead, 1966.

Evans, William McKee. *To Die Game: The Story of the Lowry Band, Indian Guerrillas of Reconstruction.* Syracuse, NY: Syracuse University Press, 1995.

Foner, Eric, ed. *America's Black Past: A Reader in Afro-American History.* New York: Harper and Row, 1970.

Franklin, John Hope, and Alfred A. Moss, Jr. *From Slavery to Freedom: A History of African Americans.* New York: McGraw-Hill, 1994.

Ginzburg, Ralph. *100 Years of Lynchings.* Baltimore, MD: Black Classic Press, 1962.

Grant, Joanne. *Black Protest: 350 Years of History, Documents, and Analyses.* New York: Ballantine Books, 1996.

Haley, Alex. *The Autobiography of Malcolm X.* New York: Grove Press, 1964.

Harris, M. A. *A Negro History Tour of Manhattan.* New York: Greenwood Publishing Corporation, 1968.

Hillard, David, and Donald Weise., ed. *The Huey P Newton Reader.* New York: Seven Stories Press, 2002.

Hine, Darlene Clark, William C. Hine, and Stanley Harrold. *The African-American Odyssey.* Upper Saddle River, NJ: Prentice Hall, 2003.

Katz, William Loren. *Black Indians: A Hidden Heritage.* New York: Aladdin Paperbacks, 1997.

Kennedy, Pagan. *Black Livingston: A True Tale of Adventure in the Nineteenth Century Congo.* New York: Viking Penguin Group, 2002.

Kinshasa, Kwando M. *The Man From Scottsboro: Clarence Norris and the Infamous 1931 Alabama Rape Trial, In His Own Words.* Jefferson, NC: McFarland, 1997.

Lamming, Lt. Colonel Michael Lee. *African Americans in the Revolutionary War.* New York: Citadel Press, 2000.

Landers, Jane. *Fort Mose: Gracia Real de Santa Teresa de Mose, A Free Black Town in Spanish Colonial Florida.* St. Augustine, FL: St. Augustine Historical Society, 1992.

Lewis, John. *Walking with the Wind: A Memoir of the Movement.* New York: Simon and Schuster, 1998.

Litwack, Leon, and August Meier., eds. *Black Leaders of the Nineteenth Century.* Chicago: University of Illinois Press, 1991.

Lofton, John. *Insurrection in South Carolina: The Turbulent World of Denmark Vessey.* Yellow Springs, OH: Antioch Press, 1964.

Marszalek, John E. *Assault at West Point: The Court Martial of Johnson Whittaker.* New York: Macmillan, 1972.

Morris, Aldon D. *The Origins of the Civil Rights Movement: Black Communities Organizing for Change.* New York: The Free Press, 1984.

Nash, Gary B. *Race and Revolution.* New York: Rowman and Littlefield Publishers, 2001.

Noble, Gil. *Black Is the Color of My TV Tube.* Secaucus, NJ: Lyle Stuart, 1981.

Quarles, Benjamin. *The Negro in the Civil War.* New York: Da Capo Press, 1953.

Smith, Rochelle, and Sharon L. Jones. *The Prentice Hall Anthology of African American Literature.* Upper Saddle River, NJ: Prentice Hall, 2000.

Trager, James. *The People's Chronology: A Year by Year Record of Human Events from Prehistory to the Present.* New York: Henry Holt and Company, 1994.

Walch, Barbara. *Frank B. Butler: Lincolnville Businessman and Founder of St. Augustine, Florida's Historic Black Beach.* St. Augustine, FL: Rudolph B. Hadley, Sr., 1992.

Wesley, Charles H. *The History of Alpha Phi Alpha: A Development in College Life.* Chicago: The Foundation Publishers, 1950.

Wiggins, Lida Keck. *The Life and Works of Paul Laurence Dunbar.* New York: Dodd, Mead, and Company, 1907.

Wilson, M. L. *Black Americans of Achievement: Chester Himes.* New York: Chelsea House Publishers, 1988.

Winch, Julie. *A Gentleman of Color: The Life of James Forten.* New York: Oxford Press, 2002.

Zinn, Howard. *A Peoples History of the United States: 1492–Present.* New York: Harpers Collins Publishers, 2003.

EDUCATIONAL AID

Catherine, G. Theodore. *A Journey into 365 Days of Black History.* Takoma Park, MD: Iokts Productions. 2005.

Easley, Arika, and Tiffany Ford. *Sparkcharts: African American History.* New York: Barnes and Noble Publication. 2004.

Mapp, Ray W., and Shannon H. Mapp. *Black Miracles: The Miracles of Black Inventors and Scientist.* Palm Coast, FL: Purpose Publishing, 2001.

WEB SITES

African American Registry. Online: http://www.aaregistry.com/african_american_history.

Antebellum Black Congregations. *The Reverend Andrew Bryan.* Online: http://www.kingtisdell.org/ante congregations.htm.

Black History, NH's "Colored Patriots" of the Revolution. Online: http://www.seacoastnh.com/blackhistory /patriots.html.

Black History Month. Net. *Black Firsts, The World's Firsts.* Online: http://www.black-history-month.net/ military.htm.

Chicago Timeline, Chicago Public Library. *1779 Jean Baptiste Point du Sable.* Online: http://www.chipublib. org/004chicago/timeline/dusable.html.

Colonial National Historical Park, National Park Service. Yorktown Historic Briefs. *The First Rhode Island Regiment.* Online: http://www.nps.gov/col/Ythanout/firstri.html.

Common-Place. Stories of Freedom in Black New York. *Black Shakespeareans in Old New York.* Online: http://www.common-place.org/vol-03/no-13/reviews/reiss.shtml.

Distinguished Women of Past and Present. Online: http://www.distinguishedwomen.com/biographies/ mahoney-me.html.

Documenting the American South. *Susie King Taylor, Reminiscences of my life in Camp with the 33rd United States Colored Troops, Late 1st S.C. Volunteers.* Online: http://docsouth.unc.edu/neh.

Electronic New Jersey: A Digital Archive of New Jersey History. *Biography: Paul Robeson.* Online: http://www. scc.rutgers.edu/njh/Paulrobeson/PRBio.htm.

Institute for Race and Justice. Online: http://www.law.harvard.edu/programs/houstoninstitute/biography. html.

Legends of America. *Lynchings & Hangings in American History.* Online: http//www.legendssofamerica.com/ LA-Lynching4.html.

Lumbee.org. *The Hero of Robeson County: The Story of Henry Berry Lowrie.* Online: http://www.lumbee.org/ hbl.htm.

Modern American Poetry. *About Countee Cullen's Life and Career.* Online: http://www.english.uiuc.edu/ maps/poets/a_f/cullen/life.htm.

National Archives Learning Curve. *Civil Rights Movement.* Online: http://www.spartacus.co.uk.

Reconstruction: A State Divided. *The Cabildo.* Online: http://Ism.crt.state.la.us/cabildo/cab11.htm.

Richard 111 Society. *The African Company Presents Richard 111.* Online: http://www.r3.org/mckellen/africa. html.

South Carolina African American History. Online: http://www.scafricanamericanhistory.com/curren- thonoree.

Today in Black History. Online: http://todayinblackhistory.blogspot.com/2004_06_01todayinblackhistory_ archive.html.

World of Education. *Opinion of the Supreme Court in United States v. the Amistad.* Online: http://library. educationworld.net/txt09/doc4.html.

INDEX

About the Author

KWANDO M. KINSHASA is Associate Professor of Sociology, and Chair, African American Studies Department, John Jay College of Criminal Justice, City University of New York. He is author of *Black Resistance to the Ku Klux Klan in the Wake of the Civil War* (2006), *The Man from Scottsboro: Clarence Norris and the Infamous 1931 Alabama Rape Trial, in His Own Words* (1998), and *Emigration vs. Assimilation: The Debate in the African American Press: 1827–1861* (1988). His research interests include 19th-century history with particular emphasis on the sociological consequences of migration and emigration patterns within African American communities.